COMPLETE EDITION

JAZZ KEYBOARD

Keyboard Workshop Book

Approved Curriculum

Beginning • Intermediate • Mastering

NOAH BAERMAN

Alfred, the leader in educational music publishing, and the National Keyboard Workshop, one of America's finest keyboard schools, have joined forces to bring you the best, most progressive educational tools possible. We hope you will enjoy this book and encourage you to look for other fine products from Alfred and the National Keyboard Workshop.

CONTENTS

Alfred Music Publishing Co., Inc.
P.O. Box 10003
Van Nuys, CA 91410-0003
alfred.com

ISBN-10: 0-7390-7890-9 (Book & CD)
ISBN-13: 978-0-7390-7890-7 (Book & CD)

Cover photographs
Clockwise from top: Michael Llewellyn; Karen Miller; Vadim Sokolov, 1993/PNI; Photodisc; Chicago Historical Society, 1995/PNI; Photodisc; Burt Glinn, 1960/PNI; (Brick wall) Jasmine, 1995/PNI

 Alfred Cares. Contents printed on 100% recycled paper.

BEGINNING JAZZ KEYBOARD

This book was acquired, edited, and produced
by Workshop Arts, Inc., the publishing arm of
the National Keyboard Workshop.
Nathaniel Gunod, acquisitions, editor
Amy Rosser, editor
ProScore, Novato, CA, music typesetter
Cathy Bolduc, interior design
Audio tracks recorded by Collin Tilton at Bar None Studio, Northford, CT

ABOUT THE AUTHOR

Noah Baerman (www.noahjazz.com) earned Bachelors and Masters degrees in Jazz Studies from Rutgers University, studying under Kenny Barron. To date, Noah has released seven jazz albums under his own name. His widely acclaimed 2003 release *Patch Kit* raised funds and awareness for Ehlers-Danlos Syndrome, a connective tissue disorder with which he was born. That album, featuring bassist Ron Carter and drummer Ben Riley, also led to an appearance for Noah on Marian McPartland's NPR program "Piano Jazz." Noah is active as an educator, teaching privately and at several institutions including Wesleyan University, where he directs the Jazz Ensemble, as well as online through WorkshopLive.com. His other instructional books for Alfred/NGW include *Jazz Keyboard Harmony* (#19414) and *The Big Book of Jazz Piano Improvisation* (#21965). His compositions have earned him First Prize awards for jazz in the Billboard Song Contest and the Unisong Contest as well as a "New Works" grant from Chamber Music America/Doris Duke Foundation. He lives in Middletown, CT with his wife, visual artist Kate Ten Eyck, and their daughters.

ACKNOWLEDGMENTS

Thank you to everyone who made this project possible (including many people who didn't make it onto this list): to Nat Gunod, Dave Smolover, Burgess Speed and everyone else at NGW and Workshop Arts; to Alfred Music Publishing; to Collin Tilton at Bar None Studios; to Dan Morgenstern, Esther Smith, and the rest of the people at the Institute of Jazz Studies; to Steve Bennett, Karl Mueller, Wynne Mun, Jeff Grace, Amanda Monaco, Damion Poirier, Jimmy Greene, Noah Richardson, Jeff Bartolotta, Roberto Scrofani, Rachel Green, the Ten Eyck family and all the rest of the friends who directly or indirectly helped me to put these books together; to all my students who taught me how to teach; to ECA and the Artists' Collective for getting me started with jazz; to the Music Department at Rutgers for all their support and training; to Eva Pierrou, Clara Shen and Wanda Maximilien for their expert piano teaching; to Mike Mossman, Sumi Tonooka, Joanne Brackeen, Larry Ridley, Phil Schaap, Ralph Bowen, and especially Ted Dunbar, George Raccio and Kenny Barron for selflessly sharing their jazz knowledge; to my dear friends and inspiring colleagues from Positive Rhythmic Force, Jason Berg, Ben Tedoff and Sunny Jain; to my family, Mom, Dad, Alison, Jennifer, Matthew and Annie for their boundless support and patience; and to Kate for everything.

00

Track 1

An MP3 CD is included with this book to make learning easier and more enjoyable. The symbol shown at bottom left appears next to every example in the book that features an MP3 track. Use the MP3s to ensure you're capturing the feel of the examples and interpreting the rhythms correctly. The track number below the symbol corresponds directly to the example you want to hear (example numbers are above the icon). All the track numbers are unique to each "book" within this volume, meaning every book has its own Track 1, Track 2, and so on. (For example, *Beginning Jazz Keyboard* starts with Track 1, as does *Intermediate Jazz Keyboard* and *Mastering Jazz Keyboard*.) Track 1 for each book will help you tune to the CD.

The disc is playable on any CD player equipped to play MP3 CDs. To access the MP3s on your computer, place the CD in your CD-ROM drive. In Windows, double-click on My Computer, then right-click on the CD icon labeled "MP3 Files" and select Explore to view the files and copy them to your hard drive. For Mac, double-click on the CD icon on your desktop labeled "MP3 Files" to view the files and copy them to your hard drive.

CONTENTS

INTRODUCTION

Welcome to *The Complete Jazz Keyboard Method,* a comprehensive series of books designed specifically for the aspiring jazz keyboardist. This method consists of three separate volumes now available in this complete edition. Each of the three volumes (*Beginning Jazz Keyboard, Intermediate Jazz Keyboard* and *Mastering Jazz Keyboard*) is an important step along the way to mastering jazz on the keyboard.

The first part, *Beginning Jazz Keyboard,* is designed to ease you into playing jazz and create a solid foundation. It assumes you have already begun your keyboard training, are familiar with reading music and have experience playing major and minor scales. Several people I've talked to, as I've been writing this, have expressed a similar interest. They say they hope that this method can help to de-mystify jazz for them. They say they've tried to play jazz before, but there is so much you need to know that it is intimidating. When they've tried to ask for help, they've gotten the impression that jazz is some kind of secret club where they can't get in unless they learn the secret handshake. *Beginning Jazz Keyboard* aims to counter these problems.

I'm not going to say that jazz is easy, and I'm not going to say that any method book can teach you everything you need to know. What the first part of this book will do, however, is teach you the basics. If you understand the basics of rhythm, harmony and improvisation, you are well on your way. In addition to preparing you for the *Intermediate* and *Mastering* sections, you'll have the information you need to play and understand jazz. The tradition of jazz education is all about learning while playing, listening and hanging out with other musicians. This first section will give you what you need to start doing those things. As you move through the second and third parts, you'll have even more information to integrate with your learned experiences.

A few pieces of advice to help you get the most out of this book:

— Play. Playing jazz is fun and satisfying, so enjoy.
— Listen. To truly understand the concepts in this book, it is absolutely essential to listen to recordings and live performances of good jazz. (See pages 96, 191 and 287 for some hints.)
— Cross-reference. When you learn a new concept, don't just use it on the tunes that relate to that concept. Try applying it to other tunes to solidify your knowledge.
— Be flexible. The cornerstone of jazz is improvisation. Very little is set in stone, and that may take some getting used to if you're not accustomed to improvising. Think of things like dynamics and phrasing marks as suggestions. For most jazz musicians, these things are instinctive and spontaneous. If you hear a different way to interpret something, trust your ears and try it.

Good luck and have fun.

CHAPTER 1

Review

This book assumes you already have some experience at the piano. You should know how to read music in both treble and bass clefs. You should also have some experience playing major and minor scales and be familiar with the differences between their sounds. In this chapter, a few basic concepts and scales that are used throughout the series will be reviewed.

Notes

Musical notes are placed on lines and spaces of the staff. The *treble clef* is usually used to notate the right hand, and the bass clef is usually used for the left hand. *Ledger lines* are little lines added above and below the staff. By extending the staff, ledger lines provide a way to indicate notes out of the range of the five-line staff.

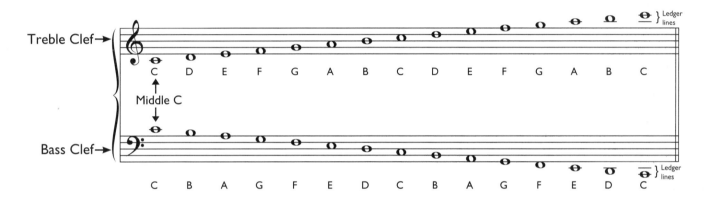

Accidentals are symbols that alter the pitch of a note. A sharp sign (♯) raises the pitch by a half step, meaning that you play a half step (the next available note) to the right of the note that comes after the sign. A *flat* sign (♭) lowers the pitch by a half step, meaning that you play a half step to the left of the note after the sign. Usually, sharps and flats are black keys. A *natural* (♮) sign cancels the preceding accidental. Sharps and flats last until the end of the measure in which they appear. When you go to a new measure, the slate is clean.

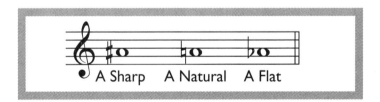

Sometimes there are different ways of writing the same note. Notes that sound the same but have different names are called *enharmonic* notes.

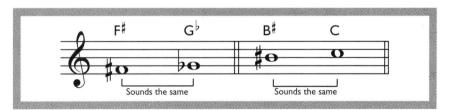

Once you know which notes to play, you need to know the *rhythm*. Rhythm is a series of various durations. It's easy...if you can count to four, then you're on the verge of mastering rhythm.

A *beat* is the basic unit of time in music. Each note is held for specific amount of time that is measured in beats. For instance, a *quarter note* ♩ lasts for one beat. *Rests*, indicating silence, are valued the same way.

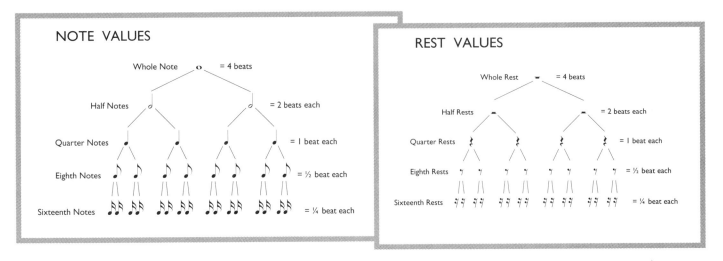

Each piece begins with a *time signature* which tells us how long each measure lasts. The bottom number shows the kind of note that equals one beat (4 means quarter note, 8 means eighth note, etc.). The top number shows how many beats are in each measure.

$\dfrac{4}{4}$ ← 4 beats per measure
← Quarter note = 1 beat

$\dfrac{3}{8}$ ← 3 beats per measure
← Eighth note = 1 beat

If you add the values of the notes and rests in a measure, you have the top number from the time signature. By counting the beats you can consistently keep track of the rhythm. You can say "one, two, three, four, one, two . . ." to yourself or just feel the pulse.

A dot after a note or rest increases its value by half. For example, a dotted half note equals three beats.

𝅗𝅥	+	♩	=	𝅗𝅥.
2		1		3

If the beats in a measure are divided (with eighth notes, sixteenth notes, etc.), you can count the *subdivisions* or fractions within the beat. With eighth notes count "one and two and three and four and ..." and with sixteenth notes count "one e and a, two e and a ..." to keep track of the rhythm.

An interval is the distance between two notes. The most basic building blocks for intervals are half steps and whole steps. A half step is the shortest distance between two notes and two of these make a whole step. The major scale is made up of this pattern of whole and half steps:

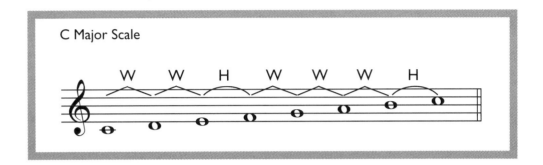

W = Whole step
H = Half step

The intervals we use have more specific names, though. Below are the intervals that make up the C Major scale. Check out the number that goes with each note and the names of the intervals.

By counting from one note to another (including the one you started on), you can find the interval that the two notes create. From F to D, count F, G, A, B, C, D - that's six, so you have a 6th. Then there are the other notes, those that don't belong to the C Major scale. Let's see what the numbers and interval names are there.

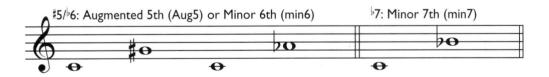

A perfect or major interval that is made a half step bigger is called augmented, and a perfect or minor interval that is made a half step smaller is called diminished. The ♯4/♭5 is sometimes called a tritone, because its size is three "tones" (the British terminology for whole steps).

Refer to this chart to remember the numbers and interval names based on their size in half steps.

Number	Number of Half Steps	Interval	Abbreviation
1	0	perfect unison	PU
♭2	1	minor 2nd	min2
2	2	major 2nd	Maj2
♭3	3	minor 3rd	min3
3	4	major 3rd	Maj3
4	5	perfect 4th	P4
♯4	6 ("tritone")	augmented 4th	Aug4
♭5	6 ("tritone")	diminished 5th	dim5
5	7	perfect 5th	P5
♯5	8	augmented 5th	Aug5
♭6	8	minor 6th	min6
6	9	major 6th	Maj6
♭7	10	minor 7th	min7
7	11	major 7th	Maj7
1	12	perfect octave	P8

Try forming each of these intervals going both up and down from different notes on the keyboard. Play them both melodically (one note at a time) and harmonically (both notes at the same time), and try to learn the characteristic sound of each interval.

INTERVAL INVERSION

Here's a neat trick to quickly figure out some of the intervals. Inversion, which means turning an interval upside down, can be used by remembering that *everything equals nine*.

If you want to find a minor 7th down from C, turn it upside down and go up a major 2nd (7 + 2 = 9) and you get the same note, D. When dealing with larger intervals like this, inversion helps you figure them out by using smaller, more manageable intervals. Take a look at the examples and at the chart below. When inverting, perfect intervals become other perfect intervals. Major becomes minor and vice versa. Augmented becomes diminished and vice versa.

From C: minor 7th down   From C: major 2nd up

From C: major 6th up   From C: minor 3rd down

Interval Inversion Chart

Perfect inverts to perfect
Major inverts to minor
Augmented inverts to diminished
2nd inverts to 7th
3rd inverts to 6th
4th inverts to 5th

KEY SIGNATURES

As we observed on page 9, the major scale always has the same pattern of whole steps and half steps: whole, whole, half, whole, whole, whole, half. That's why the major scale always has a certain sound no matter what the starting pitch is. Key signatures are derived from scales and tell us which notes have to be raised (with sharps) or lowered (with flats) throughout a piece. Sometimes a scale or piece will be in a minor key rather than a major one. If we play the major scale beginning on the sixth degree of the scale instead of the first degree, the new scale that is produced is called the *relative minor*. The relative minor always has the same key signature as the major scale it comes from.

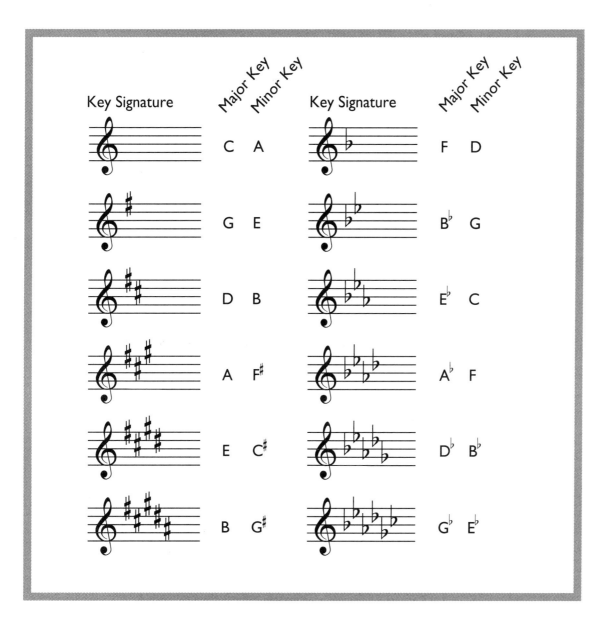

Look at the key signatures on the previous page. Note that with the sharp keys, every time you move up the *interval of a 5th* (a distance of 3½ steps, or 7 half steps) you add a sharp. With the flat keys, every time you move down a 5th you add a flat. This brings us to the circle of 5ths. This circle organizes scales and key signatures in 5ths. As you will see, the scales and keys that are most closely related are not the ones that are close together on the keyboard, but rather, the ones that are close together on the circle of 5ths.

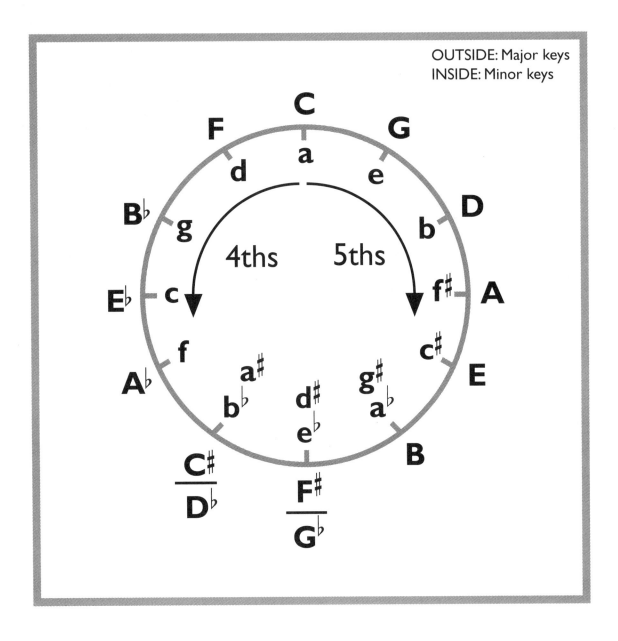

MAJOR SCALES

Here is a review of the twelve major scales. Right hand fingerings are shown above the scale and Left hand fingerings are shown below the scale. Play the left hand scale one octave (8va) lower.

R.H. = Right hand
L.H. = Left hand

C MAJOR (No #'s, no ♭'s)

G MAJOR (One sharp: F#)

D MAJOR (Two sharps: F# and C#)

A MAJOR (Three sharps: F#, C# and G#)

① Menka
② Roses From the South
③ Cancan
④ The Firebird

F MAJOR (One flat: B♭)

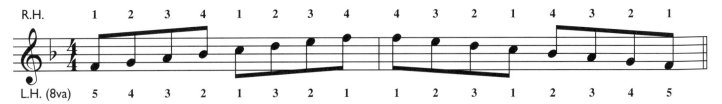

B♭ MAJOR (Two flats: B♭ and E♭)

E♭ MAJOR (Three flats: B♭, E♭ and A♭)

A♭ MAJOR (Four flats: B♭, E♭, A♭ and D♭)

D♭ MAJOR (Five flats: B♭, E♭, A♭ D♭ and G♭)

G♭ MAJOR (Six flats: B♭, E♭, A♭, D♭, G♭ and C♭)

NATURAL MINOR SCALES

The natural form of the minor scale contains 8 notes and has the following pattern of whole steps and half steps: whole, half, whole, whole, half, whole, whole. The natural minor scale has a ♭3, ♭6, and ♭7 compared to its parallel major scale. Parallel keys share the same tonic note but have completely different key signatures. For example, A minor has no sharps or flats in its key signature but its parallel key, A major, has three sharps.

A MINOR, relative of C Major (No #'s, no ♭'s)

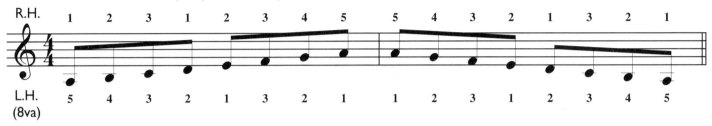

E MINOR, relative of G Major (One sharp: F#)

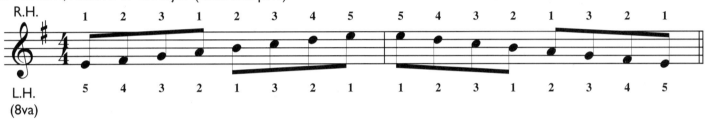

B MINOR, relative of D Major (Two sharps: F# and C#)

F# MINOR, relative of A Major (Three sharps: F#, C# and G#)

C# MINOR, relative of E Major (Four sharps: F#, C#, G# and D#)

G# MINOR, relative of B Major (Five sharps: F#, C#, G#, D# and A#)

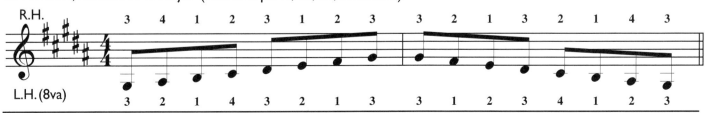

D MINOR, relative of F Major (One flat: B♭)

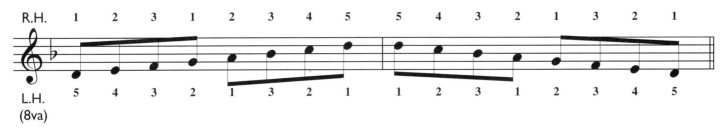

G MINOR, relative of B♭ Major (Two flats: B♭ and E♭)

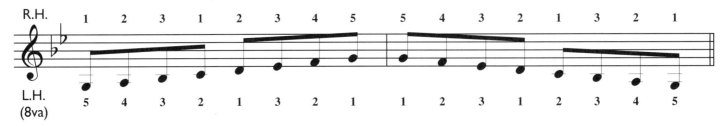

C MINOR, relative of E♭ Major (Three flats: B♭, E♭ and A♭)

F MINOR, relative of A♭ Major (Four flats: B♭, E♭, A♭ and D♭)

B♭ MINOR, relative of D♭ Major (Five Flats: B♭, E♭, A♭, D♭ and G♭)

E♭ MINOR, relative of G♭ Major (Six Flats: B♭, E♭, A♭, D♭, G♭ and C♭)

HARMONIC MINOR SCALES

The harmonic minor is an important scale. As the name implies, we use it to derive harmonies.
It has a raised 7 compared to the ♭7 in the natural minor.

A MINOR, relative of C Major (No #'s, no ♭'s)

E MINOR, relative of G Major (One sharp: F#)

B MINOR, relative of D Major (Two sharps: F# and C#)

F# MINOR, relative of A Major (Three sharps: F#, C# and G#)

C# MINOR, relative of E Major (Four sharps: F#, C#, G# and D#)

G# MINOR, relative of B Major (Five sharps: F#, C#, G#, D# and A#)

✖ = *Double sharp.* Raise note one whole step (two half steps)

D MINOR, relative of F Major (One flat: B♭)

R.H.

L.H.
(8va)

G MINOR, relative of B♭ Major (Two flats: B♭ and E♭)

R.H.

L.H.
(8va)

C MINOR, relative of E♭ Major (Three flats: B♭, E♭ and A♭)

R.H.

L.H.
(8va)

F MINOR, relative of A♭ Major (Four flats: B♭, E♭, A♭ and D♭)

R.H.

L.H.
(8va)

B♭ MINOR, relative of D♭ Major (Five flats: B♭, E♭, A♭, D♭ and G♭)

R.H.

L.H.
(8va)

E♭ MINOR, relative of G♭ Major (Six flats: B♭, E♭, A♭, D♭, G♭ and C♭)

R.H.

L.H.
(8va)

CHAPTER 2

Intro to Harmony

Have you ever played more than one note at a time on the keyboard? If so, you have had hands-on experience with harmony. On the most basic level, harmony is anything that involves two or more notes sounding at the same time. Most of the harmony we'll be using involves *chords*, stacks of three or more notes. Guitarists and keyboardists are fortunate to play instruments that allow us to play chords as well as melodies. Some great pianists like Bill Evans and George Shearing are known for using rich chords with many notes, while others like Count Basie and Thelonious Monk made use of simple, sparse harmonies, sometimes using only two or three notes in a chord. Either way, an understanding of harmony is a priceless tool for all of us.

TRIADS

Chords are built using the intervals of the major and minor 3rd. *Triads* are three-note chords. Most Western music, from classical to rock, is based on triads. Triads are built by stacking 3rds derived from the scale. To build a C Major chord, use the first degree of the C Major scale, C, the third degree of the scale, E, and the 5th, G. Starting from the bottom, the notes of the triad are referred to as the root, the 3rd and the 5th. In a major chord, the intervals above the root are a major 3rd (C to E) followed by a minor 3rd (E to G). The interval from the root to the 5th is a perfect 5th.

To build a *minor triad*, take a major triad and flat (lower) the 3rd by a half step, leaving the root and 5th the same. The order of the intervals in a minor chord is a minor 3rd followed by a major 3rd. The perfect 5th remains the same as in the major chord.

To build an *augmented triad*, take a major triad and sharp (raise) the 5th by a half step. The order of the intervals is a major 3rd followed by another major 3rd. The perfect 5th has changed to an augmented 5th.

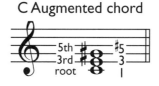

To build a *diminished triad*, take a minor triad and flat the 5th by a half step. The order of the intervals is a minor 3rd followed by another minor 3rd. The perfect 5th has been changed to a diminished 5th.

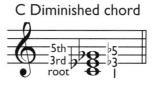

Another type of triad you might encounter is the suspended triad. This is an honorary member of the triad family, not typically mentioned in the same breath as the "big four." The suspended triad has a perfect 4th and a perfect 5th, but no 3rd. The typical use of this chord is for the 4th to resolve to the 3rd of a major triad with the same root, although this chord is sometimes found by itself.

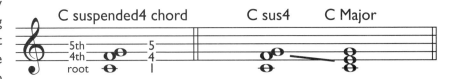

This chart shows the abbreviated symbols which are used to notate each type of chord. In each case, the first symbol listed is the one that will be used in this series. Chord symbols are a shorthand way of indicating what chord is to be played.

Chord	Possible Symbols	Formula
C Major	C, CMaj, CM, C△	1, 3, 5
C minor	Cmin, Cmi, Cm, C-	1, ♭3, 5
C Augmented	CAug, C+	1, 3, ♯5
C diminished	Cdim, C°	1, ♭3, ♭5
C Suspended4	Csus4, Csus	1, 4, 5

In Harmony will give you a chance to play some triads. Practice the chords first and then add the melody. Look at the chord symbols and notice what chords you are playing.

IN HARMONY

Track 2

INVERSIONS

The notes C, E and G, form a C Major triad. This is true regardless of the order of the notes. A chord with the root on the bottom is in *root position*. A triad whose lowest note isn't the root is in an *inversion*. A triad with the 3rd on the bottom is in *1st inversion*. If the 5th is on the bottom, the chord is in *2nd inversion*.

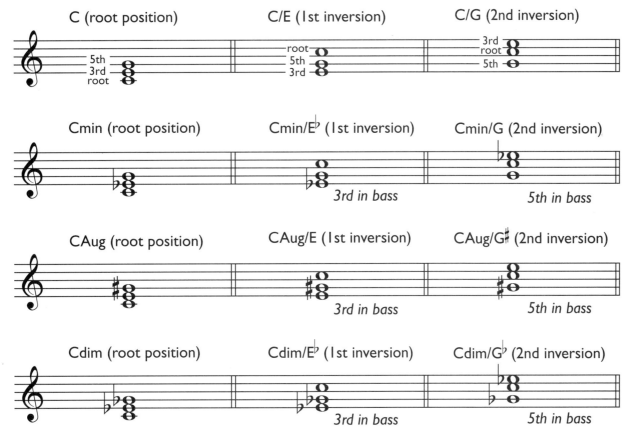

Inverted chords are usually notated as *slash chords*. Slash chords are chords where some note other than the root is the bass (lowest) note. The chord comes before the slash (/) and the bass note comes after the slash. For example, a C/G indicates a second inversion C chord.

VOICING

Voicing is the specific way that the notes in chords are arranged. As mentioned above, any chord is valid as long as it contains all of the notes in that chord. Inversions are used to create smoother and more melodic voice leading. By putting the root in the bass, we can maintain the root position sound. Check out these different ways to voice a C Major triad in root position.

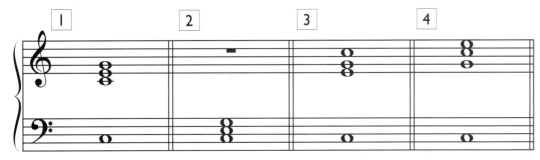

The third and fourth voicings use inversions in the right hand. These are root position chords because the left hand is still playing the root of the chord in the bass. In voicings 1, 3, and 4, the root is played twice, once in each hand. This is called *doubling* that note.

Twilight in Sandy Hook uses inversions to voice triads, and includes a few inversions (where the root isn't in the bass). As with *In Harmony*, pay attention to the chord symbols as you play so you're aware of what chord you're playing at any moment. Play this slowly, at first, to thoroughly hear the harmony, and gradually bring it up to tempo.

Pianists often release and depress the pedal as the chords change. This is a little tricky, so practice slowly with the pedal in mind.

Notice the ♩ = 92 marking at the beginning of the piece. This indicates the tempo (speed). Once you are sufficiently comfortable with the notes, set your metronome to 92, count each click as a quarter note and off you go.

TWILIGHT IN SANDY HOOK

Track 3

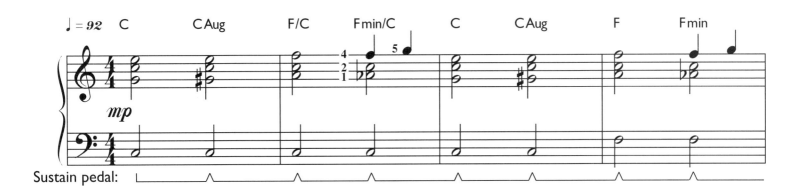

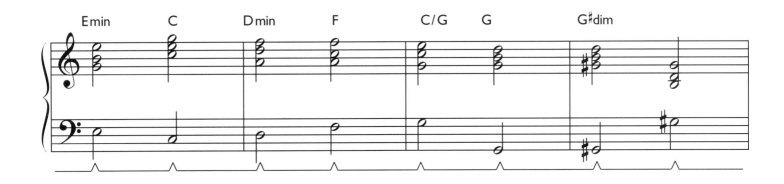

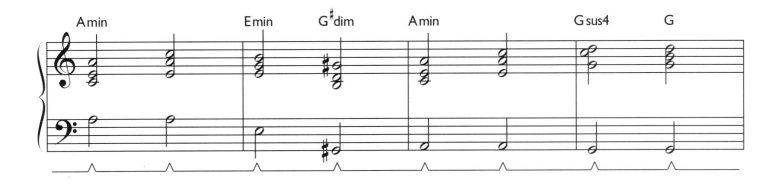

DIATONIC HARMONY

Diatonic means "of the scale." When we refer to diatonic harmony, we mean chords built from a particular scale. The most common way to build these chords is by stacking 3rds from each degree of the scale (through the simple process of skipping every other note). Here are the diatonic chords in the key of C Major derived in this way.

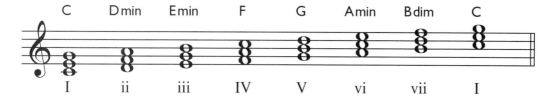

The quality of the chord built on each degree is the same in every major key. We use Roman numerals to signify the scale degree a chord is built on, since that notation is not limited to a particular key (I is I in every key). We use upper case Roman numerals for major and augmented chords and lower case Roman numerals for minor and diminished chords. Here's a quick review of these Roman numerals and their Arabic equivalents.

I	or	i	=	1		V	or	v	=	5
II	or	ii	=	2		VI	or	vi	=	6
III	or	iii	=	3		VII	or	vii	=	7
IV	or	iv	=	4						

In every major key, the type of chord built on each degree is the same:

I	Major		V	Major
ii	Minor		vi	Minor
iii	Minor		vii	Diminished
IV	Major			

When looking for the chords in a particular key, you can refer to the following chart which shows the diatonic chords that belong to each of the twelve keys.

Key	I	ii	iii	IV	V	vi	vii
C	C	Dmin	Emin	F	G	Amin	Bdim
G	G	Amin	Bmin	C	D	Emin	F♯dim
D	D	Emin	F♯min	G	A	Bmin	C♯dim
A	A	Bmin	C♯min	D	E	F♯min	G♯dim
E	E	F♯min	G♯min	A	B	C♯min	D♯dim
B	B	C♯min	D♯min	E	F♯	G♯min	A♯dim
G♭	G♭	A♭min	B♭min	C♭	D♭	E♭min	Fdim
D♭	D♭	E♭min	Fmin	G♭	A♭	B♭min	Cdim
A♭	A♭	B♭min	Cmin	D♭	E♭	Fmin	Gdim
E♭	E♭	Fmin	Gmin	A♭	B♭	Cmin	Ddim
B♭	B♭	Cmin	Dmin	E♭	F	Gmin	Adim
F	F	Gmin	Amin	B♭	C	Dmin	Edim

When you see a good movie, you go for a ride. There are moments of tension and excitement along the way but they're usually resolved by the end. If the tension was constant and unresolved, you'd be edgy and tense driving home from the theater. Without any tension, you'd be bored. Like movies, music has to go somewhere to be interesting. Movement in music creates interest and excitement when it builds and releases tension at the right moments. A *chord progression* is a series of chords that go somewhere. In jazz we sometimes call the chords in a tune *the changes*, since the change in sound as one chord moves to another defines the sound of a progression.

Each chord in a key has a particular sound and function in the context of the other chords in that key. Roman numerals and the chart on the previous page come in handy as we look at chord progressions. A Roman numeral indicates both the type and function of a chord in a key, and the function of a particular numeral carries over to all other keys. Let's look at the most significant chords for a jazz musician in any major key: I, ii and V.

The leading tone, or 7th degree of the major scale, is a very unstable note sounding like it wants to resolve up a half step to the *tonic* (1st degree). In addition, the ear expects to hear root movement downward in 5ths.

When you play the V chord (or dominant):

1) The ear wants to hear the leading tone (the 3rd of the V chord) resolve to the tonic.
2) The ear wants to hear the root of the dominant chord resolve down a 5th to the tonic.

These two elements lead us to the I chord. The sound of V-I is the single most common source of tension and resolution in Western music.

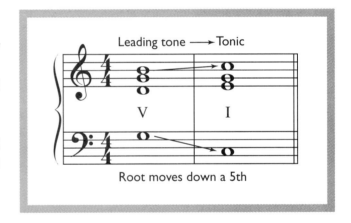

If we use the ii chord before the V chord, we have another instance of downward root movement in 5ths. When the ii moves to the V it's often an upward 4th. By consulting our interval inversion chart, we see that we wind up with the same note and therefore the same effect. The use of the ii chord before the V builds up more tension and intensity, making the resolution to I that much stronger. The ii-V-I progression is the most common progression in jazz. Play the example on the right a few times to get the sound in your head.

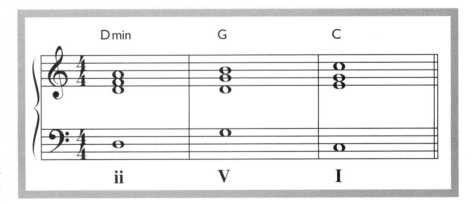

The chart below maps out the basic function of each chord in a major key. Notice that some chords can be substituted for other chords, taking their place in a progression because they have a similar function.

Table of Chord Functions		
I	Tonic	Home. The most stable chord in a key
ii	Supertonic	Gravitates towards V
iii	Mediant	Can substitute for I (though less stable), or gravitate downward a 5th to vi
IV	Subdominant	Can substitute for ii, gravitating towards V. Commonly used in this way in pop/rock tunes
V	Dominant	Gravitates towards I
vi	Submediant	Can substitute for I (relative minor) or gravitate downward a 5th to ii
vii	Leading Tone	Can substitute for V, gravitating towards I

Enough charts and diagrams for now, let's play and hear what's really going on here. *Ton Doo* uses all 7 chords of the major scale, in this case G Major. Notice how each chord sounds in context, and refer back to the table of chord functions afterward to compare notes between what's on the chart and what you heard. The sound is what will really make the chart (or any other bit of theory) make sense.

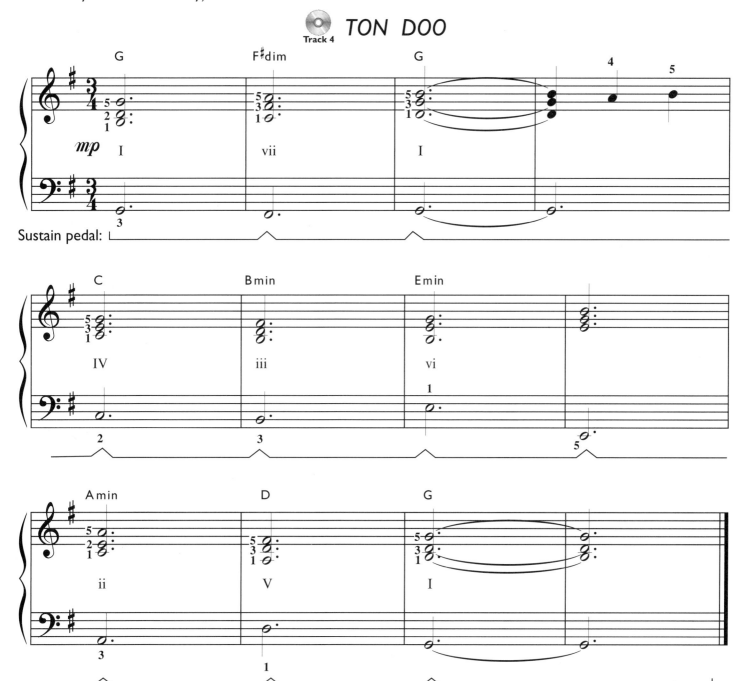

TON DOO
Track 4

One of the biggest sources of tunes for a jazz player is the "fake book" (sometimes called a "real book"), a book of music that generally crams in as many tunes as possible by giving just enough information for us to figure out what to play. Therefore, we have to learn how to read *lead sheets*. A lead sheet gives us the melody and the chord symbols, and lets us voice the chords as we see fit. As we learn more kinds of voicings, that increases our range of choices as we flesh out a lead sheet.

For example, if we saw this four-bar fragment from a lead sheet . . .

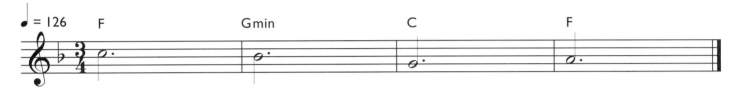

...we might voice it like this, playing the roots in the left hand and using the right hand to play whichever inversion puts the correct melody note on top.

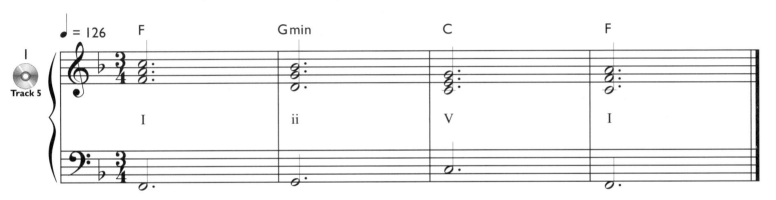

Below is *Ton Doo* in lead sheet form. Try playing through it by just looking at the lead sheet. Form your chords with the bass notes in the left hand and with your right hand play whichever inversion has the melody note on top. In this example, the left hand will always be playing the roots. Once you've tried this, check it against the fully written out version on page 25. Every note doesn't have to match up exactly, but the sound should be similar. Keep going back and forth between the two until you get the hang of it. Notice from the version on page 25 that you need only play one chord per measure, even if there are several notes in the melody. This is only one of the numerous ways to make music from a lead sheet.

TON DOO (LEAD SHEET STYLE)

To play something in a minor key, find the relative major key (the one with the same key signature), and borrow its chords, shifting the Roman numerals to match the key.

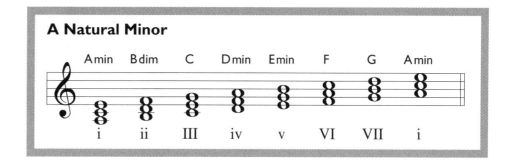

A Natural Minor

Traditionally, the harmonic minor (see p. 17-18) is used for minor key harmony; the same method of stacking 3rds is used, but with the raised 7th in the picture instead of the usual ♭7. Compare the chords of A Natural Minor and A Harmonic Minor.

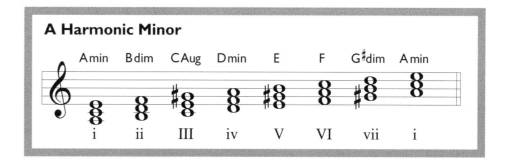

A Harmonic Minor

The most notable difference is the V chord. The major V in the harmonic minor gives a much stronger pull back to i (the minor tonic). This gravity pulling toward i is the main reason for using the harmonic minor. In pop and jazz, the two scales are both used, often interchangeably, and where the chords differ, it simply becomes a matter of choice.

Nellie's Woe is notated here in lead sheet style. Try voicing it with the same method you used for *Ton Doo*. The tune is in the key of A Minor, using both natural and harmonic minor harmonies. Notice in particular the difference in the sounds and impacts of the V chords, E (from A Harmonic Minor) and Emin (from A Natural Minor). The next page has the tune written out.

NELLIE'S WOE (LEAD SHEET)

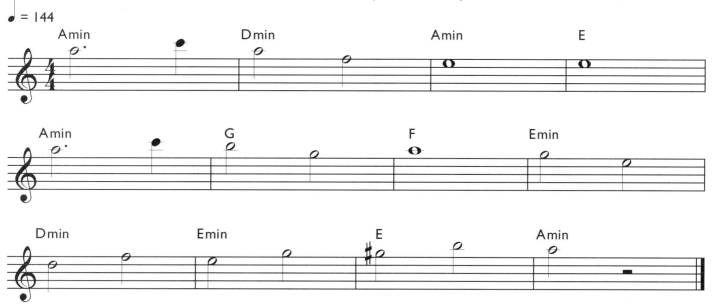

As a reward for your efforts on the previous page, here is *Nellie's Woe* written out fully. Like you did with *Ton Doo*, go back and forth between the lead sheet and the written out music a few times until you become comfortable with the lead sheet.

NELLIE'S WOE

Track 6

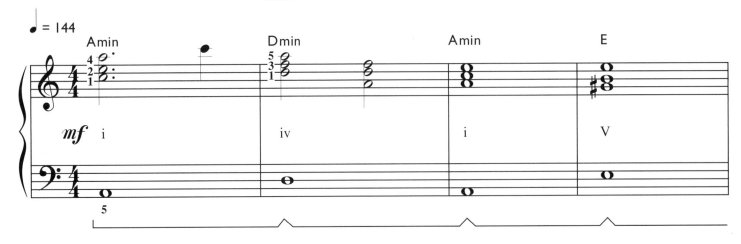

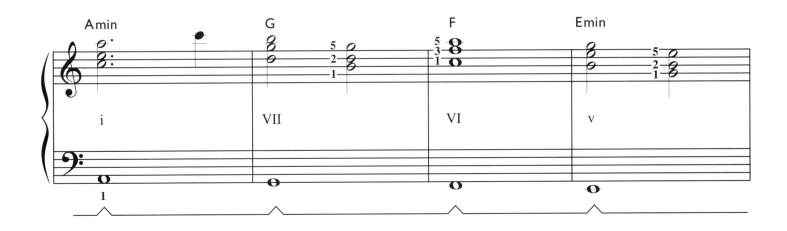

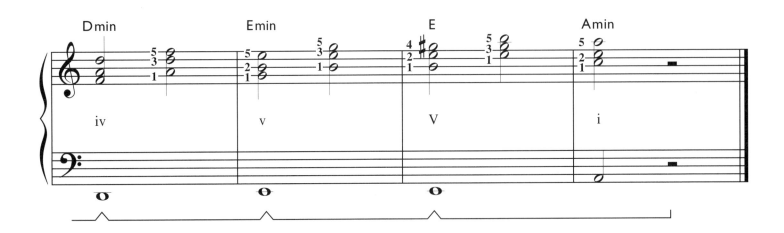

Remember, when playing chords, the pedal can change whenever the chords change. The pedal does not necessarily change when inversions of the same chord are used.

BLUES PROGRESSIONS

The most common chord progression in jazz (or blues or rock) is the twelve-bar blues. In its most basic form, it consists of three four-bar sections:

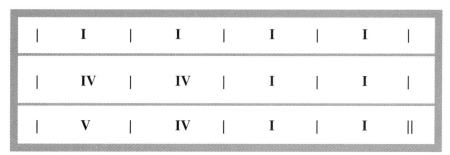

Traditionally, a blues melody presents a four bar phrase, repeats that four bar phrase starting on the IV chord, and then answers it with another four bar phrase starting on the V chord.

> "I got the lonesome purple blues, blues with a little red. (Sho 'nuff baby)
> I
> I got the lonesome purple blues, blues with a little red.
> IV   I
> My bloodshot eyes have been cryin' from all those things you said"
> V   IV   I

Play this progression slowly in a few different keys. Refer back to the diatonic chord chart on page 23 to figure out which chords match up with the numerals for a given key. Once the sound of the progression is in your head, you'll notice how much of the music you hear is based on these chords.

Purple Blues is a twelve-bar blues in F. This time, try playing the chords entirely with the left hand, voiced in root position. The right hand can play the melody. It may be helpful to learn each hand separately first and then put them together. The fully-notated version appears on the next page.

PURPLE BLUES (*LEAD SHEET*)

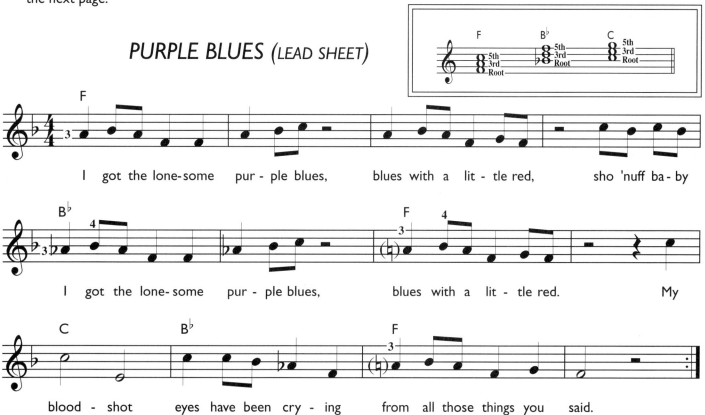

PURPLE BLUES

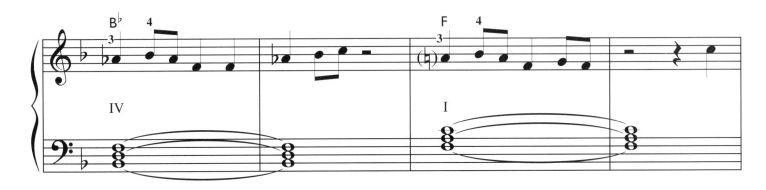

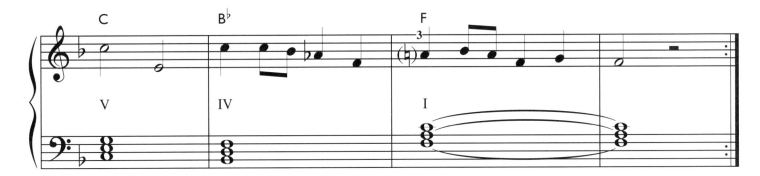

Note:

When playing more involved single-note lines like those in *Purple Blues*, the pedal is used infrequently (or not at all), as it would make the lines sound muddy.

*Born in 1894, **James P. Johnson** became known as the father of stride piano. In the 1920s his popularity flourished. He was also a prolific composer of songs, piano pieces and concert music.*

CHAPTER 3

Feel, Scales and Soloing

It's fun. It's creative. It's liberating. It's expressive. It's in the here and now. It's fundamental to the world of jazz and to life itself. It's *improvisation*! Improvisation is the act of spontaneously playing music, making up the things you play as you go along. If you've ever had a conversation, you have used the skill of improvisation. You can't have a real conversation if you plan out everything you're going to say beforehand. You need to be in the moment and respond to whatever is being said. Your control of the language allows you to spontaneously express your thoughts.

Jazz improvisation is no different. You use whatever information you have at your disposal to put your ideas and feelings into music. This music is generally not pulled out of thin air. Instead, the jazz musician learns a musical language of scales, chords, rhythms and so on. When it's time to "speak," this knowledge acts as the foundation for improvised expression.

The most dramatic use of improvisation is the solo. If you listen to live or recorded jazz, it often revolves around solos. The *head*, which is the basic melody of a tune, is played at the beginning and the end of a piece. In between, you hear some or all of the players improvise solos. The chance to solo is a wonderful opportunity for a jazz musician. Not only are your ideas in the forefront, but they are the ideas that you have right at that moment.

PHOTO COURTESY OF THE INSTITUTE OF JAZZ STUDIES

Earl "Bud" Powell, an important bebop innovator, set the standard for modern jazz keyboard soloing in the 1940s.

STYLE

Imagine a room with four people in it. One is from New York, one is from Texas, one is from London and one is from Dublin, Ireland. All four speak the same language, yet each one sounds very distinct. None of them are speaking more or less correctly than the others, but the accents are different.

Jazz "feel" is like a distinct dialect within the language of music. No scholar is likely to accurately describe how to phrase in a jazz style, but that style does exist. The key is to listen. You couldn't imitate a Scottish accent if you'd never heard one. Likewise, you need to hear jazz to play and understand its rhythms, feel and phrasing. Check out the list of recommended albums on page 96, seek out a jazz-loving friend, teacher, librarian or record store employee, and go hear the best jazz players in your area. Soak in everything you can. The more good stuff you have in your ears, the easier it is to phrase in a jazz style. As you hear more and learn more, you'll begin making choices. You may dig one keyboardist's style and be less into another's. In the end, you ultimately sound like yourself, a personalized mixture of everything you've heard and everything you like.

Okay, quiz time.

Swing is:

   a) A popular sub-style of jazz that had its heyday in the 1930s.

   b) A kind of rhythm that serves as a common thread in most jazz phrasing.

   c) A really good feeling that all jazz musicians strive for.

   d) All of the above and more!

If you guessed "d," you are an astute jazzhead well on your way to being righteously swingin'!

The term "swing" was popularized in the 1930s, particularly with big bands. The most respected and popular jazz musicians were praised with names like "the King of Swing" (Benny Goodman), and "the Swinginest Band in All the Land" (Count Basie's). Even as big bands declined in popularity, the feeling of swing remained as a fundamental part of jazz, one that has been there since its early days.

To understand the swing feel, we need to look at the *triplet*. When we divide the beat in two, we get eighth notes. When we divide an eighth note in two, we get sixteenth notes. With triplets, we divide the beat in three. We can count "one-and-a, two-and-a, three . . ." to keep track of the beat.

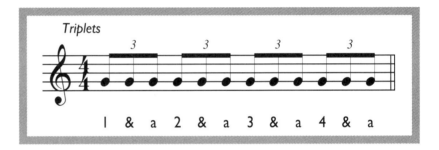

Jazz is usually played and notated using *swing eighth notes*. A pair of swing eighths sounds like a triplet with the first two notes tied together (a tie makes a note last as long as both tied notes combined, without repeating the note).

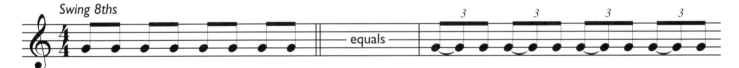

Unless you're told otherwise, assume that all of the following pieces from here on are to be played using swing eighths. Listen to the way different players play their eighth notes. Many old-style players hold the first eighth in a pair for even longer than the $^2/_3$ of a beat shown above, whereas some players play them more evenly. Use the above triplet-based method as a basic guideline for playing swing eighths, but keep your ears open, too. Like jazz style in general, swing is a concept that is hard to notate but it is very important. If someone says you're swingin', you've just been given one of the highest compliments a jazz musician can receive.

You're about to appreciate the time you've put into practicing the major scale, because you're going to use it to begin improvising. First, practice the left hand part below (a four-bar pattern in C Major) until it is comfortable. Then add the right hand, playing the C Major scale up and down on top of the chords. Repeat this exercise in a continuous loop until it is comfortable enough that you can keep it going without much effort or thought. Remember to swing the eighths.

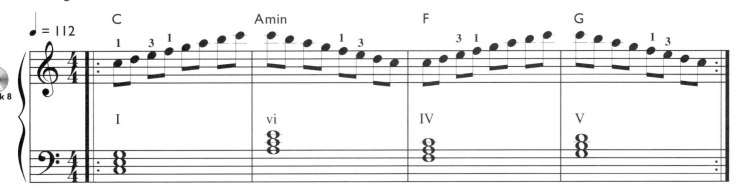

Now let's try improvising over these changes (chords). Like the exercise above, we'll play up and down the scale as the chords go by. This time, however, we'll try changing the rhythm here and there to keep it interesting (making sure that the right hand doesn't overlap with notes in the left hand's chords). Here is how that might sound.

That already sounds pretty good, but now let's try adding some leaps (notes that aren't next to each other in the scale) and some repeated notes.

Sponge on a Stick is in the key of D Major, and the melody uses only the D Major scale. Once you've learned the tune, go back and try the techniques from the previous page to solo with the D Major scale. Keep the left hand the same and remember to swing the eighth notes!

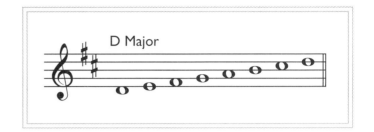

SPONGE ON A STICK

Track 11

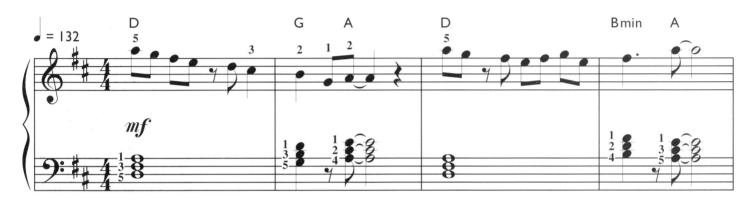

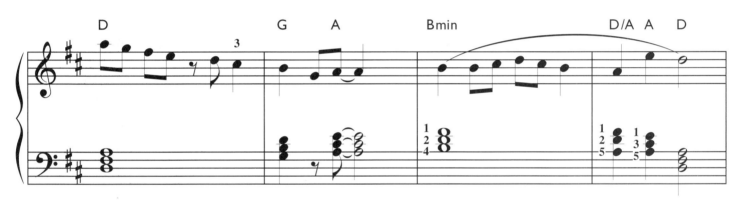

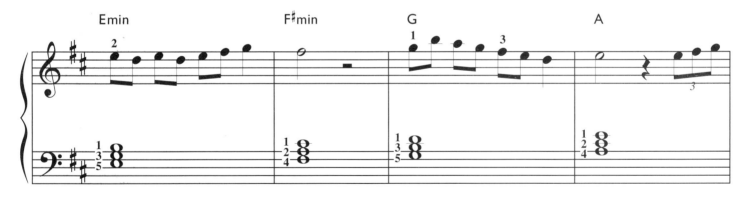

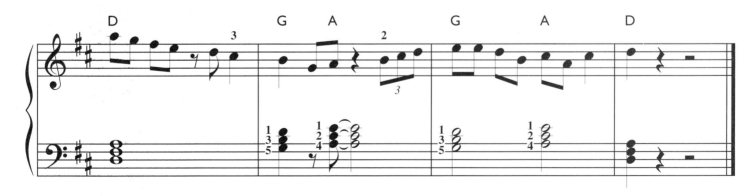

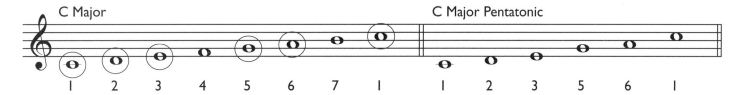

THE MAJOR PENTATONIC SCALE

In Greek, *Penta* means "five," and *tonic* means "tone." A pentatonic scale is any scale with five different notes (all the scales we've learned so far have seven). The *major pentatonic scale* is derived from the major scale. To find any major pentatonic scale, simply take the major scale in the same key and eliminate the 4th and 7th degrees. You're left with 1, 2, 3, 5 and 6.

The pentatonic scales are probably the handiest scales for an inexperienced improviser to know, because if you use them over diatonic progressions, it's very hard to play anything that sounds like a wrong note. The pentatonic sound is very accessible. Once you have the scale under your fingers and the sound in your head, you'll be improvising catchy melodies in no time.

Dedicated to pioneering jazz pianist Earl "Fatha" Hines, *Fatha Fatha* is in the key of F Major and uses the F Major Pentatonic scale. When you know the melody, try improvising over the chords using the F Major Pentatonic scale.

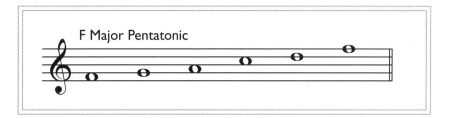

FATHA FATHA

Track 12

Syncopation is emphasizing the weak beats and weak parts of the beat instead of the strong beats. In jazz that especially means playing "off" the beat (on the "&'s") instead of consistently landing on the downbeats. Notice the difference below.

In the syncopated example, notice the note on the "&" of four of the first bar (tied to the beginning of the second bar). This is called *anticipation*, because it anticipates the next bar by half a beat. An anticipated note can be tied over to the beat it anticipates or there can be a rest on the beat being anticipated. Either way the ear will still hear the note as relating to the beat it anticipates, but with an added rhythmic bite. When you listen to jazz, be aware of anticipations and other syncopation.

When you're dealing with syncopation, it becomes even more important than usual to keep track of the beat, because the rhythm in the music is less predictable and you don't want it to throw you off. When you encounter music with a lot of syncopation, learn it slowly. Count every beat and division of the beat. Sing or clap the rhythm as you count. Jazz rhythm thrives on syncopation. As you become more comfortable playing both on and off the beat, you will inevitably become much more swingin'.

The example below shows a solo over *Fatha Fatha,* still derived entirely from the F Major Pentatonic scale. Much of it is syncopated, particularly from the use of anticipations. Take your time learning it. Pay attention to the difference in feel between a note landing on the beat and one that anticipates that beat. Syncopations are highlighted in grey.

SOLO ON FATHA FATHA

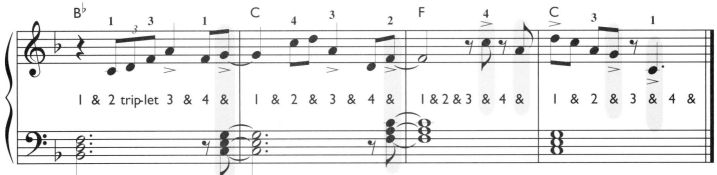

Note:

When anticipation occurs, the chord symbol is placed over the beat that is anticipated, not over the anticipated note itself. This helps to keep track of where the fundamental rhythm is.

The *minor pentatonic scale* has a lot in common with the major pentatonic scale. It has five notes, is derived from a scale we already know, and it can be an easy to use tool for convincing improvisation. The scale is derived from the natural minor scale by omitting 2 and ♭6 and playing only 1, ♭3, 4, 5 and ♭7.

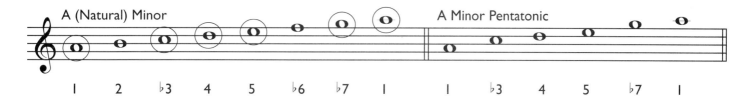

This scale is very useful with minor chord progressions, whether they're based on the natural or harmonic minor. To perhaps an even greater extent than with the major pentatonic scale, it is very hard to play anything that sounds like a wrong note when you use this scale over minor-key changes.

EMBELLISHING A MELODY

One of the earliest forms of jazz improvisation was the embellishment of written melodies. Rather than improvising a melody completely from scratch, players would take a pre-existing melody and change it around — maybe change the rhythm here, add a couple notes there, leave a couple out over here and so on. Let's look at a phrase in G Minor, using the G Minor Pentatonic scale.

6a
Track 15

Now that we have this little chunk of melody, we can play around with it almost endlessly to come up with new material. Check out some examples, still using the G Minor Pentatonic scale.

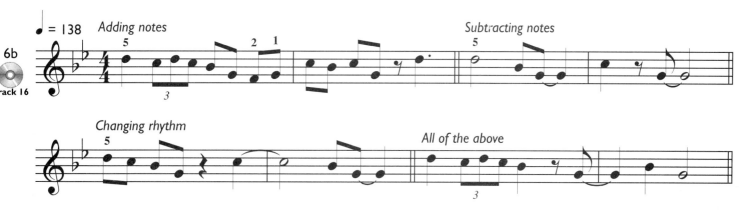

6b
Track 16

Here's *Basie's Minor Boogie*, dedicated to Count Basie. Once again, learn the written melody first, then try improvising over the chords. Try embellishing the melody, and also try improvising completely new melodies. All the while, use the G Minor Pentatonic scale.

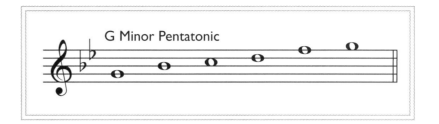

BASIE'S MINOR BOOGIE

Track 17

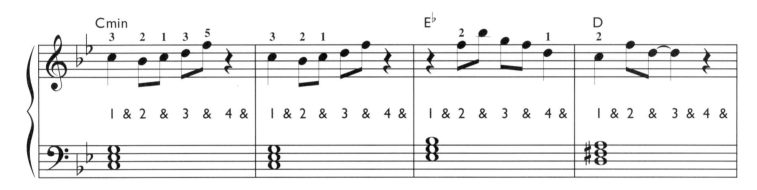

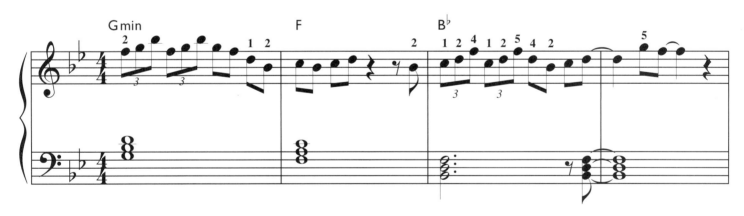

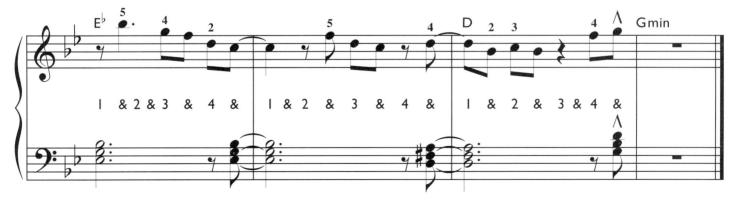

THE BLUES SCALE

In analyzing African-American spirituals, blues, and jazz, certain notes in a scale are called *blue notes* since they are said to have a distinctly mournful, emotive, "bluesy" quality. Some notes are just more blue than others. The notes in any key or scale that are most commonly called *blue notes* are the ♭3, ♭5 and ♭7. The pentatonic minor scale already has a ♭3 and a ♭7, but doesn't have a ♭5. To derive the *blues scale*, we take the pentatonic minor scale and add a ♭5 in between the 4 and the 5, giving us all three blue notes in one six-note scale. To build any blues scale, use 1, ♭3, 4, ♭5, 5 and ♭7.

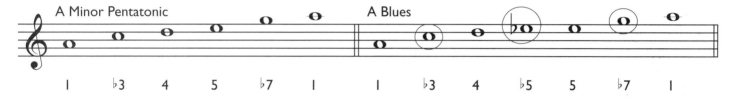

You can use the blues scale in the same places as the minor pentatonic scale: in minor-key progressions. Sometimes you can use it over other progressions, particularly blues progressions, to add a distinctively bluesy, gritty sound. For example, you could noodle over the chords from *Purple Blues* (p. 29) using the F Blues scale. In jazz, blues, and rock music, this scale is indispensable. Some guitarists and keyboardists have built reputations and careers with solos using little or nothing else besides the blues scale. And if you combine this scale with a good groove, it's unstoppable.

TWO AND FOUR

Another key to swinging is recognizing the importance of beats two and four in a bar of $\frac{4}{4}$ time. If you listen to the drum beat on virtually any rock tune, you'll hear the drummer accenting the 2nd and 4th beat of every bar on the snare drum. This is called the *backbeat*. In jazz, the backbeat is generally more subtle, but the players hear it even if nobody is explicitly playing it. To practice, try playing simple rhythms or tunes you know well at the piano. On the two and four, tap your foot or snap your fingers on your free hand (if you have one).

You'll often see jazz players (or hip fans) snapping their fingers on the two and four, a sign that they feel the pulse of the music rocking off the backbeat. Often, watching or hearing the click of the drummer's hi-hat cymbals will clue you in as to where the backbeat is on a swinging tune. Develop your ability to feel and hear this backbeat naturally.

Note:

A common and effective way to practice feeling the backbeat is to set your metronome at half the normal tempo for a quarter note and think of the clicks as the two and four.

Yes, Les McCann Can is dedicated to the great jazz keyboardist Les McCann, who made much use of the blues scale over the years. And yes, he can play the blues. The melody is based on the E Blues scale. Learn it well, and then try playing it with your right hand while snapping or tapping the backbeat. And, of course, solo over the chords with the E Blues scale.

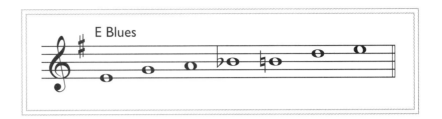

YES, LES McCANN CAN

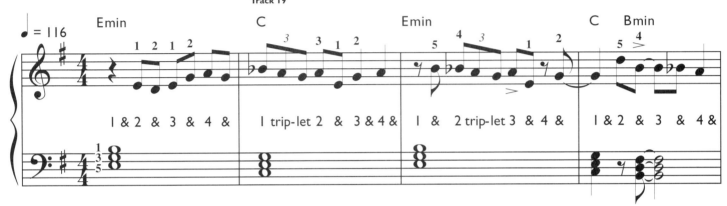

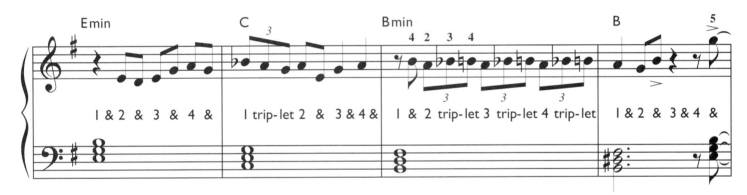

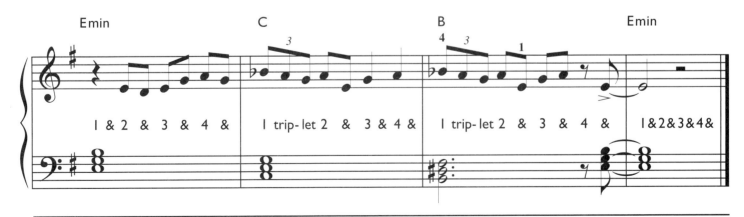

CHAPTER 4

Intro to Four-Note Chords

In Chapter 2, we learned how to formulate triads, three-note chords made up of root, 3rd and 5th. 7th chords are formed the same way but they have four notes: root, 3rd, 5th and 7th. If you're used to triads, the sound will take some getting used to, but 7th chords are colorful, versatile and much more common in jazz than triads.

We can find each of the 5 main types of 7th chords by taking a triad we already know and adding a note.

The *major 7th chord* takes a major triad and adds a major 7th on top.
The formula is 1, 3, 5, 7.

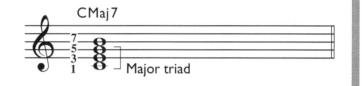

The *dominant 7th chord* takes a major triad and adds a minor 7th. It is called dominant since it is generally built on the 5th (dominant) degree of a scale or key.
The formula is 1, 3, 5, ♭7.

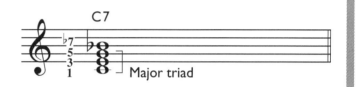

The *minor 7th chord* takes a minor triad and adds a minor 7th.
The formula is 1, ♭3, 5, ♭7.

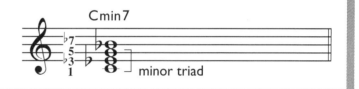

The *minor 7th flat five* (or "half-diminished") chord takes a diminished triad and adds a minor 7th. The name half-diminished means that the 5th is diminished but not the 7th (as opposed to the "fully diminished" chord below).
The formula is 1, ♭3, ♭5, ♭7.

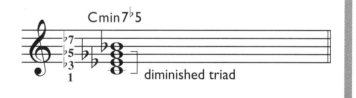

The *diminished 7th chord* takes a diminished triad and adds a diminished 7th. The diminished 7th on top is enharmonically equivalent to a major 6th. **The formula is 1, ♭3, ♭5, 6 (or ♭♭7).***

*Rather than use the ♭♭7, we will substitute the equivalent 6th spelling for simplicity.

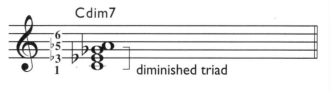

6th chords are another kind of four-note chord that we use in jazz. Rather than being built as root, 3rd, 5th, 7th, a 6th chord is root, 3rd, 5th and <u>6th</u>. We can find and build 6th chords the same way we built 7th chords, starting with a triad and adding a note on top.

The *Major 6th chord* takes a major triad and adds a major 6th.
The formula is 1, 3, 5, 6.
The major 6th chord and major 7th chord are interchangeable with regard to their function.

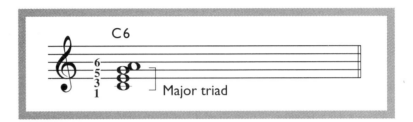

The *minor 6th chord* takes a minor triad and adds a major 6th.
The formula is 1, ♭3, 5, 6.
The minor 6th chord is often used

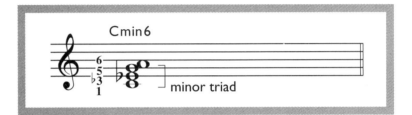

This chart shows the common symbols used for the different types of 7th and 6th chords. As with the triads, the first symbol listed for each chord is the one that will be used in these books.

Chord	Possible Symbols	Formula
C Major 7th	CMaj7, CM7, C△7	1, 3, 5, 7
C Major 6th	C6, CMaj6, CM6, C△6	1, 3, 5, 6
C Dominant 7th	C7	1, 3, 5, ♭7
C Minor 7th	Cmin7, Cmi7, Cm7, C-7	1, ♭3, 5, ♭7
C Minor 6th	Cmin6, Cmi6, Cm6, C-6	1, ♭3, 5, 6
C Minor 7th (flat 5)	Cmin7♭5, Cmi7♭5, Cm7♭5, C-7♭5, Cm7-5, Cø	1, ♭3, ♭5, ♭7
C Diminished 7th	Cdim7, C°7	1, ♭3, ♭5, 6 (♭♭7)

Try playing each of these chords starting on any note. Pick a root and use the formula for each chord to play all seven of these chords from that root. Also, you can pick a chord type and play it through the circle of 5ths.

The exercise below will take you through all seven of these chord types. Play it as written, and then play it an octave lower with your left hand so that each hand gets a chance to play the chords. Make sure to look at the chord symbols and be aware of which chords you're playing.

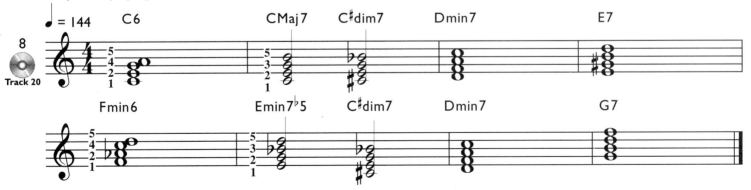

Inversion of four-note chords is done the same way as with triads, but now we have four forms of each chord. The intervals are inverted too, so you'll notice that the 7ths become 2nds in the inverted 7th chords, often giving the chords an intense, biting sound.

Note:

Notice that the 3rd inversion C6 chord has the same notes as a root position Amin7 chord. Likewise, the 3rd inversion Cmin6 chord has the same notes as a root position Amin7♭5 chord. In jazz harmony, you will often find instances where a single harmony could have several names and functions. This isn't supposed to be bewildering, it is actually a source of freedom. When you're in that situation, the chord can be whichever you want it to be at that moment.

Inversions of these chords, like triad inversions, can also be used in the right hand over roots in the left hand (or, as we'll see, in the left hand over roots played by a bassist) to give us a greater variety of root position chord voicings. This will be your greatest use for the inversions. It is uncommon to find 7th chords with non-root bass notes in jazz tunes, but the need for inversions in voicings will arise often. Here are some examples of a C7 chord voiced this way.

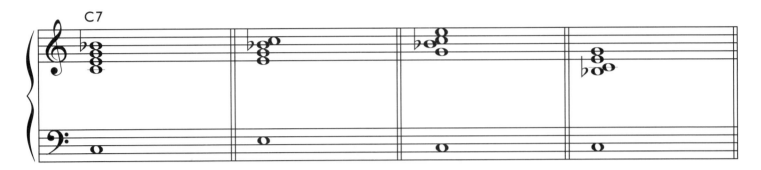

Play *All You Need Is Seven* for some more practice playing 7th and 6th chords. Like you did with *Twilight in Sandy Hook* (page 22), play it slowly to get the sound of each chord in your ears and then increase the tempo to get your hands used to the movement. Many of the chords will be voiced with inversions in the right hand and with the left playing roots as bass notes. Watch the chord symbols to make sure you always know what chords you're playing as you play them. The changes are in the style of the standard tune *Don't Blame Me*, popularized by Charlie Parker.

ALL YOU NEED IS SEVEN
Track 21

DIATONIC HARMONY WITH 7TH CHORDS

We build diatonic 7th chords in a key the same way we build triads. The only difference is that we stack an extra note on top.

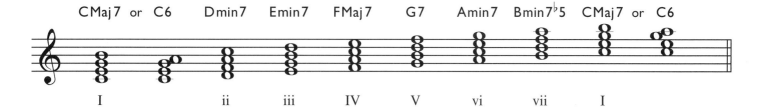

In every major key, the following 7th chords are built from each degree of the scale:

I	Maj7		V	(Dominant) 7
ii	min7		vi	min7
iii	min7		vii	min7♭5
IV	Maj7			

This chart shows the diatonic 7th chords in every key:

Key	I	ii	iii	IV	V	vi	vii
C	CMaj7	Dmin7	Emin7	FMaj7	G7	Amin7	Bmin7♭5
G	GMaj7	Amin7	Bmin7	CMaj7	D7	Emin7	F♯min7♭5
D	DMaj7	Emin7	F♯min7	GMaj7	A7	Bmin7	C♯min7♭5
A	AMaj7	Bmin7	C♯min7	DMaj7	E7	F♯min7	G♯min7♭5
E	EMaj7	F♯min7	G♯min7	AMaj7	B7	C♯min7	D♯min7♭5
B	BMaj7	C♯min7	D♯min7	EMaj7	F♯7	G♯min7	A♯min7♭5
G♭	G♭Maj7	A♭min7	B♭min7	C♭Maj7	D♭7	E♭min7	Fmin7♭5
D♭	D♭Maj7	E♭min7	Fmin7	G♭Maj7	A♭7	B♭min7	Cmin7♭5
A♭	A♭Maj7	B♭min7	Cmin7	D♭Maj7	E♭7	Fmin7	Gmin7♭5
E♭	E♭Maj7	Fmin7	Gmin7	A♭Maj7	B♭7	Cmin7	Dmin7♭5
B♭	B♭Maj7	Cmin7	Dmin7	E♭Maj7	F7	Gmin7	Amin7♭5
F	FMaj7	Gmin7	Amin7	B♭Maj7	C7	Dmin7	Emin7♭5

These diatonic chords function in a similar way to their respective triads (p. 22), with the notable exception of the min7♭5 built on vii. The min7♭5 doesn't generally gravitate to the I chord; its most common function is in minor keys, and will be discussed in a couple of pages.

Play the following tune in the key of G Major, and notice the way the chords function as they lead us away from our home of G and back again. The last two measures are a *turnaround*, a chord progression that creates motion bringing us back to the top (beginning) of the tune. We could just play G6 for those two measures, but by the time we got back to the top, we'd have been "home" for three bars, and might get a bit stir crazy. The I-vi-ii-V progression builds anticipation so that when we get back to the first bar on the repeat, we're more excited to be there.

A JOG AROUND THE BLOCK

Track 22

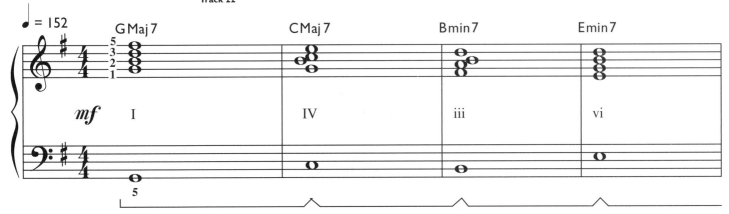

Note:

The pedaling guidelines discussed in Chapter 2 still apply with 7th chords.

*The great pianist **Teddy Wilson** was famous for his work with Benny Goodman, Billie Holiday and Lester Young. In 1935, he joined Goodman's Trio, the first significant integrated performing ensemble in jazz.*

MINOR HARMONY WITH 7TH CHORDS

When playing 7th chords in a minor key, we generally use a mixture of the harmonic minor and natural minor scales to derive our harmony, with the harmonic minor taking precedence because of the V and vii chords it gives us. Check this out in A Minor.

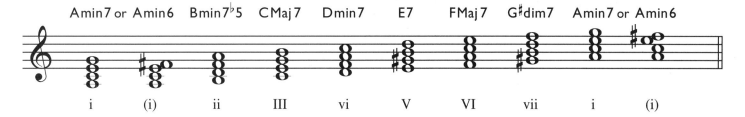

What you see above uses some exceptions to the rule of using the harmonic minor. The min7 chord on i is derived from the natural minor, to avoid having a minor chord with a major 7th (a real chord, but one we're not going to deal with until the *Intermediate* section). The min6 option on the i chord is not from either the harmonic or natural minor scale but is still used sometimes, particularly to prevent clashes between the root and 7th. And the III chord is borrowed from the natural minor. If we used the harmonic minor there, we'd have a Maj7 with a ♯5 (another chord that is way down the road in our studies).

As mentioned on the previous page, this is where the min7♭5 chord is most useful. On page 24, we looked briefly at the ii-V-I progression (in a major key), the most common chord combination in jazz. The ii sets up the V, and the built-up tension is released as V resolves to I. With the min7♭5 chord as our ii chord, we have a colorful and very useful ii-V-i for minor keys. Check out the sound of the minor ii-V-i in A Minor.

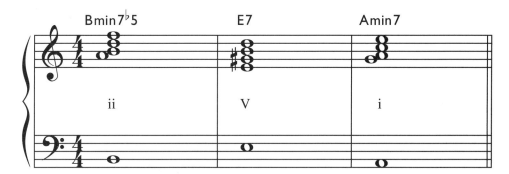

Virtuoso pianist, **Erroll Garner** *became immensely popular in the 1950s and was the composer of the jazz standard* Misty *.*

95° in the Shade is an exercise in minor harmony in D Minor. The chords are in the style of the classic Gershwin tune *Summertime*, which has been recorded in jazz versions by John Coltrane, Miles Davis, Sidney Bechet, Louis Armstrong and many others. Once you've played this tune a bit, the minor ii-V-i sound will become a more familiar sound to you. Note that in bars 12 & 13 the chords hint at the relative major key (F), and the final i chord replaces the minor 7th chord with a minor 6th chord.

95° IN THE SHADE

Track 23

CHAPTER 5

Voicing 7th Chords

7th chords open up a whole new world of possibilities. It's funny to think that just one extra note per chord can greatly alter the sound, but dealing with 7th chords does just that. Voicing becomes much more important now that we're using 7th chords. More notes create more voicing possibilities. As jazz keyboardists, we strive to learn what those possibilities are, how to execute them and what impact each one may have on the overall sound.

VOICE LEADING

Play these two examples of voicings for a ii-V-I progression in B♭ Major.

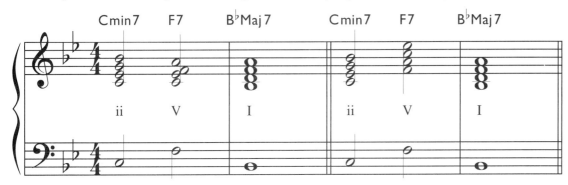

The first example makes more sense. Each voicing flows smoothly to the next one, and the hands have to move very little to play the progression. In the second example the sound is broken up, and the right hand has to jump around to play the chords. The difference is that the first example uses good voice leading. *Voice leading* is the smooth movement of voices (notes) from one chord to the next. If your hands are jumping all over the place, you're probably not using good voice leading, and the music is unlikely to sound smooth or cohesive. To voice lead well, your hands should expend the least possible amount of energy. Imagine that, the easier it is to play, the better it sounds!

Check out this example of a iii-vi-ii-V-I progression in F Major with good voice leading.

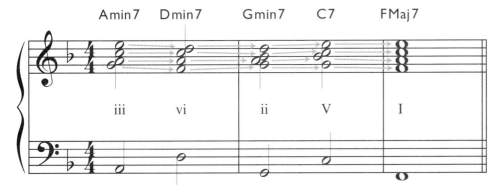

Each of the four voices in the right hand moves very little as the chords change. Just like the individual singers in a choir, who can't jump around too much without getting tired and confused, the voices in a chord should avoid leaps whenever possible. The bass notes move around more but that's inevitable when the roots are moving in large intervals like 4ths and 5ths. Since the left hand is playing one note at a time, it is not difficult to play.

We have more freedom with voicing when the left hand plays the roots. So far, we've been playing four notes at a time in the right hand whenever we play 7th chords. Now that we're getting the hang of them, we can eliminate one of those notes. The right hand can play the 3rd, 5th and 7th of each chord and the left hand can take care of the roots.

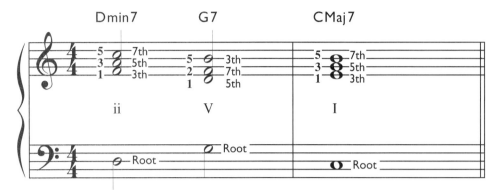

With this kind of voicing, the sound becomes more open. We don't lose the fullness because all four notes of each chord are still being played. We still use the same method of voice leading, simply omitting the root from the right hand. Let's take the following progression in B Minor (the vertical slash marks underneath each chord are shorthand indicating the number of beats devoted to each chord).

Bmin7	Emin7	Bmin7	GMaj7	C#min7♭5	F#7	Bmin7
/ /	/ /	/ /	/ /	/ /	/ /	/ / / /

Let's voice the progression in this style with roots in the left hand, and 3rds, 5ths and 7ths in the right hand with smooth voice leading.

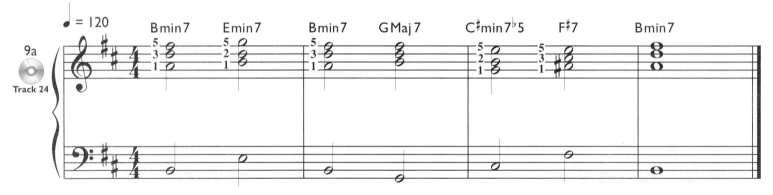

If we begin the progression with a different voicing for the first Bmin7 chord, then the voice leading will naturally lead to other voicings for the rest of the chords, since other voicings will be within easier reach. Here's another way of voicing the same changes with the same technique.

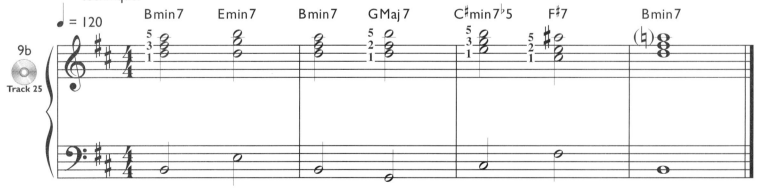

Well, How About Bridgeport? is a chordal study in the style of the changes to *Afternoon in Paris* by John Lewis of the Modern Jazz Quartet. All the chords have the root in the left hand and the other three voices in the right hand. The only exceptions come when the melody note is also the root, in which case both hands play the root and the right hand plays the other three notes of the chord underneath. Notice the smooth voice leading.

This song is in *AABA form*, a common song structure where the first section (A-section) is repeated twice, followed by a bridge (B-section), and another repeat of the A-section (*D.C. al Fine). The sum of all this is a *chorus*, which in jazz means once through the entire song form.

*D.C. al Fine (*Da Capo al Fine*) means to go back to the beginning and play until the *Fine*.

The concept of reading 7th chords in lead sheet is the same as reading triads (see Chapter 2, page 19). You're given a melody and chord symbols, and it is up to you to flesh it out. Once you've chosen a method of voicing (such as roots in the left hand and 3rds, 5ths and 7ths in the right hand) often the voicings choose themselves based on the melody notes.

In this example, the first note is F#. The most sensible way to voice the chord is to put the F# on top, and stack the other voices underneath. The melody note for Emin7 is G so we put that note on top and stack the other chord tones underneath.

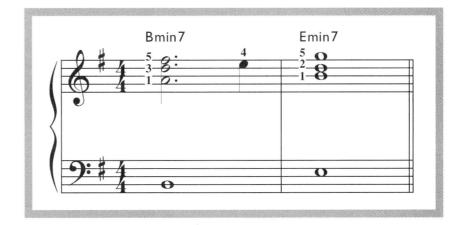

The melody leaps down a 5th at the change to Amin7 so the voicing should leap down with it. When voicing a lead sheet, it is good to focus on voice leading when the melody doesn't move around too much. Don't worry when the melody leaps. Simply begin voice leading again when the melody returns to stepwise motion.

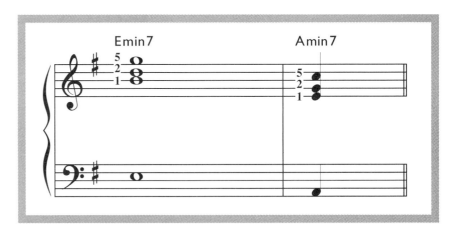

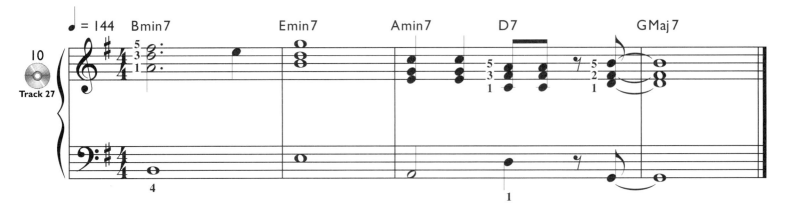

This is the lead sheet for *Bouncin' With Bill E.*, dedicated to the great Bill Evans. The changes are loosely based on the standard tune *I'll Remember April.* Learn it well because most of the remaining voicing lessons in this chapter will be based on this tune. Begin by voicing it with roots in the left hand and 3rds, 5ths and 7ths (plus the melody note if it isn't already one of these) in the right hand. Check it against the written-out music on page 54. If you encounter a bar with rests instead of notes, simply voice the chord(s) however you see fit.

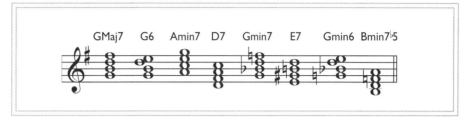

BOUNCIN' WITH BILL E. (*LEAD SHEET*)

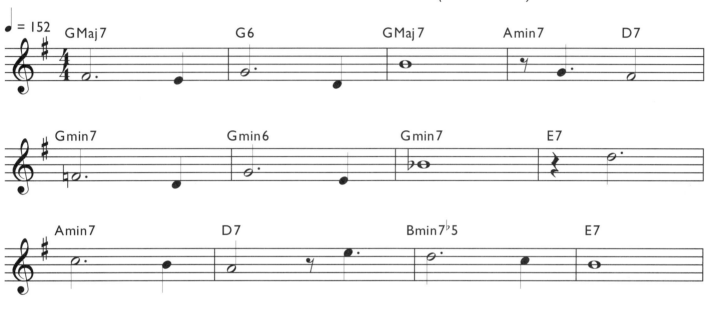

*Pianist **Bill Evans** was a master of harmony and improvisation. His work has been a source of inspiration to jazz musicians and fans since the 1950s.*

Here's a fully voiced version of *Bouncin' With Bill E.* What you play from the lead sheet should be similar to this, but don't worry if there are voicings here and there that don't match exactly. You should be playing the correct notes in the chords, of course, but beyond that we can be somewhat flexible since there are many different ways to voice a chord.

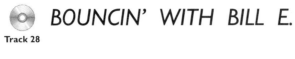

Track 28

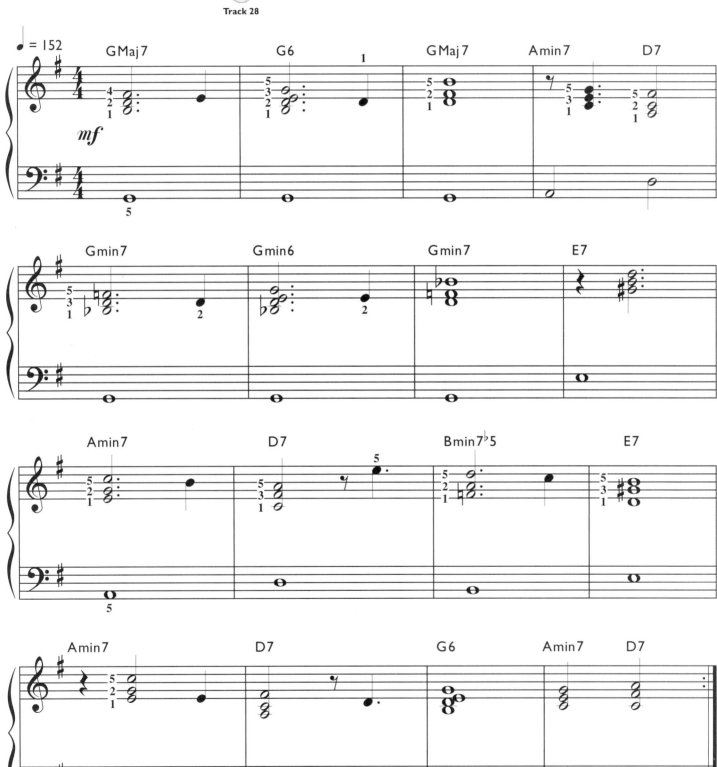

SHELL VOICINGS

As the Declaration of Independence says, all people are created equal. The same can't be said for chord tones, however. Some are more important than others. Let's line up the three most common 7th chords (major, minor and dominant) from a root of D, and take a look:

We know the root is important since that is what defines the chord. The 3rd and 7th are not the same from chord to chord so we need those to determine the chord quality. The 5th, however, is another story. The major, minor and dominant 7th chords all have perfect 5ths. That means we could leave the 5th out entirely and still know which of these three chords was being played.

To play *shell voicings*, we use the same concept we've been using but leave out the 5th of each chord; the roots go in the left hand and the right hand takes the 3rds and 7ths. If the melody note is the 3rd or 7th of a chord, we have three-note chords; if not, we add the melody note on top and have a four-note chord. Either way, this is a very sparse, compact way to voice chords without losing the character of the changes. Play this I-vi-ii-V-I in G Major.

These voicings just get easier and easier on the hands, don't they? In the above example, the right hand barely has to move at all. This ease in voice leading is common with shell voicings whenever the roots are moving down in 5ths (or up in 4ths). In these cases, the most you'll have to move to get from the 7th of one chord to the 3rd of the next is a whole step, sometimes only a half step. To get from the 3rd of one chord to the 7th of the next, you often need only to repeat the same note!

Here we have *Bouncin' With Bill E.* voiced with shells. Pay attention to the places where the 3rd or 7th is in the melody and only three notes are needed for the voicings. Since you won't have to move your hands much, use your extra energy to notice the smooth voice leading.

BOUNCIN' WITH BILL E. (SHELL VOICINGS)

Track 29

BEBOP STYLE LEFT-HAND VOICINGS

When we discussed soloing in Chapter 3, the examples divided the roles of the hands; the right hand soloed, the left hand played chords. This is a common division of labor in modern jazz keyboard. Earl "Fatha" Hines, Teddy Wilson and Nat "King" Cole were all pioneers in soloing with the right hand while allowing the left to fill in the harmony, and they usually did this with an ornate left hand style. In the *bebop* era (starting in the 1940s), horn players like trumpeter Dizzy Gillespie and saxophonist Charlie "Bird" Parker developed a new, exciting style of soloing. The solo lines in bebop tended to be so full of rhythmic and harmonic ideas that there was less need to fill in space with thick chords. Bebop pianists, led by Earl "Bud" Powell, began to use simple, skeletal voicings with their left hands, often with only two notes per chord.

And we thought that shell voicings were sparse! Bebop style left hand voicings consist of either the root and 3rd or root and 7th of a chord. These voicings by themselves don't sound full enough to define the chords. Having just D and F♯ is not enough information to know that you have a D7 chord. However, when you combine these voicings in the left hand with melodies and solos in the right hand, the sound begins to fill out, and the left hand is better able to stay out of the right hand's way.

A great benefit of these voicings is improved voice leading. In Chapter 3, our left hands were jumping all over the place to get from one root position chord to the next but with triads we could get away with it. With 7th chords, that would be too clunky but the extra note gives us more voice leading options. To play bebop style voicings, think of "voicings on the half shell": shell voicings with one of the two non-root tones taken away. So if you play root-7th on one chord (and the root is going down a 5th), you'll play root-3rd on the next and vice-versa.

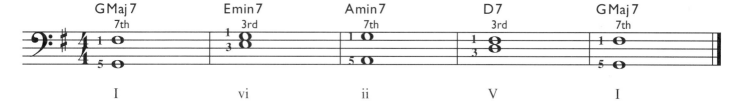

None of the notes in the above voicings go above the G below middle C which leaves the right hand plenty of room to solo without any overlapping of the hands. As long as you keep the non-root tones at or above the D below middle C, it shouldn't sound muddy.

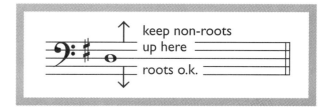

If you have big hands, one way to enrich the sound of bebop style voicings is by playing the root-3rd voicings with the root an octave lower. This gives you the interval of a 10th (an octave plus a 3rd), a fuller sound than the 3rd. If you feel an uncomfortable stretch when you reach a 10th, don't do it. It is not worth getting tendonitis to liven up your voicings.

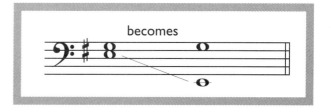

Bouncin' With Bill E. is found here with bebop style voicings in the left hand. To make things a little more interesting, the melody in the right hand is embellished a bit. Practice one hand at a time if you find it helpful. If your left hand can handle it, try stretching the 3rds into 10ths. Pay attention, as always, to the voice leading in the left hand.

BOUNCIN' WITH BILL E. (BEBOP STYLE LEFT-HAND VOICINGS)

Track 30

ROOTLESS LEFT-HAND VOICINGS

Many inventions through time have given musicians the freedom to better express themselves. The invention of the phonograph allowed musicians to be recorded so that a piece could be listened to over and over. The invention of radio allowed musicians to be heard in places where they could never actually travel. And we jazz keyboardists should give a hearty pat on the back to whoever invented bass players!

With all the voicing types we've discussed so far, we've had to play the root in the left hand. Without the root down below, a chord usually sounds vague. But nobody said that we had to always be the ones playing the roots. Most jazz groups include a bassist (either bass guitar or acoustic "upright" bass), and usually the bassist's job includes keeping a solid pulse and laying down the roots of the chords. We can leave the roots to the bassist and worry only about the rest of the notes.

Let's take the same I-vi-ii-V-I in G Major that we've used for the last couple of examples and look at it voiced with *rootless voicings* in the left hand.

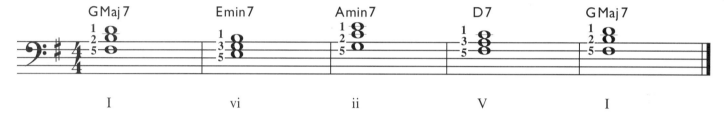

Here we begin with the same voicing concept that we introduced on pages 49 and 50, where we put the root on the bottom (with the left hand) and added the 3rd, 5th and 7th on top (with the right hand). Instead, though, we let the bass player take over the duties of the left hand and let the left hand play what the right hand would be playing. This leaves the right hand free to solo (or grab a sandwich, if so inclined).

The sound and feel of rootless voicings may take some getting used to, especially if you don't have the opportunity to play with a bassist. Have no fear, though. It will be very helpful to be comfortable with rootless voicings, and in time you will get used to the sound and hear the harmonic movement even if the roots aren't being played by anybody. For now, if you don't feel grounded as you play rootless voicings, slow down, hit the sustain pedal, and reach over with your right hand to play the roots underneath. Here are the changes for the first five bars of *Well, How About Bridgeport?* (page 51) voiced with left hand rootless voicings.

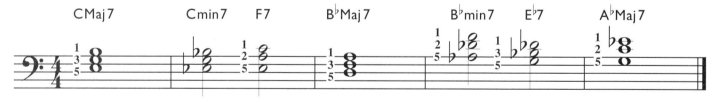

At the change from B♭Maj7 to B♭min7, the voicing leaps up rather than continuing the voice leading. This makes sense here since going below that D with anything but the root will muddy the sound, as we saw with bebop style voicings.

It is still possible to play root position chords with a bass player present, but the common technique in contemporary jazz is to let the bassist have the roots and stay out of his way. Rootless voicings can be a nice change of pace even in solo playing, and when you find yourself in an ensemble situation, you'll be very glad to know them.

Yet again, *Bouncin' With Bill E.*, this time with the right hand taking the melody and the left hand playing three note (3rd, 5th and 7th) rootless voicings underneath.

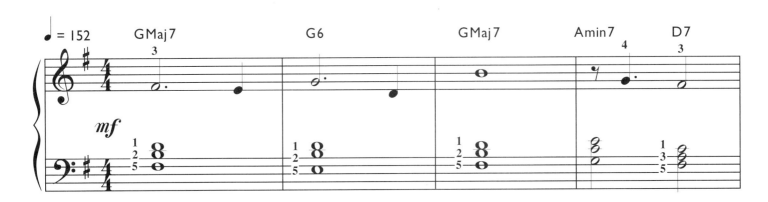

BOUNCIN' WITH BILL E. *(ROOTLESS LEFT-HAND VOICINGS)*

Track 31

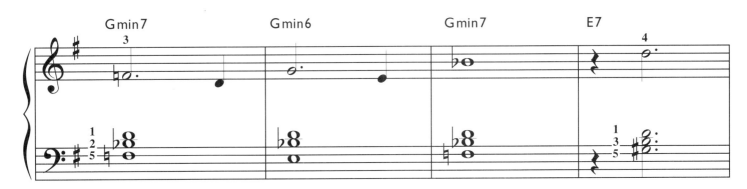

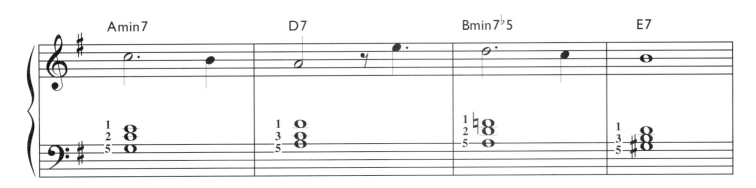

Rootless shell voicings are simply a combination of the concepts of rootless voicings and shell voicings. The left hand plays the 3rd and 7th of each chord, allowing the bassist to play the roots and giving the right hand freedom to do its thing.

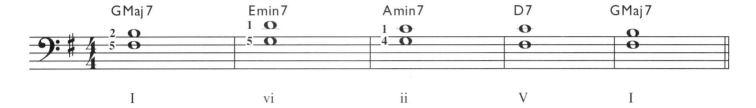

When we voiced these changes with shells on page 55, we used a different voicing for the Emin7. This version has the 7th on top in the Emin7 chord, whereas the one on page 55 had the 3rd on top. Either way is valid. Your goal is to voice the chord so that it generally avoids the notes beneath the D below middle C, which would produce a muddy sound.

By looking ahead to the length of a progression and how much downward motion in 5ths you'll have, you can judge the range in which you should begin voicing to avoid the muddy notes and awkward leaps.

*The one and only **Thelonious Monk** (1917-1982), who thrived on sparse voicings like these, was a brilliant artist and guru to many important jazz musicians.*

Now that you can play the melody to *Bouncin' With Bill E.* in your sleep, we're going to make things more interesting in the left hand. The rendition below has the left hand playing rootless shell voicings. Rather than using half and whole notes, the rhythms are varied to resemble a typical left hand accompaniment. Work on the left hand separately if you need to, working out the syncopated rhythms precisely and with a good swing feel.

BOUNCIN' WITH BILL E. (ROOTLESS SHELL VOICINGS)

Track 32

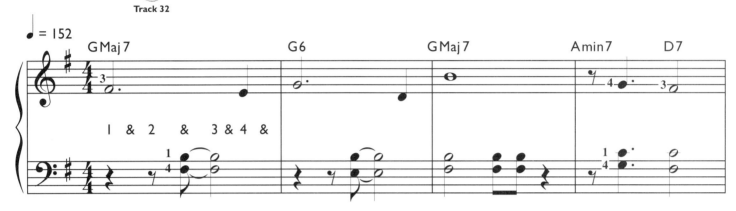

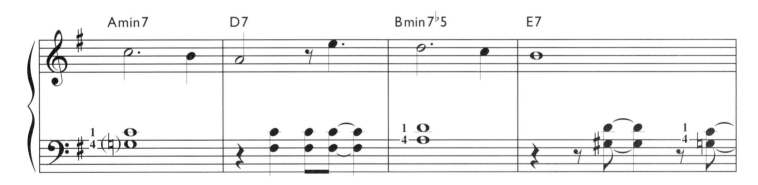

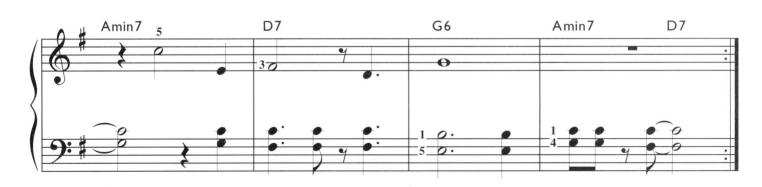

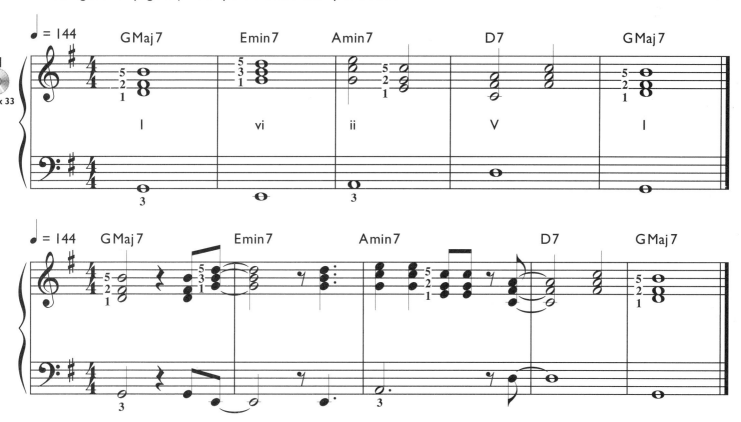

COMPING

Comping is jazz lingo for the chordal accompaniment a pianist or guitarist provides during a melody or solo. Some say it is short for "accompanying" and some say it is short for "complementing." In fact, comping is both of those things. You can comp behind another player or you can use your left hand to comp for your right hand while you solo or play a melody.

The next time you listen to a jazz group, be aware of the comping. Some compers, like Horace Silver, take control of the music with their aggressive comping. Others, like Wynton Kelly, let the soloists take control, choosing instead to punctuate the soloists' statements. There are no hard and fast rules about what approach to take except one: listen! Your ears and sensitivity will be the keys to successful comping. If a soloist is playing softly and you're banging, something's wrong. Likewise, if the soloist is building a solo's energy level higher and higher and you're playing the same stuff you were two minutes ago, you're probably not listening. Great compers like Wynton Kelly, Red Garland, Cedar Walton and Kenny Barron often sound like mind readers. They listen to the soloist so well that they're always playing the right thing, and they can even predict where the soloist is going and comp accordingly.

Among the elements of good comping, good rhythm is about on a par with listening. The jazz *rhythm section* usually consists of bass, drums and keyboard (most often piano, sometimes organ, occasionally electric piano or synthesizer). Other possible rhythm section instruments include percussion, guitar and vibraphone. The rhythm section listens to and responds to the soloist, but first and foremost their job is to set a groove that feels great (refer to the explanation of swing feel on page 32). Compare the two examples below.

The first example is fine, especially in a laid back, reserved setting (for example, the saxophone solo has just begun softly and sparsely). The second example (with the same voicings but different rhythms) is much more propulsive and exciting, appropriate for a high energy situation. Syncopation (note especially how the Emin7 and D7 are anticipated by half a beat) adds a lot of drive to your comping. Listen attentively to the way the great compers do it and you'll get the sound in your head.

One more time! Here we have a sample solo over the changes to *Bouncin' With Bill E.* with the left hand comping underneath using the three types of left hand voicings we've studied. Learn each hand separately if you need to and pay close attention to the rhythms between the two hands. Sometimes the left hand emphasizes the rhythms that the right hand plays; other times the left hand punctuates where the right hand is less rhythmically active. Remember to swing!

BOUNCIN' WITH BILL E. *(SAMPLE SOLO WITH COMPING)*

Track 34

All Hail the King, dedicated to the great pianist Nat "King" Cole, is in the style of the changes to Kurt Weill's *Mack the Knife*. Louis Armstrong, Dick Hyman and Sonny Rollins are among those who have recorded great jazz versions of that tune. Here, we're in the key of A Major, and in sixteen bars we'll go through all the voicing types discussed in this chapter.

ALL HAIL THE KING

Track 35

Tommy's Touch, a tribute to pianist Tommy Flanagan, is presented here in lead sheet form. The tune uses harmony from the keys of B♭ Major and its relative, G Minor, which share the same key signature of two flats. Familiarize yourself with the melody and the changes. Then go through each voicing method discussed in this chapter and work out the tune with each method. This tune is in the style of the changes to the standard *Autumn Leaves*, which has been recorded successfully by the likes of Bill Evans, Erroll Garner and Julian "Cannonball" Adderley.

TOMMY'S TOUCH

Track 36

CHAPTER 6

Scales and Soloing, Part Two

Now that we're using 7th chords, our sound is getting more colorful. Naturally we want our soloing to move forward as well. In this chapter we're not going to look at any scales we haven't already learned. Instead we're going to take the scales we already know and learn how to apply them in some new ways.

To prepare to dig into soloing, review all the scales we've looked at so far:

Major

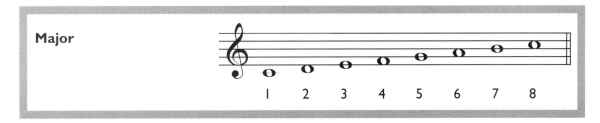

Major Pentatonic

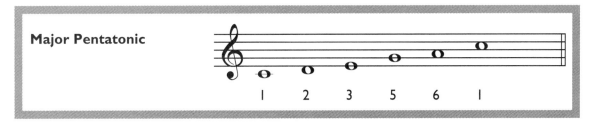

Natural Minor

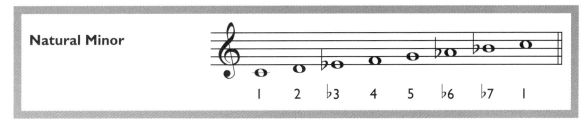

Harmonic Minor

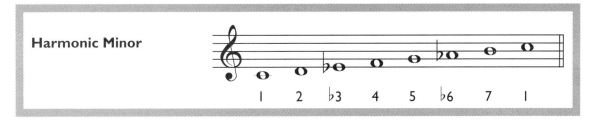

Minor Pentatonic

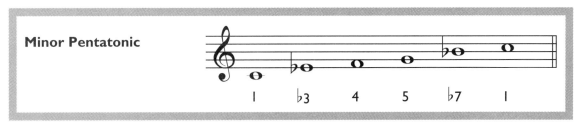

Blues

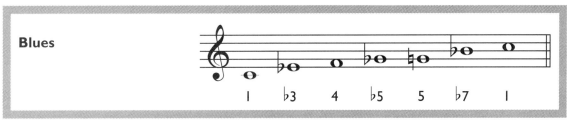

Harmonic analysis is taking a set of changes and figuring out what they mean. Let's say you open up a chart and see the following progression:

| **Amin7** | **Dmin7** | **Gmin7** | **C7** | **FMaj7** |

It is time for you to solo and you're trying to make heads or tails of the changes. Luckily, you have the chord chart from page 45 (perhaps by now you've tattooed it onto your arm) and scanning it, you realize that all these chords fit into the key of F Major. So, you take a pencil and jot down the key and the Roman numerals associated with each chord.

F: iii	vi	ii	V	I
Amin7	**Dmin7**	**Gmin7**	**C7**	**FMaj7**

Now you can go your merry way, soloing in F Major (using the F Major scale or the F Major Pentatonic scale) and keeping track of how the harmonic drama unfolds as the vi leads to ii which leads to V, and so on. Look for clues in the changes.

If you see a min7 moving to a 7 down a 5th, then you've got a ii-V, and that tells you (at least for the moment) what key you're in.

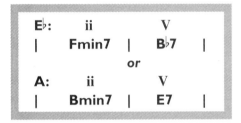

If those same changes then go to a Maj7 chord down a 5th, that's a dead giveaway. The iii-vi-ii-V-I is another common pattern that makes it clear what key you're in.

D: ii	V	I
Emin7	**A7**	**DMaj7**

or

A♭: iii	vi	ii	V	I
Cmin7	**Fmin7**	**B♭min7**	**E♭7**	**A♭Maj7**

The tunes in this chapter are examples of what you can do when you're in control of the changes and know where they come from. The left hand is given voicings and rhythms for comping but you're encouraged to play around with them, trying different voicings and rhythms for more personalized comping. Most importantly, have fun noodling around with the scales and chords. Improvising is loads of fun, and you should enjoy the opportunity to play your own melodies as they come into your head.

The melody and changes to *Pebble Hill* are based on the A Major scale. Learn the melody and use the A Major scale to solo. You can use the written comping pattern or use your own. Keep swinging the eighth notes but since the tune is in $\frac{3}{4}$ time, there is a slight difference to the rhythmic feel (you can't emphasize the two and four if there is no four!). The written left hand part shows examples of typical $\frac{3}{4}$ rhythms. The parentheses around the final E7 imply that you should use that change on a turnaround to bring you back to the top of the tune, but when you end the tune leave it out and end on the AMaj7.

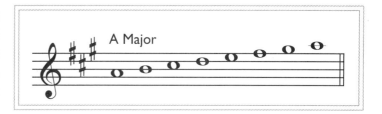

PEBBLE HILL

Track 37

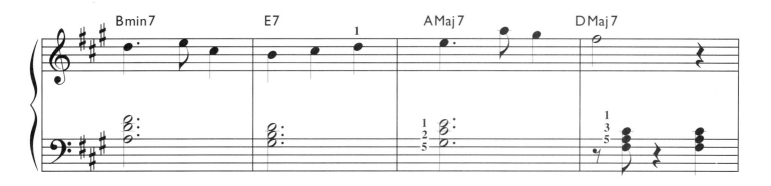

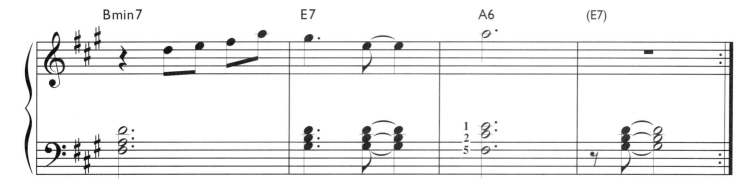

This piece is dedicated to the intensely swingin' organists Jack McDuff and Shirley Scott. It's in the key of E♭ Major, and the melody is derived entirely from the E♭ Major Pentatonic scale, so you can try soloing just from that scale. The song is in AABA form.

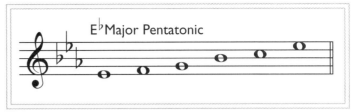

BROTHER JACK AND SISTER SHIRLEY

Track 38

HARMONIC ANALYSIS IN MINOR KEYS

Just as there are ways to tell what major key you're in, the same opportunity exists for minor keys. Let's start by looking at this progression:

| B♭Maj7 | FMaj7 | Emin7♭5 | A7 | Dmin7 ||

Because the first chord is B♭Maj7, we might instinctively assume that we're in the key of B♭ major. But in jazz harmony, where you start is less important that where you're going. As the progression moves further along we see it moving us to Dmin7 and realize that all the chords relate to the key of D Minor.

Dmin: VI	III	ii	V	i
B♭Maj7	FMaj7	Emin7♭5	A7	Dmin7 ||

As with major keys, there are certain chord patterns in minor keys that clearly point you towards recognizing the key.

If you see a min7♭5 chord moving down a 5th to a 7th chord, that is a sign you're in a minor key.

Emin:	ii	V
	F♯min7♭5	B7

If you have the same progression and the 7 chord goes down a 5th to a min7 or min6 chord, then it is even more clear that you're in a minor key.

B♭min:	ii	V	I
	Cmin7♭5	F7	B♭min6

If you see a Maj7 chord move down a half step to a dominant chord, that is another good sign that a 5th below the 7th chord lies the i chord in the present minor key.

Fmin:	VI	V	(i)
	D♭Maj7	C7	(Fmin7)

Sometimes a tune passes freely between relative major and minor keys, like *Tommy's Touch* on page 66, which goes back and forth between B♭ Major and its relative minor, G Minor. This makes which key we're in a bit more ambiguous. Not to worry, though, you can change your thinking whenever the changes hint more at one than the other. This will be addressed further on page 75 when we discuss modulations and pivot chords.

Tommy's Touch

E♭: ii	V	I	IV	Cmin: ii	V	i
Fmin7	B♭7	E♭Maj7	A♭Maj7	Dmin7♭5	G7	Cmin7 ||

Blue Drew is in the key of B Minor and the melody uses the
B Minor Pentatonic scale and the B Blues scale. The only
difference is the F natural in the B Blues scale. These scales
give us a funky, blues-based sound. Use each of these scales
when you solo. Then begin to mix them up, adding the ♭5
from the blues scale when the mood strikes. This tune is
dedicated to Kenny Drew who was one of the great pianists
of modern jazz and an expert at this type of funky playing.

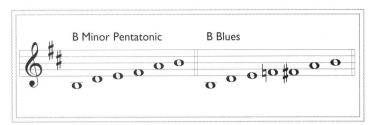

BLUE DREW

Track 39

NATURAL MINOR VS. HARMONIC MINOR: THE CHOICE

We know by now that the harmony in a minor key is derived from the harmonic minor scale, but with some significant borrowing from the natural minor for certain chords. When it comes time to solo over a minor progression, the issue of which scale to use arises. Let's compare the two, using the first chord progression from page 71, voiced in the left hand with three-note rootless voicings. If we run the D Natural Minor scale over these changes, it sounds like this:

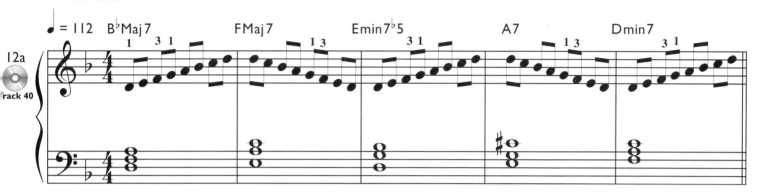

Not bad, but when we get to the ii-V, there is a little problem. The C♯ in the A7 chord, a crucial part of the progression, clashes with the C natural in the D Natural Minor scale. So now let's try the D Harmonic Minor scale, which has the missing C♯ we seek.

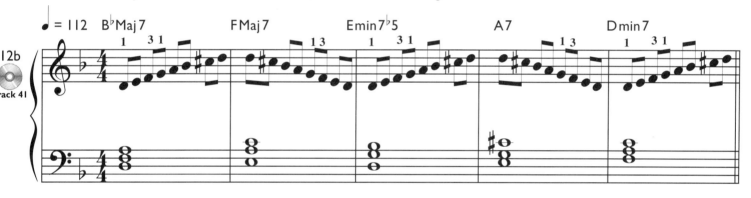

With this scale we solve one problem but add two more. The C♯ that we needed for the A7 clashes with the C naturals in the FMaj7 and Dmin7 chords.

The solution is to be flexible. If you want to use these scales, use the harmonic minor whenever you encounter a V or ii-V, and use the natural minor the rest of the time. This way you can "make the changes" (play melodies that match up with the chords going by).

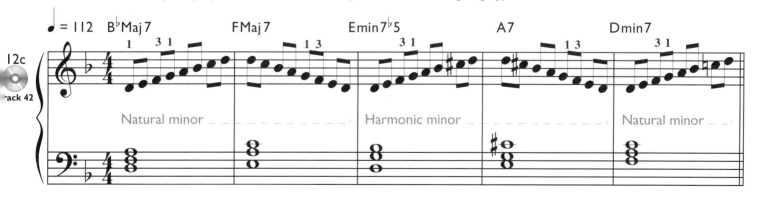

Mingus Reincarnated, a tribute to the great bassist/composer/bandleader Charles Mingus (himself a great pianist), is in the key of G Minor. The natural and harmonic minor are both used, changing wherever it is appropriate. When you solo, use the same scales as in the melody.

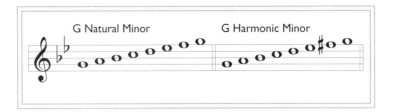

MINGUS REINCARNATED

PROGRESSIONS WITH MODULATIONS

So you've decided to go back and try soloing on some of the tunes that came earlier in this book. Go back to page 51 and try to solo on the changes to *Well, How About Bridgeport?*

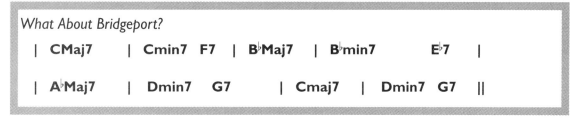

The key signature has no sharps or flats and the first chord is CMaj7, so it seems like it is in C Major. But starting on the second measure, many of the chords don't fit with C Major. What you're encountering is *modulation*, the changing of keys. *Well, How About Bridgeport?* begins in C Major but it doesn't stay there. Look at the harmonic analysis for these changes:

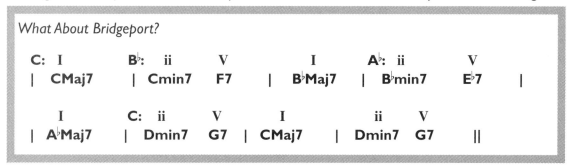

So actually the tune passes through the keys of C Major, B♭ Major and A♭ Major. No one scale is going to work soloing over the whole tune. You can use the major (or major pentatonic) scale that corresponds with each key while you're there, and then move on to the next when it's time.

Sometimes, as in *Tommy's Touch*, there is an overlap of chords as the modulation occurs.

<table>
<tr><td colspan="10">Tommy's Touch</td></tr>
<tr><td>E♭:</td><td>ii</td><td>V</td><td>I</td><td>IV</td><td>vii</td><td>Cmin: V</td><td></td><td>i</td></tr>
<tr><td>or</td><td></td><td></td><td></td><td></td><td></td><td></td><td></td><td></td></tr>
<tr><td>Cmin:</td><td>iv</td><td>VII</td><td>III</td><td>VI</td><td>ii</td><td>V</td><td></td><td>i</td></tr>
<tr><td></td><td>| Fmin7</td><td>| B♭7</td><td>| E♭Maj7</td><td>| A♭Maj7</td><td>| Dmin7♭5</td><td>| G7</td><td>|Cmin7</td><td>||</td></tr>
</table>

The first five chords in this progression could be analyzed as relating to either of the two keys, E♭ Major and C Minor. These chords are examples of *pivot chords*. A pivot chord is a chord that functions in two keys and helps provide a smooth transition in the modulation from one key to the next. When pivot chords arise, you have a choice whether to think in the key you're coming from or the one you're going to. Either is fine, as long as you're prepared for the modulation.

The key to modulation is awareness. Stay on your toes as a tune goes along and keep looking out for cues that will help you determine what key you're in at that moment. Once you've determined that you're temporarily in a certain key, you can do the same things to solo that you would do if you were in that key for a whole tune.

Bright Red was composed in memory of pianist Red Garland. This tune modulates repeatedly. The melody is derived from the major scale of whichever key the tune is in at a given moment. Use this tune to practice your ability to quickly shift gears as your solo accounts for each modulation by changing the scale you use.

BRIGHT RED

Track 44

You Neeque uses changes in the style of the standard tunes *There Will Never Be Another You* and *You're a Weaver of Dreams*. These changes modulate repeatedly, usually using pivot chords for smooth transitions. Learn the tune, familiarizing yourself with the changes and the keys the tune passes through. Whenever pivot chords come up, the primary numeric symbol is from the key the chord is leading to. The numeric symbols in parentheses indicate the functions of the chords if you relate them to the key you're leaving (the key you were just in).

YOU NEEQUE

Track 45

Here's a sample chorus-long solo over the changes to *You Neeque* using scales appropriate to the keys through which the tune passes.

YOU NEEQUE (SAMPLE SOLO)

Track 46

MEMORIZING CHANGES

In addition to guiding your scale choices for a solo, harmonic analysis is an indispensable tool in helping you memorize changes. Imagine if you had to memorize directions to a place one word at a time: "Go . . . down . . . the . . . block . . . and . . .." Similarly, if we had to memorize the changes to the A-section of *Well, How About Bridgeport* by thinking "C Major 7 to C Minor 7 to F7 . . ." our brains would run out of space long before we got to the end of the tune. By using Roman numerals, we can condense changes into bigger chunks of information. Instead of thinking of each chord one at a time, we can think:

"I in C to ii-V-I in B♭ to ii-V-I in A♭ to ii-V-I in C . . ."

Here we just took ten chords and condensed them into four pieces of information to remember. As we get used to common chord progressions, it will be easier to condense the information in the same way that we think of "Take a left at the stop sign" as one piece of information and not seven.

Oscar Peterson, *often compared with Art Tatum, was born in Montreal in 1925. Peterson was highly influential throughout his long career for his mixture of stunning technique and elegant swing.*

TRANSPOSING CHANGES

Another way in which Roman numerals help is with transposition, playing something in another key. Unless you plan to always keep one hand on the "pitch modulation" button of your synthesizer, this is a skill worth developing. Sometimes a singer's voice range doesn't fit the key you're used to using; sometimes somebody will just want to play something in a different key. Let's say somebody wants to play *Well, How About Bridgeport* in F Major. Instead of trying to of bring every chord up a 4th, think of the Roman numerals. We know we have I in the home key, followed by ii-V-I down a whole step, ii-V-I down another whole step and then ii-V-I back in the home key. In F, that would be:

F: I	E♭: ii	V	I	D♭: ii	V	I	F: ii	V	I
| FMaj7	| Fmin7	B♭7	| E♭Maj7	| E♭min7	A♭7	| D♭maj7	| Gmin7	C7	| FMaj7 ||

Señor Ruiz, dedicated to pianist Hilton Ruiz, is a tune with a Latin feel, so play the eighth notes straight (don't swing them). The changes are in the style of the harmony from the modern jazz classic *Blue Bossa* by trumpeter Kenny Dorham. On this tune, learn (and try to memorize) the changes based on the Roman numerals. Notice that it modulates from C Minor up a half step to D♭ Major. Once you have it down, slowly work on transposing it into the other eleven keys. You can choose the keys by going up or down in half steps or by going around the circle of 5ths (see page 12 if you need help remembering the circle).

SEÑOR RUIZ

Track 47

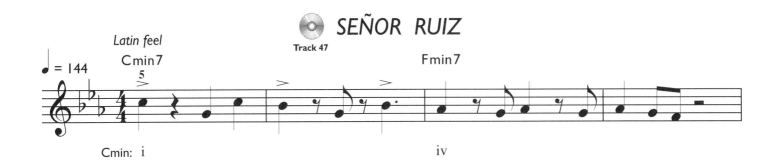

CHAPTER 7

More Soloing

MELODIC SCALE PATTERNS

If someone says "don't forget that this weekend is Groundhog Day," you may or may not remember. If a little while later, they say "remember this weekend," you'll be more likely to remember. *Repetition* is a great tool in jazz improvisation as well, allowing you to make the most out of every musical idea and giving listeners something to latch onto so that they'll remember your musical statements.

Melodic scale patterns are a good source of musical repetition. Most musicians practice patterns like these as technical exercises. The *Virtuoso Pianist* by Hanon (Alfred #616), used by many keyboard students, is a book of technical exercises based on these sorts of patterns. There are many other books like it.

♩ = 120

If you played the above examples verbatim over a tune in C Major, it would sound . . . well, boring. Kind of like hearing "Don't forget Groundhog Day" every minute for an hour, which would probably make you less interested in groundhogs after a while. Therefore, we have to be a bit creative about how we dress up the patterns to keep them interesting (see the exercise on the next page).

Still, practicing straight patterns can be a technical and musical boost, even if you're not going to play them verbatim in a solo. You're encouraged to check out Hanon or another pattern book and use it to build your chops and give you some ideas for patterns to play.

Here we use the pattern from the previous page, example ①, with the C Major scale. The pattern is kept intact but the rhythm in which it is played is varied throughout, and it is used over repeated ii-V-I's in C. This serves as an introduction to using patterns creatively in a jazz context. Voice the changes in the left hand in whatever style you like.

*Born in 1928, **Horace Silver** made a big splash with his playing, composing and band leading in the 1950s and '60s. His use of blues and gospel devices in jazz has made him one of our most influential players.*

PHOTO COURTESY OF THE INSTITUTE OF JAZZ STUDIES

ARPEGGIOS

An *arpeggio* is a "broken chord." We've been playing all the notes in our chords simultaneously (*block chords*) but we can also *arpeggiate* the chords and play one note at a time.

Arpeggios give us yet another melodic possibility when we solo. They are particularly useful in "making the changes." Playing scales over a progression addresses the key of the changes but not necessarily the individual chord. Arpeggios, on the other hand, lay out the sound of each and every chord that is arpeggiated.

The principles of voice leading are still very important when playing arpeggios in a jazz solo. Compare these two arpeggiations of a iii-vi-ii-V-I in E♭ Major.

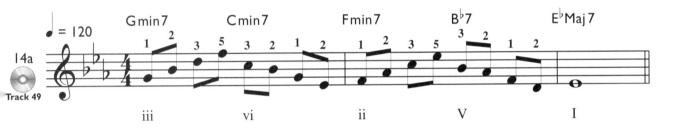

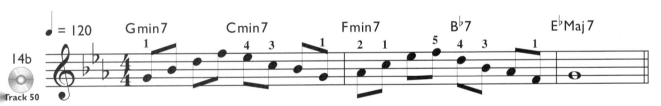

In example 14a, each arpeggio begins with the root, but there are awkward leaps from the Gmin7 to the Cmin7 and from the Fmin7 to the B♭7. In example 14b, a nearby chord tone is played at every chord change, resulting in a smoother sound. Practice the smooth linking of arpeggios over whatever changes you're trying to solo on.

As with patterns, smooth can be dull after a certain point. Once you're able to smoothly link arpeggios, you can throw in some leaps to mix things up.

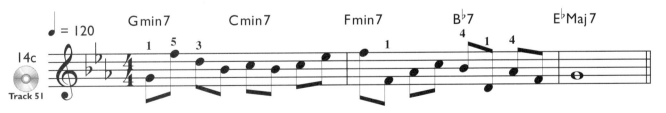

The three exercises that follow all use the same changes, ii-V-I's going counterclockwise around the circle of 5ths (therefore making it a circle of 4ths) through all twelve major keys. Practice the right hand alone at first so you can get used to hearing the sound of the changes from the arpeggios themselves. Once you're comfortable with the right hand, you can choose your own left hand voicings to play underneath.

This exercise deals with the smooth linking of arpeggios. Remember to swing those eighth notes; just because it is an exercise doesn't mean it shouldn't swing.

This exercise keeps the same constant eighth-note rhythm and the same goal of smoothly linking the arpeggios. Although the arpeggios lead smoothly into one another and only chord tones are played, there is more freedom to the melodic contour, compared to the "straight up and down" nature of the last exercise.

This exercise is freer still, allowing for rhythmic variety as well as variety in melodic contour.
The sound gets more and more musical and we're still only using chord tones.

It is very difficult to play an engaging solo using just one technique. Scales, chords, arpeggios and melodic patterns can all be interesting and musical, but after a couple choruses of any one of them, boredom is likely to set in. Using all of these elements in a single solo makes it much easier to keep things interesting. Let's look at a I-vi-ii-V-I in G Major using several different elements.

The G Major Scale

The G Major Pentatonic Scale

Arpeggios

Melodic Scale Patterns

All of these sound fine, but let's extend the progression (by repeating it once) and try using all of these elements.

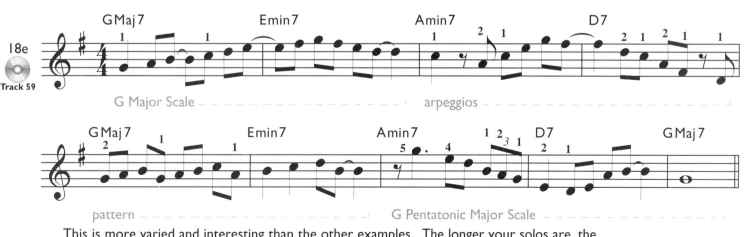

This is more varied and interesting than the other examples. The longer your solos are, the more important it is to have this kind of variety to maintain interest.

We're going to take a more in-depth look at how to combine the elements we've studied in this book, using the tune *Wonder-ful* as the basis. *Wonder-ful* is in the style of the progression in Stevie Wonder's *You Are the Sunshine Of My Life*, which has been recorded in a jazz style by the likes of Mal Waldron, Phineas Newborn, Jr. and Ella Fitzgerald. Learn the tune well, especially the changes, before moving on to the next few pages. In pencil, write out a harmonic analysis over the chords in this lead sheet.

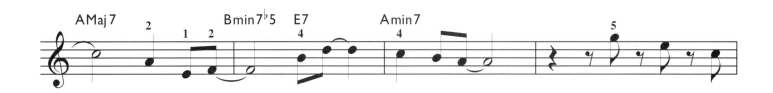

Here is a sample solo over a chorus of *Wonder-ful* using a variety of elements. Once you've learned this solo, try taking your own solo using the same elements. Try choosing for yourself which elements you're going to use where. There are no wrong choices, so explore!

(SAMPLE SOLO #1 ON) WONDER-FUL

Track 61

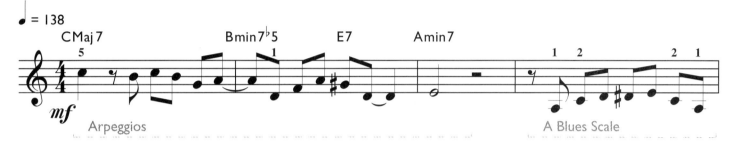

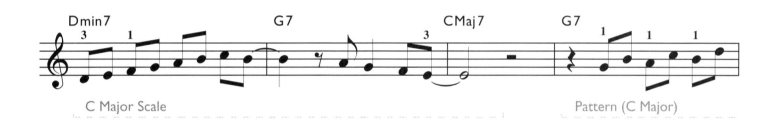

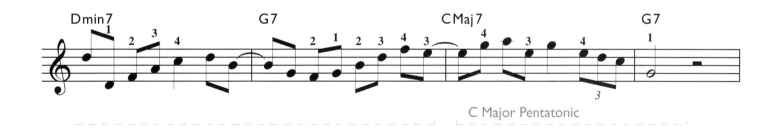

Continued on next page

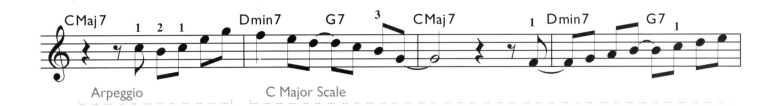

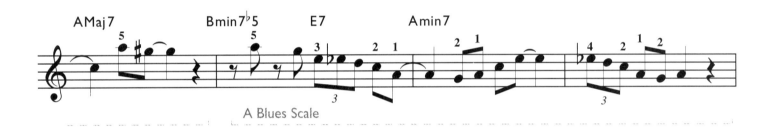

* The C# in the seventh measure of the second page of this tune is in the key of this phrase (A Major), but is not a member of the Bmin7 chord being arpeggiated at the moment. This kind of mixture of scale and arpeggio is common in jazz.

Here is another solo chorus on *Wonder-ful*, still using a variety of elements. This time the focus is on the left hand. Dig into the left hand here, noticing the types of voicings used, the rhythms and the way the comping interacts with the solo.

(SAMPLE SOLO #2 ON) WONDER-FUL (WITH COMPING)

Track 62

Continued on next page

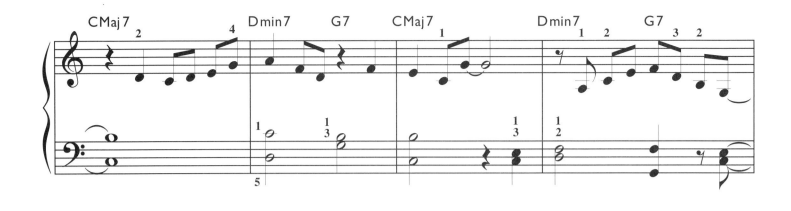

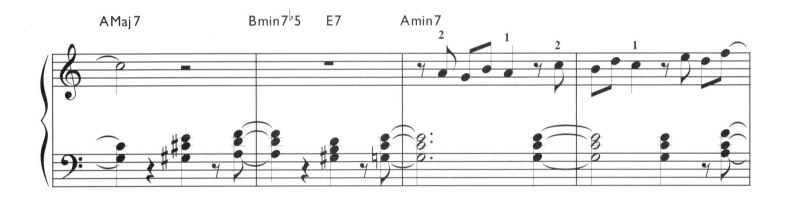

CHAPTER 8

Afterword

EAR TRAINING

You may have thought that the fingers were the most important part of a jazz keyboardist's anatomy. Fingers are near the top of the list, definitely, but the ears win out. The tradition of jazz is an aural tradition and even if we use written music, we are always depending on our ears. *Ear training* is the practice of learning to hear things. A seasoned jazz musician can hear just about anything whether at the keyboard or away from it. Here are some ways to practice your ear training.

1) **Practice identifying sounds.** If you hear the interval of a minor 2nd, do you recognize it? How about a min7♭5 chord? If the answer is no, not really or sometimes, this would be useful to practice. Focus on one thing at a time — intervals, triads, 7th chords, chord progressions, etc. Have a friend play different intervals (or whatever you're focusing on) and try to identify them. If you don't have anyone else around, record examples on a tape recorder or sequencer and wait a few days until you've forgotten what you played. Or simply pop in a CD or turn on the radio and try to figure out what is going on by ear. Strive for a level where it is second nature to be able to hear and identify anything.

2) **Play along.** Put on an album you like and play along with it. Don't worry about getting every note or even most of them. Just practice hearing things and trying to play them back instantly. After a while your ability to recreate what you hear will improve. Anything you want to play along with is fine, as long as it is not so fast and complex that you can't keep up. Particularly useful is playing along with improvisations on tunes you already know.

3) **Transcribe.** Take a recording of a solo or some chord voicings that you particularly like. Begin by listening several times so that the sound is firmly in your head and all you need to do is figure out what the notes are. Then sit down at the keyboard with the recording and figure out exactly what they're doing. You can write it down or try to memorize it right from the record. You will gain some insight into that player's style, and instead of blowing fifteen bucks on a transcription, you'll have the satisfaction of knowing you did it yourself and improved your ears in the process.

4) **Sight sing.** Take a lead sheet to a tune you don't know. Give yourself the starting pitch at the keyboard and see if you can sing the rest. When your ears are well developed, this will be perfectly natural.

Note:

In many music magazines there are advertisements for methods of attaining *perfect pitch*. Perfect pitch is the ability to identify any note out of thin air. *Relative pitch,* on the other hand, is the ability to hear the relationships between notes. With relative pitch, you may not immediately know what the first note of a melody is, but if someone tells you, you can figure out the rest of the notes by how they sound in relation to the first one and to each other. Perfect pitch can certainly help but relative pitch is much more useful to a jazz musician.

"Keyboard" can have many different meanings. Traditionally, the acoustic piano is by far the most common jazz keyboard instrument. Coming in second is the organ — in the 1950s, Jimmy Smith and others legitimized the Hammond B-3 as a modern jazz instrument. In the '60s and '70s, people began to experiment with electric pianos like the Wurlitzer and the Fender Rhodes. Then, beginning in the '70s, more jazz musicians began to use synthesizers. Affordable synthesizers were eventually built that tried to simulate the sounds and effects of the more traditional instruments. These are still popular.

Nowadays, we have several options for keyboards to play and/or purchase.

1) **Acoustic piano.** After all these years, the piano is still the King of Keyboards in straight-ahead jazz. The tone, touch and responsiveness of a good piano are unmatched. On the downside, a good piano is neither cheap nor portable. Therefore, many contemporary keyboardists find themselves looking at other options in addition to or instead of pianos.

2) **Organ.** A Hammond B-3 is cheaper and more portable than a piano, but not by much. Also, since the sound of the organ is less common than that of the piano, investing in an organ means committing to that sound.

3) **Electric piano.** You or someone you know may own an old Fender Rhodes and you can probably find one in the want ads pretty cheap. They are heavy but portable enough to take to a gig and the touch and responsiveness are often great. The sound of the Rhodes and other electric (not electronic) pianos, however, seems to scream "70s!" If you and the people you're playing with don't have a problem with this, then it might not be a bad choice. Another thing to keep in mind is that most electric pianos are no longer manufactured so getting them repaired can be difficult.

4) **Digital piano.** Many companies now manufacture digital pianos. The sounds are similar to piano sounds, the feel (with weighted "piano-like" keys) is similar to a piano and it is cheaper and more portable than a piano. These instruments aren't quite the "real thing," but all things considered, they're often worthy substitutes.

5) **Synthesizer.** There is a broad range of synthesizers out there with a range of prices and capabilities. For the sake of playing jazz, the most important feature is touch sensitivity (having the dynamic level of a note change depending on how hard you hit the key). Without that, it is hard to play jazz expressively. If you can get weighted or semi-weighted keys, that is helpful, too. Another important feature is having enough polyphony (notes you can play at once) to not run out of notes when you play big chords or use the sustain pedal. It is hard to get by with less than sixteen note polyphony. Finally, sounds are important but so many affordable MIDI (Musical Instrument Digital Interface) modules are available with good sounds that you can always upgrade your sounds later on, as long as your synth is MIDI compatible.

TUNES

If you are comfortable with most of the concepts in this book, you are ready to learn some tunes.

You should save a few dollars and buy yourself a *fake book*. A fake book (sometimes called a "real book") is a book of lead sheets to commonly played tunes.

Fake books can be found at virtually any music store. Sometimes the tunes are typeset and easy to read, other times they are handwritten. The charts vary from painstakingly accurate to thumbnail sketches. No book of this type tries to put all the tunes you will ever need into one book, emphasizing quality over quantity.

Build a library of tune sources. This way you can cross-reference between books to figure out the "correct" way to play a tune. If you can only get one fake book, the choice depends on your needs.

Once you have some tunes, PLAY THEM. Go to some jazz gigs and jam sessions and see what tunes people are playing. If you hear a particular tune often, learn it. If there is a tune that keeps showing up on records you have, learn it. If you don't have a lead sheet, ask a musician who knows it to show it to you. Or, if your ears are up to the task, try taking the tune off a record. Begin by trying to hear the roots in the bass. Then, see if you can figure out the changes. Go back and figure out the melody.

Also, try sight-reading lead sheets out of fake books. See if you can quickly (if not necessarily perfectly) take a tune you don't already know and play the melody, the chords and a solo. This way you will be exposed to more tunes and you will get into the practice of sight reading tunes. When you play with other people, you are likely to play tunes you don't already know and it is very useful to be able to read them like this.

Make tunes a focal point of your jazz education. When you learn a new concept or technique, try applying it to a tune. Make it a goal to learn enough tunes so that you can go out and play with other people. Playing with other people is where you will get your most important training.

RECORDINGS

The following is a list of recordings that are well worth checking out. This is not a comprehensive list by any means. These albums are simply a good place to start listening to great jazz. These recordings will help reinforce the ideas from this book. Enjoy!

— Cannonball Adderley: *Somethin' Else* (with Hank Jones on piano)
— Louis Armstrong and Earl Hines: *Louis Armstrong and Earl Hines*
— Kenny Barron: *Live at Bradley's*
— Count Basie: *The Complete Count Basie on Decca*
— Count Basie: *The Atomic Basie*
— Art Blakey and the Jazz Messengers: *Three Blind Mice* (with Cedar Walton on piano)
— Nat "King" Cole: *Transcriptions*
— John Coltrane: *Blue Train* (with Kenny Drew on piano)
— Miles Davis: *Milestones* (with Red Garland on piano)
— Miles Davis: *In A Silent Way* (with Chick Corea, Herbie Hancock and Joe Zawinul on keyboards)
— Duke Ellington: *Piano Reflections*
— Duke Ellington: *Duke Ellington at Newport*
— Bill Evans: *Portrait in Jazz*
— Erroll Garner: *Concert By the Sea*
— Stan Getz: *Sweet Rain* (with Chick Corea on piano)
— Benny Goodman: *After You've Gone* (with Teddy Wilson on piano)
— Dexter Gordon: *A Swingin' Affair* (with Sonny Clark on piano)
— Herbie Hancock: *Takin' Off*
— Ahmad Jamal: *But Not For Me – Live at the Pershing*
— Jo Jones: *Jo Jones Trio* (with Ray Bryant on piano – also available as part of *The Essential Jo Jones*)
— Wynton Kelly Trio with Wes Montgomery: *Smokin' at the Half Note*
— Ramsey Lewis: *The In Crowd*
— Les McAnn and Eddie Harris: *Swiss Movement*
— Charles Mingus: *Blues & Roots* (with Horace Parlan and Mal Waldron on piano)
— Thelonious Monk: *Monk's Dream*
— Phineas Newborn, Jr.: *A World of Piano*
— Charlie Parker: *The Complete Savoy & Dial Master Takes* (various pianists)
— Oscar Peterson Trio: *We Get Requests*
— Bud Powell: *Jazz Giant*
— Sonny Rollins: *Saxophone Colossus* (with Tommy Flanagan on piano)
— Horace Silver: *Finger Poppin'*
— Jimmy Smith: *Organ Grinder Swing*
— McCoy Tyner: *Inception*
— Art Tatum: *Piano Starts Here*
— Mary Lou Williams: *Live at the Cookery*
— Lester Young and Teddy Wilson: *Pres and Teddy*

Dig into any of these albums you can get your hands (and ears) on, and enjoy! We'll meet again in *Intermediate Jazz Keyboard.*

INTERMEDIATE JAZZ KEYBOARD

This book was acquired, edited, and produced
by Workshop Arts, Inc., the publishing arm of
the National Keyboard Workshop.
Nathaniel Gunod, acquisitions, editor
Amy Rosser, editor
ProScore, Novato, CA, music typesetter
Cathy Bolduc, interior design
Audio tracks recorded by Collin Tilton at Bar None Studio, Northford, CT

CONTENTS

Contents   **99**

INTRODUCTION

Welcome to the *Intermediate* section. If *Beginning Jazz Keyboard* was designed to get your feet wet playing jazz, this section assumes you've enjoyed the water and want to plunge into the deep end. The information will build upon the foundation you've established and help make you performance-ready. Once you've spent some time shedding (a.k.a. "woodshedding," the jazz term for practicing) the concepts and techniques in this section, you'll be quite ready to get out and play. In fact, if you made it through the *Beginning* section, you could start playing out already. By the time you learn about modes, extended and altered chords, substitution, making the changes, the blues, and comping, you'll be prepared for a great many performance situations. You may not know everything, but you'll be able to supplement your studies in this book with some on-the-job training, and that's how you'll really integrate this information.

As with *Beginning Jazz Keyboard,* you're encouraged to cross-reference within this section. For example, when you learn chord extensions in Chapter 3, go back and use them on the modal tunes in Chapter 2. All the while, keep learning tunes (see the list in Chapter 9) and applying the new concepts to them. And, as you keep listening to great jazz, the things you're learning will help you begin to identify and understand what's going on. Have fun and I'll see you on the bandstand.

ACKNOWLEDGMENTS

Thank you to everyone who made this project possible (including many people who didn't make it onto this list): to Nat Gunod, Dave Smolover, Burgess Speed and everyone else at NGW and Workshop Arts; to Alfred Music Publishing; to Collin Tilton at Bar None Studios; to Dan Morgensen, Esther Smith and the rest of the people at The Institute of Jazz Studies; to Steve Bennett, Karl Mueller, Wynne Mun, Jeff Grace, Amanda Monaco, Damion Poirier, Jimmy Greene, Noah Richardson, Jeff Bartolotta, Roberto Scrofani, Rachel Green, the Ten Eyck family and all the rest of the friends who directly or indirectly helped me to put these books together; to all my students who taught me how to teach; to ECA and the Artists' Collective for getting me started with jazz; to the Music Department at Rutgers for all their support and training; to Eva Pierrou, Clara Shen and Wanda Maximilien for their expert piano teaching; to Mike Mossman, Sumi Tonooka, Joanne Brackeen, Larry Ridley, Phil Schaap, Ralph Bowen, and especially Ted Dunbar, George Raccio and Kenny Barron for selflessly sharing their jazz knowledge; to my dear friends and inspiring colleagues from Positive Rhythmic Force, Jason Berg, Ben Tedoff and Sunny Jain; to my family, Mom, Dad, Alison, Jennifer, Matthew and Annie for their boundless support and patience; and to Kate for everything.

00

Track I

An MP3 CD is included with this book to make learning easier and more enjoyable. The symbol shown at bottom left appears next to every example in the book that features an MP3 track. Use the MP3s to ensure you're capturing the feel of the examples and interpreting the rhythms correctly. The track number below the symbol corresponds directly to the example you want to hear (example numbers are above the icon). All the track numbers are unique to each "book" within this volume, meaning every book has its own Track I, Track 2, and so on. (For example, *Beginning Jazz Keyboard* starts with Track I, as does *Intermediate Jazz Keyboard* and *Mastering Jazz Keyboard*.) Track I for each book will help you tune to the CD.

The disc is playable on any CD player equipped to play MP3 CDs. To access the MP3s on your computer, place the CD in your CD-ROM drive. In Windows, double-click on My Computer, then right-click on the CD icon labeled "MP3 Files" and select Explore to view the files and copy them to your hard drive. For Mac, double-click on the CD icon on your desktop labeled "MP3 Files" to view the files and copy them to your hard drive.

CHAPTER 1

Review

The material in this section begins where *Beginning Jazz Keyboard* left off. This chapter will provide a quick review of some of the concepts and techniques covered in that first section. If anything seems hazy to you as you go through the review, go back and look over the original, more thorough explanation. The review won't cover more abstract issues like swing feel, syncopation in solo lines and melodic embellishment, since those are things we're all constantly working on regardless of our level.

INTERVALS

An interval is the distance between two notes. Intervals have formal names from classical music theory (minor 2nd, Perfect 4th, Augmented 5th), and they can also be named as scale degrees using the number system ($\flat$2, 4, $\sharp$5).

Number	Number of ½ Steps	Interval	Abbreviation
1	0	Perfect unison	PU
$\flat$2	1	Minor 2nd	min2
2	2	Major 2nd	Maj2
$\flat$3	3	Minor 3rd	min3
3	4	Major 3rd	Maj3
4	5	Perfect 4th	P4
$\sharp$4	6 ("tritone")	Augmented 4th	A4
$\flat$5	6	Diminished 5th	dim5
5	7	Perfect 5th	P5
$\sharp$5	8	Augmented 5th	Aug5
$\flat$6	6	Minor 6th	min6
6	9	Major 6th	Maj6
$\flat$7	10	Minor 7th	min7
7	11	Major 7th	Maj7
1	12	Perfect octave	P8

We can also turn the intervals upside down using interval inversion and find equivalents of each interval.

Interval Inversion Chart
Perfect inverts to perfect
Major inverts to minor
Augmented inverts to diminished
2nd inverts to 7th
3rd inverts to 6th
4th inverts to 5th

TRIADS

A chord is a structure built from three or more notes. The most basic type of chord is a triad, a three note chord. A triad is built with a root (1), 3rd (3) and 5th (5). We learned five types of triads.

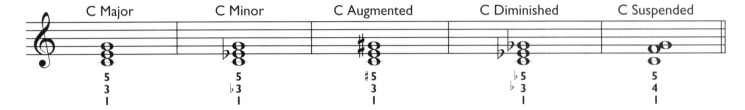

Each triad has a chord symbol associated with it, a shorthand way of notating the chord. There are different possible symbols for each chord, but the first one listed for each chord type is the symbol used in this series.

Chord	Possible Symbols	Formula
C Major	C, CMaj, CM, C△	1, 3, 5
C Minor	Cmin, Cmi, Cm, C-	1, ♭3, 5
C Augmented	C+, Caug	1, 3, ♯5
C Diminished	Cdim, C°	1, ♭3, ♭5
C Suspended	Csus, Csus4	1, 4, 5

The notes that make up a chord can be played in any order. Playing a chord with a note other than the root as the bass (bottom) note is called an inversion. A chord with the root on the bottom is said to be in root position. A chord with the 3rd on the bottom is in 1st inversion. A chord with the 5th on the bottom is in 2nd inversion. *Slash notation* is often used to indicate an inversion. For instance, C/G indicates a 2nd inversion C Major triad (G is the bass).

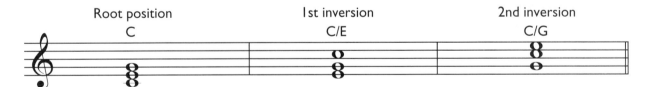

If an inversion is played in the right hand and the root is played with the left hand, it is still a root position chord. Playing inversions in the right hand over roots in the bass allows us more variety of chord sounds. The specific way we arrange the notes in a chord is called *voicing*.

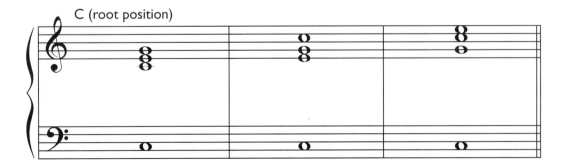

7TH CHORDS

7th chords are four note chords that add a 7 on top of the 1, 3 and 5 of triads. 7th chords consist of root, 3rd, 5th and 7th. There are five main types of 7th chords: Major 7th, Dominant 7th, minor 7th, minor 7th ♭5 (half diminished) and diminished 7th.

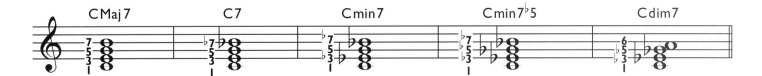

Another type of four note chord is the 6th chord. These chords are the same as 7th chords except that a Major 6th replaces the 7th. The 6th in a 6th chord functions the same way as the 7th in a 7th chord. There are two types: Major 6th and minor 6th.

These are the common symbols used for the different types of 7th and 6th chords. As with the triads, the first symbol listed for each chord is the one used in these books.

Chord	Possible Symbols	Formula
C Major 7th	CMaj7, CM7, C△7	1, 3, 5, 7
C Major 6th	C6, CMaj6, CM6, C△6	1, 3, 5, 6
C Dominant 7th	C7	1, 3, 5, ♭7
C Minor 7th	Cmin7, Cmi7, Cm7, C-7	1, ♭3, 5, ♭7
C Minor 6th	Cmin6, Cmi6, Cm6, C-6	1, ♭3, 5, 6
C Minor 7th (flat 5)	Cmin7♭5, Cø, Cmi7♭5, Cm7♭5, C-7♭5	1, ♭3, ♭5, ♭7
C Diminished 7th	Cdim7, C○7	1, ♭3, ♭5, 6 (♭♭7)

DIATONIC HARMONY

Diatonic is Greek for "of the scale" and diatonic harmony refers to the chords associated with a given scale or key. If we stack thirds and build 7th chords from each note in the C Major scale, we wind up with this:

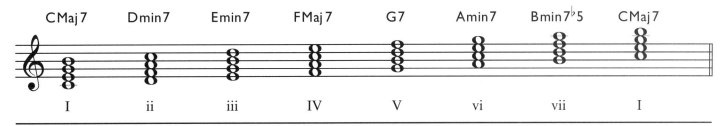

The chords are labeled with Roman numerals to indicate the scale degree. In general, uppercase Roman numerals are used for chords with Major 3rds (Maj, Maj7, Maj6 and dominant 7th) and lowercase Roman numerals are used for chords with minor 3rds (min, min7, min6, min7♭5 and dim7).

Here is a Roman numeral review:

I	or	i	=	1		V	or	v	=	5
II	or	ii	=	2		VI	or	vi	=	6
III	or	iii	=	3		VII	or	vii	=	7
IV	or	iv	=	4						

The same chord types are always associated with the same numerals regardless of the key. In any major key, 7th chords are built from each degree of the scale as follows:

I	Maj7		V	(Dominant) 7
ii	min7		vi	min7
iii	min7		vii	min7♭5
IV	Maj7			

Here are the diatonic 7th chords in all twelve keys.

Key	I	ii	iii	IV	V	vi	vii
C	CMaj7	Dmin7	Emin7	FMaj7	G7	Amin7	Bmin7♭5
G	GMaj7	Amin7	Bmin7	CMaj7	D7	Emin7	F♯min7♭5
D	DMaj7	Emin7	F♯min7	GMaj7	A7	Bmin7	C♯min7♭5
A	AMaj7	Bmin7	C♯min7	DMaj7	E7	F♯min7	G♯min7♭5
E	EMaj7	F♯min7	G♯min7	AMaj7	B7	C♯min7	D♯min7♭5
B	BMaj7	C♯min7	D♯min7	EMaj7	F♯7	G♯min7	A♯min7♭5
G♭	G♭Maj7	A♭min7	B♭min7	C♭Maj7	D♭7	E♭min7	Fmin7♭5
D♭	D♭Maj7	E♭min7	Fmin7	G♭Maj7	A♭7	B♭min7	Cmin7♭5
A♭	A♭Maj7	B♭min7	Cmin7	D♭Maj7	E♭7	Fmin7	Gmin7♭5
E♭	E♭Maj7	Fmin7	Gmin7	A♭Maj7	B♭7	Cmin7	Dmin7♭5
B♭	B♭Maj7	Cmin7	Dmin7	E♭Maj7	F7	Gmin7	Amin7♭5
F	FMaj7	Gmin7	Amin7	B♭Maj7	C7	Dmin7	Emin7♭5

In a minor key, we derive harmony in the same way. We have the natural minor and the harmonic minor from which to stack our 3rds. The harmony we usually use takes some chords from each. The i and III chords are taken from the natural minor, the V and vii chords are taken from the harmonic minor and the ii, iv and VI chords are the same in both. Here are the chords in the key of A Minor:

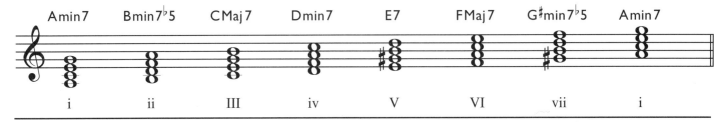

VOICINGS

In the *Beginning* section we examined a few different ways to voice 7th chords. The fundamental concept behind all of these voicing methods is *voice leading*, the smooth movement of the notes in one voicing to the notes in the next voicing. We want the hands to have to move as little as possible going from one chord to the next. That makes life easier on our hands and it sounds better, too. We will look at the different voicing methods as they might be used on a iii-vi-ii-V-I progression in the key of B♭.

FOUR-NOTE VOICINGS

For these voicings, we play the root in the left hand and the 3rd, 5th and 7th in the right hand. The left hand will leap around a bit but we try to keep the right hand as smooth as possible.

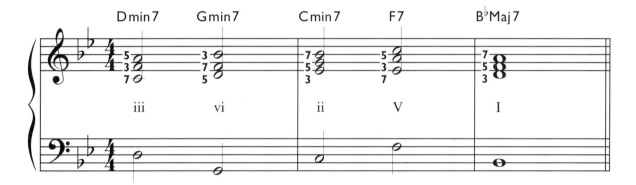

SHELL VOICINGS

Since the perfect 5th is present in Maj7, 7 and min7 chords, we don't need it to define the sound of the chord. Therefore, we can play these economical voicings with the roots in the left hand and the 3rd and 7th in the right hand. When the roots move down in 5ths (or up in 4ths), the voice leading in the right hand is very smooth.

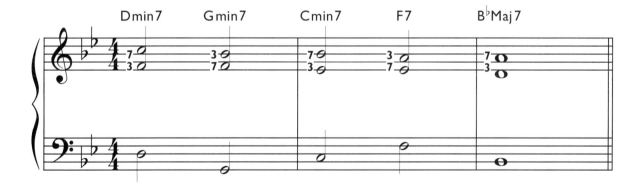

BEBOP-STYLE LEFT-HAND VOICINGS

Bebop-style left hand voicings, popularized by Bud Powell, are about as simple and skeletal as they come, designed to serve as simple root-position voicings for the left hand while the right hand plays a melody or improvised solo. You play the root and then the 3rd or 7th above it, depending on which note provides the smoothest voice leading.

THREE NOTE ROOTLESS VOICINGS

When you play with a bass player (which is the case in most jazz group settings), there is already someone playing the roots so you needn't play them yourself. To play three note rootless voicings, simply take the four note voicings from the previous page and let your left hand play the 3rd, 5th and 7th instead of the right. The roots are omitted.

ROOTLESS SHELL VOICINGS

Here again we give the right hand part of a voicing method to the left hand and leave out the roots, leaving the right hand free. Take regular shell voicings and put the 3rd and 7th in the left hand.

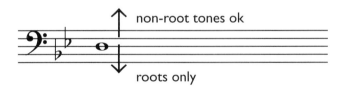

Note:

Voicings get muddy when non-root tones are played too low. In general, keep everything but the roots at or above the D below middle C, especially on rootless voicings (where anything played that low will sound like a root).

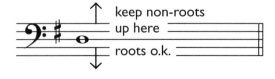

HARMONIC ANALYSIS

Harmonic analysis is figuring out what key (or keys) a set of changes is in and how the chords relate to the key of the moment. If you saw these changes . . .

| Bmin7 | Emin7 | Amin7 | D7 | GMaj7 |

... you would realize that they all function within the key of G, so you would analyze them like this, perhaps even writing this analysis on top of the changes in pencil:

G: iii	vi	ii	V	I
Bmin7	Emin7	Amin7	D7	GMaj7

Now, when you go to solo, you know what key you're in and can choose your scales accordingly. The same can be done with minor keys:

Gmin: i	iv	ii	V	i
Gmin7	Cmin7	Amin7♭5	D7	Gmin6

Modulation is the changing of keys. Quite often, a tune will modulate meaning that you have to shift your harmonic thinking to match up with the changing of keys. On page 51, we learned the tune *Well, How About Bridgeport?* which modulates to three different keys in the A-section. When you solo, you simply shift your thinking (and scale choices) to each new key whenever there is a modulation.

C: I	B♭: ii	V	I	A♭: ii	V
CMaj7	Cmin7	F7	B♭Maj7	B♭min7	E♭7

I	C: ii	V	I	ii	V
A♭Maj7	Dmin7	G7	CMaj7	Dmin7	G7

Look out for common harmonic patterns to clue you in about what key you are in. The most common pattern in jazz is the ii-V-I so if you see a ii-V-I or any variation thereof (ii-V, minor ii-V-i, iii-vi-ii-V-I), take it as a cue for the key you are in at that moment.

B♭min: ii	V	i
Cmin7♭5	F7	B♭min7

E: ii	V
F#min7	B7

SCALES

We learned the following scales for use with soloing in a key. The major and major pentatonic work with major keys and the other four apply to minor keys.

Major

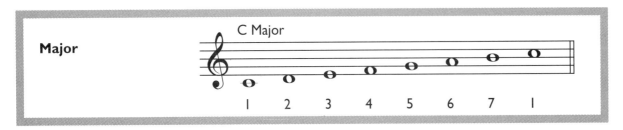

Major Pentatonic

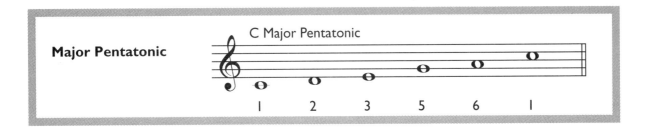

Natural Minor

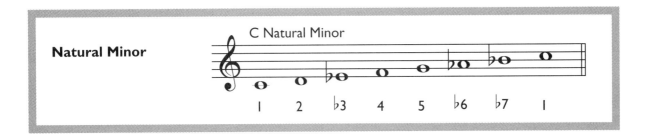

Harmonic Minor

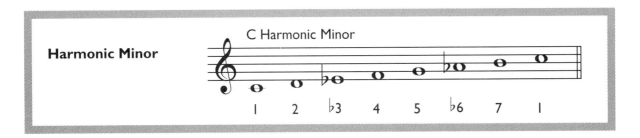

Minor Pentatonic

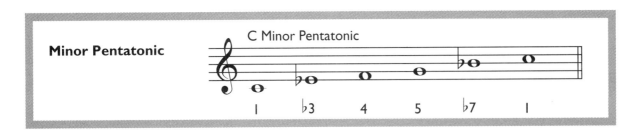

Blues

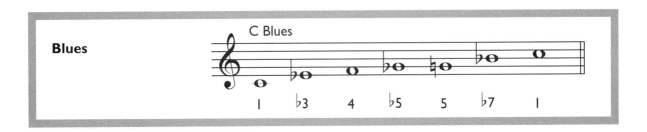

ARPEGGIOS

In addition to using scales to solo in a key, we can play the notes of the chords by using arpeggios (which we will re-examine on page 141). In the context of jazz soloing, think this way: when a chord is occurring, solo based on the notes in that chord. When the chord changes, shift to the notes of the new chord. Beyond that, be creative.

LEAD SHEETS

In jazz, we don't often get fully-written-out keyboard parts. More commonly we read lead sheets, especially when we're playing tunes out of fake books. A lead sheet gives us the melody and the chord symbols to a tune and leaves the rest to us. To flesh out a lead sheet, we can do one of two things (or switch between the two):

1) Figure out chord voicings that put the melody note on top.
2) Play the melody in the right hand and voice the chords in the left hand.

Try playing through the lead sheet below in both of these ways.

TREKKIN' (LEAD SHEET)

If you could get through this lead sheet with both of these methods, then it looks like you're ready to move on to the world of modes, extended chords, substitutions and making the changes. The next two pages show the lead sheet realized with each method. Your versions don't have to match with them exactly. They are just examples.

Track 2

TREKKIN' *(TWO-HANDED CHORDS WITH MELODY ON TOP)*

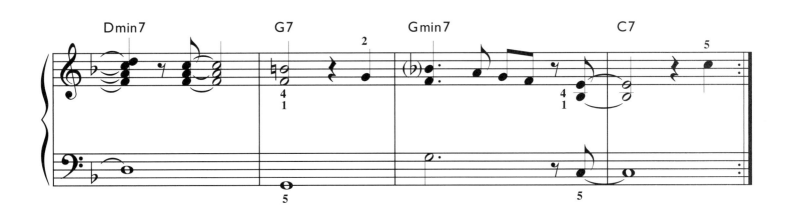

Track 3

TREKKIN' (MELODY IN RIGHT HAND, CHORDS IN LEFT)

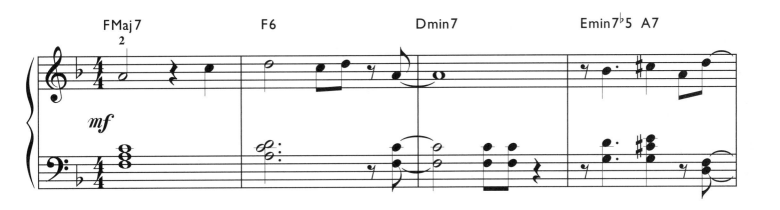

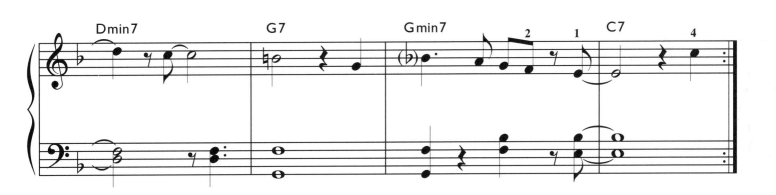

CHAPTER 2

Modes of the Major Scale

Beginning in the mid to late 1950s, jazz musicians like George Russell, Miles Davis, Bill Evans and John Coltrane began to experiment with *modes*. Far from a revolutionary new sound, these Greek-named modes had simply been neglected since the Renaissance. Classical composers rescued the modes of the major scale from obscurity in the late 19th and early 20th centuries and in the 1950s jazz musicians saw how useful they could be in modern jazz.

The concept behind modes is quite simple. A major scale is a series of eight notes with a specific order of half steps and whole steps. If we start the scale from a different note, we get a different sound even though we still have the same eight notes. We have already encountered this with the relative minor, in which we start a major scale on its 6th (not 1st) degree and wind up with a completely different sound.

A mode of the major scale is simply that scale begun from a different note. If we use C Major as our parent scale (scale from which other things are derived), the modes are as follows.

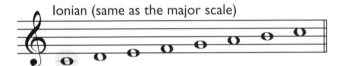

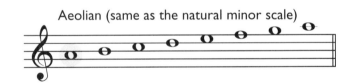

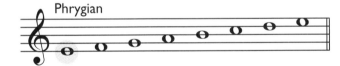

You can use this little phrase to help remember the order of the modes. Just think about how you are working to develop your own style and not simply imitate jazz keyboard greats of the past like Thelonious Monk or Lennie Tristano. Then declare to the world:

("**I** **D**on't **P**lay **L**ike **M**onk **A**nd **L**ennie!")

Just to drive the point home, let's also take a look at the modes of the F and G major scales.

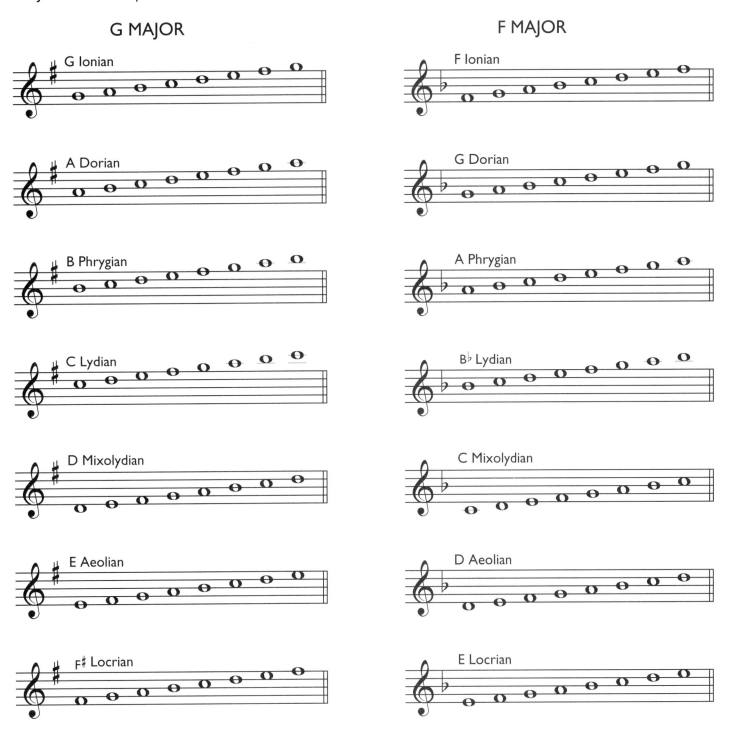

G MAJOR

- G Ionian
- A Dorian
- B Phrygian
- C Lydian
- D Mixolydian
- E Aeolian
- F# Locrian

F MAJOR

- F Ionian
- G Dorian
- A Phrygian
- B♭ Lydian
- C Mixolydian
- D Aeolian
- E Locrian

Each mode, in addition to being another way to play the major scale, is a valid scale in its own right. The terms "scale" and "mode" are basically interchangeable. They're both scales and the term "mode" simply implies that it has been derived from another scale (just like the relative minor). As you learn the modes, practice playing and thinking about them in both of these ways. Know the modes that go with a particular parent scale but also learn each mode as a scale all its own. When we look at modes as autonomous scales, we find that they all resemble scales we already know.

Up until now, we've been using scales only to solo over an entire key center. The only way we have been able to deal with each chord individually has been with arpeggios. The modes of the major scale are very useful in giving us scales that we can associate with specific chords. As you check out each mode, pay attention to which type of chord it relates to.

The Dorian mode, built from the 2nd degree of the major scale, implies a minor 7th chord (the circled notes). The notes in the mode are the same as a natural minor scale with a raised 6th.

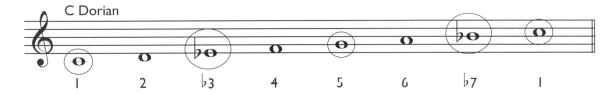

This mode sounds great over virtually any min7 chord. Since it is based on the 2nd degree of the major scale, it is particularly useful over ii chords in major keys.

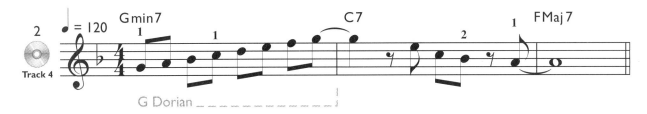

To play the Dorian mode from any note, find the natural minor scale from that note and raise the 6th degree by a half step.

Iceberg is a tune using the Dorian mode. The melody is based on the Dorian mode starting from each of the min7 chords' roots. When you solo, use the Dorian mode that corresponds with each min7 chord.

ICEBERG

THE LYDIAN MODE

The Lydian mode, built from the 4th degree of the major scale, implies a major 7th chord. The notes in the mode are the same as a major scale with a raised 4th.

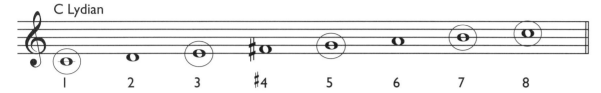

The Lydian mode is often the modern jazz musician's first choice for a scale to match up with a Maj7 chord, even when the major scale would seem to be the logical choice. The ♯4 gives the mode a very open sound, unlike the natural 4th of the Ionian mode (major scale), which has a strong pull to the 3rd.

To play the Lydian mode from any note, find the major scale from that note and raise the 4th degree by a half step.

The melody for *Courtesy Call* uses the Lydian mode on all the Maj7 chords, and you should do the same as you improvise. Once you feel comfortable, try substituting the major scale periodically, just to notice the difference in sound. And don't forget that you are in $\frac{3}{4}$ time.

COURTESY CALL

The Mixolydian mode, built from the 5th degree of the major scale, implies a dominant 7th chord. The notes in the mode are the same as a major scale with a lowered (flatted) 7th.

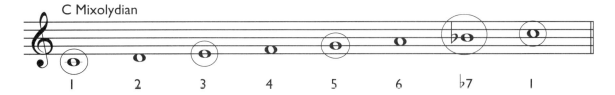

The Mixolydian mode is the most common scale choice for dominant chords. This is true on V chords that resolve to I, and also on more free-floating dominant chords like those you would find in a blues (such as *Blues in Bloom* below).

To play the Mixolydian mode from any note, find the major scale from that note and lower the 7th degree by a half step.

Blues in Bloom is a twelve bar blues in G based on the Mixolydian mode. Use the Mixolydian mode on each of the dominant chords when you solo.

BLUES IN BLOOM

Track 9

THE PHRYGIAN MODE

The Phrygian mode, built from the 3rd degree of the major scale, implies a minor 7th chord. The notes in the mode are the same as a natural minor scale with a lowered (flatted) 2nd.

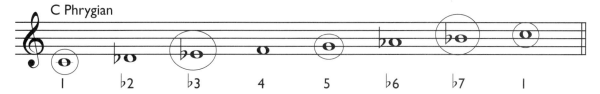

Although you can derive a min7 chord from the Phrygian mode, it is a less common sound than the Dorian. The ♭2 gives it an exotic (some say Middle Eastern) flavor that's a bit strong for most situations where you encounter min7 chords (i chords in minor keys, ii chords, etc.). Some modern tunes like Wayne Shorter's *Infant Eyes* and John Coltrane's *After the Rain* use the Phrygian sound for an open, mysterious feeling. The Phrygian mode can also be used on the iii chord in a major key, since it is derived from the 3rd degree of the major scale.

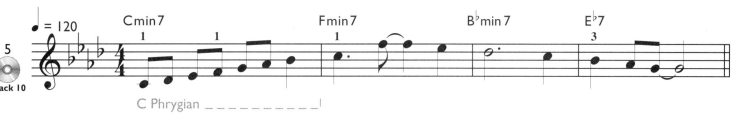

To play the Phrygian mode from any note, find the natural minor scale from that note and lower the 2nd degree by a half step.

THE LOCRIAN MODE

The Locrian mode, built from the 7th degree of the major scale, implies a minor 7th ♭5 (half-diminished) chord. The notes in the mode are the same as a natural minor scale with a lowered (flatted) 2nd and a lowered 5th.

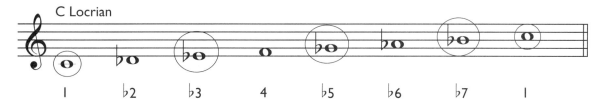

The Locrian mode gives us a scale to use with min7♭5 chords. Sometimes this chord will appear as the vii chord in a major key, but we most commonly find the min7♭5 as the ii chord in a minor key. The Locrian mode sounds fine when we insert it into that setting.

To play the Locrian mode from any note, find the natural minor scale from that note and lower both the 2nd and 5th degrees by a half step.

THE IONIAN AND AEOLIAN MODES

The Ionian mode and Aeolian mode are simply the old Greek names for the major and natural minor scales, respectively. At one time, they were just two among the seven modes but they eventually became the most popular, and consequently, the other five were temporarily forgotten.

The funny thing is that modern jazz musicians have changed this hierarchy around somewhat. The uses for the major and natural minor scales that we learned in the *Beginning* section still apply and are still very useful. However, the modes give us access to colors that are sometimes more useful than these. The Dorian mode is more commonly used in modern jazz soloing than the Aeolian (natural minor). Even on the i chord in a minor key, notice the difference.

Both lines sound fine, but the Dorian one has a more open, flexible sound. And notice that the raised 6th in the Dorian matches up with the 6th in a min6 chord; if you or someone you were playing with wanted to use a min6 for the i chord in a minor key, Dorian would match up perfectly.

Likewise, the Ionian mode (the almighty major scale) sounds fine over diatonic progressions and over major chords. However, the Lydian sound is more open and flexible over a major chord than the Ionian.

Of course, there will be times when the sound of Ionian or Aeolian is exactly what you want to hear at that moment but you will be glad to have the others at your disposal. Allow yourself time to get used to these sounds. Most of us are used to playing music that relies heavily on the more traditional scales (major and natural minor), so it can take some time to learn to hear modes like Dorian and Lydian as comfortable sounds. Be patient and listen to the greats of modern jazz to hear the modes being put to good use.

One very useful way to use the modes is to match them up with the diatonic chords in a key. Since both the modes and the diatonic chords in a major key are derived in basically the same way, the relationship is clear. Look at the relationships in the key of B♭ major.

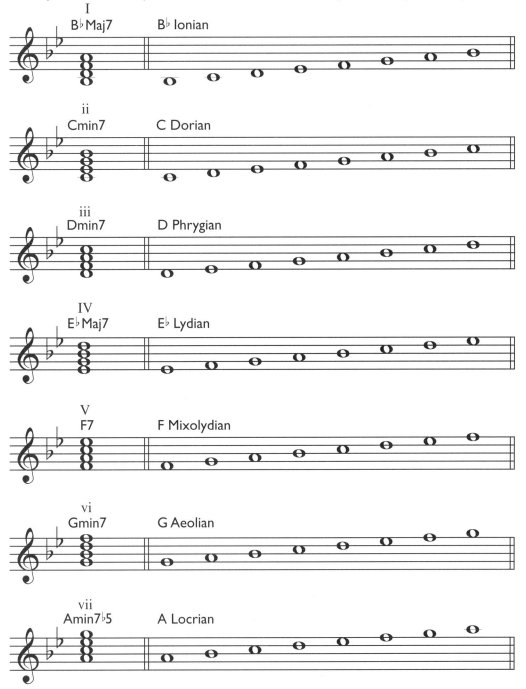

Armed with this knowledge, you can solo over changes in a key and immediately know which mode may be the most appropriate over any individual chord. For example:

iii	vi	ii	V	I
D Phrygian	**G Aeolian**	**C Dorian**	**F Mixolydian**	**B♭ Ionian**
| Dmin7	| Gmin7	| Cmin7	| F7	| B♭Maj7 ||

We may choose to substitute other modes for these (for example, using Lydian instead of Ionian on the I chord) based on the sounds we want to hear, but this is a surefire way to find modes that fit the changes and sound great.

Struttin' with Fats, dedicated to keyboardist and composer Fats Waller, is in the key of A Major using all the modes derived from that key. Notice that for a moment it modulates to D Major, temporarily using the modes from that key instead. When you solo, use the modes that correspond to the diatonic chords.

STRUTTIN' WITH FATS

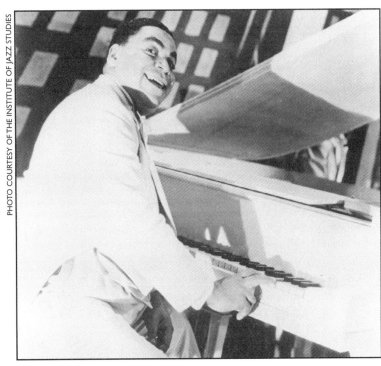

Thomas "Fats" Waller *is best known for late 1920s compositions like* Ain't Misbehavin' *and* Honeysuckle Rose, *but he was also a superb keyboardist.*

Rather than dealing with diatonic harmony, the melody of *Still Waiting. . .* simply matches the Dorian mode with all the min7 chords, Mixolydian with all the dominant 7 chords, and Lydian with all the Maj7 chords. When you solo, do the same to get more practice with these three indispensable modes. The changes are in the style of *Nardis,* a Miles Davis tune that has been recorded by Bill Evans, Cannonball Adderley and Joe Henderson, among others.

STILL WAITING . . .

Track 15

CHAPTER 3

Chord Extensions

Let's say we're in C Major. We're on the 4th degree, F natural, and we want to form the triad built from that degree. So, we stack a couple 3rds and wind up with an F major triad.

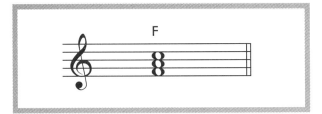

Then we decide that we want more color, so we look for the 7th chord built from the same degree. We take the triad we've already found and stack another 3rd on top of that, giving us FMaj7.

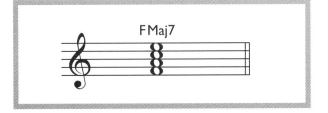

Since that sounds good, let's keep stacking more 3rds, alternating every other note until we repeat one. Now that's one big, fat, colorful chord.

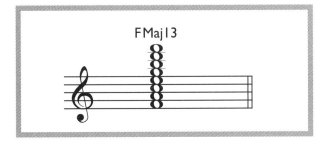

This is the basic concept behind *chord extensions*. The four notes that make up a chord aren't the only notes that sound good when played with that chord. Chord extensions are extra notes stacked on top of a chord to give it extra color.

Below is a two-octave C major scale, labeled by scale degree. Since the new notes we are talking about are extensions, we need the second octave to distinguish them from the chord tones (which would be in the first octave).

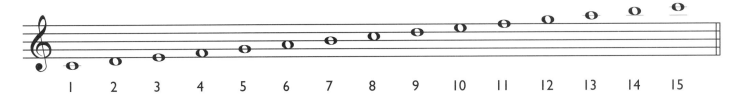

If we stack 3rds from C, we wind up with this voicing. The Root, 3rd, 5th and 7th are there as usual with the addition of the 9th, 11th and 13th. 9ths, 11ths and 13ths are typically the extensions you will be dealing with. The others are simply repetitions of chord tones. The distinction is important; calling the D in this chord the 9th and not the 2nd indicates that it is an extension and not a fundamental part of the chord. In other words, extensions are always a higher number than 7.

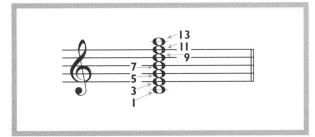

Sometimes these extensions will be specifically notated. The typical way to do so is to name the chord by the highest extension in the voicing. For example, a Cmin9 is a Cmin7 with only an added 9th (D natural), but Cmin11 could also have a 9th in addition to the 11th.

This chart shows some of the chord symbols you could encounter in a lead sheet (each with C as its root), along with the chord each symbol is based on, the implied extension, and other possible extensions. You don't need to study this chart now but it is here as a reference for when you encounter chord symbols with extensions.

Chord Symbol	Begin with	add	can also add
CMaj9 (C△9)	CMaj7	9	
CMaj7♯11 (C△7♯11)	CMaj7	♯11	9
CMaj13 (C△13)	CMaj7	13	9, ♯11
C6/9	CMaj6	9	
C9	C7	9	
C7sus (C7sus4)	C7	4 (11) replaces 3	9, 13
C13	C7	13	9, ♯11
C7♭9	C7	♭9	
C7♭13	C7	♭13	
Cmin9 (C-9)	Cmin7	9	
Cmin11 (C-11)	Cmin7	11	9
Cmin6/9 (C-6/9)	Cmin6	9	
Cmin/Maj7 (C-△7)	Cmin	(Maj)7	
Cmin9/Maj7 (C-9△7)	Cmin/Maj7	9	
Cmin9♭5 (Cø9)	Cmin7♭5	9	
Cmin11♭5 (Cø11)	Cmin7♭5	11	9
Cdim9 (C○9)	Cdim7	9	
Cdim11 (C○11)	Cdim7	11	9
Cdim7♭13	Cdim7	♭13	9, 11
Cdim/Maj7 (C○△7)	Cdim7	7 (14)	9, 11, ♭13

More often, chord extensions are not notated specifically but rather left to the discretion of the player. The next few pages are devoted to exploring the common extensions and their uses.

PHOTO COURTESY OF THE INSTITUTE OF JAZZ STUDIES

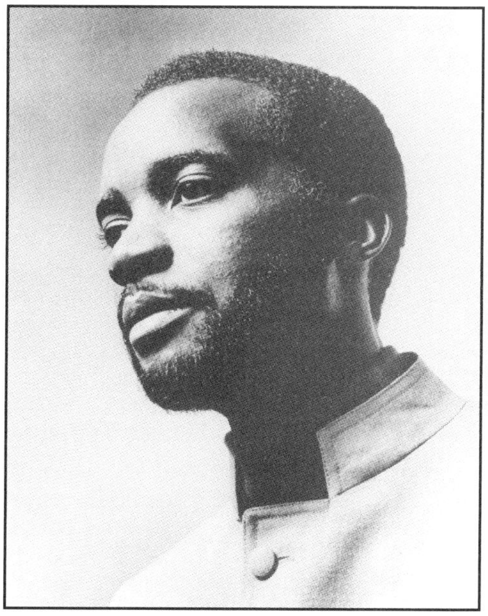

***Ahmad Jamal's** playing style underwent several changes after his emergence in the early 1950s, but his rich chord voicings remained a constant.*

When you see the symbol C7, there are many things you can do to color the chord, and you don't have to wait for the symbols "C9" or "C13" to do them. Here are some suggestions.

When you encounter a dominant chord, you can generally add the 9th and it will sound great. Note that in the third example, the 5th of the chord is omitted. With shell voicings (page 55) we learned that the root, 3rd and 7th are the key notes to the sound of a chord and the 5th can sometimes be left out. When voicing chords with extensions, the 5th is often left out to allow us to add more color without cluttering the voicings with too many notes.

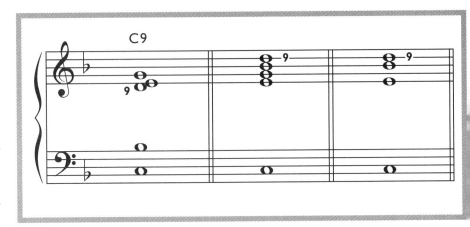

The 13th is another common extension on dominant chords. The second example contains the 9th as well, and the third example has the 9th, #11th, and 13th. In fact, the symbol C13 implies all three of these extensions (it's just a simpler symbol than "C9,#11,13"). We don't usually play all three of those extensions in each voicing, since that many notes can clutter the sound and make voice leading more awkward. The #11 is used because the natural 11 would clash with the 3rd of the chord. If you see a natural 11, it will most likely be in a C7sus4 chord. This chord is simply a

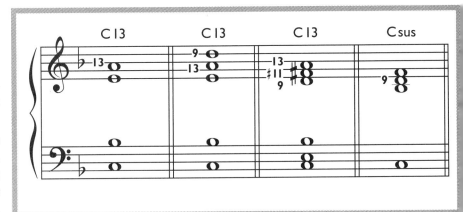

dominant 7th chord with the 3rd replaced by the 4th, just like a suspended triad. The fourth example above shows a C7sus4 chord with an added 9th, an extension we can freely use on this chord.

So far the dominant extensions we've looked at have related to the major scale. When we're in a minor key, some notes are different and the extensions don't always correspond. If the C7 were the V chord in F minor (not F major), then the most compatible 9th would be a half step lower, a ♭9. Likewise, the 13th would be a ♭13 (also a half step lower).

Note: to play any of these as rootless voicings, simply leave out the root (the bottom note in the left hand).

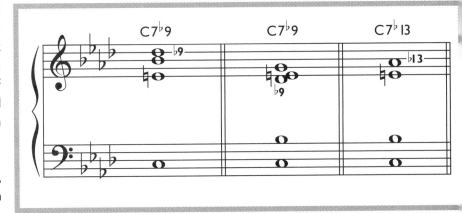

Flex, Extend is a tune chock full of dominant extensions. Play the tune in tempo but also go back and play each dominant chord by itself to get the colors in your ears.

FLEX, EXTEND
Track 16

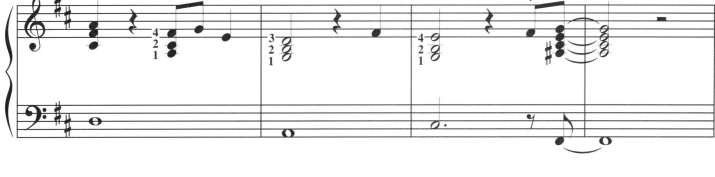

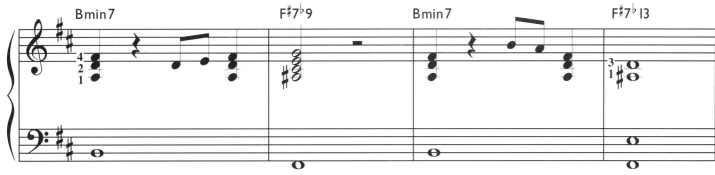

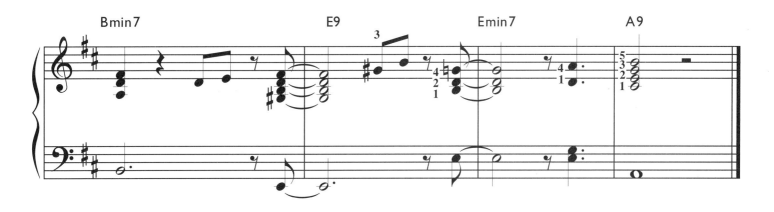

We have many opportunities to take an ordinary chord symbol and spice it up. In this case, we'll use CMaj7.

Here we have CMaj7 voiced with 9th extensions in the same three basic ways that we voiced the C9 on page 124. Two of the three voicings include the 5th. Since we're only using one extension, and the 9th and 5th are far enough apart that they aren't dissonant, there's less need to eliminate the 5th. When the voicings get denser, the 5th is typically omitted.

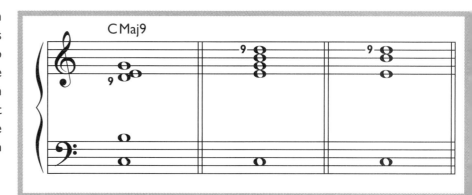

Here we have three voicings for CMaj7 with a ♯11 extension. As with the dominant extensions, the natural 11 would clash with the 3rd, so the ♯11 is used. The ♯11 is also in keeping with the Lydian sound, which we've already learned to be useful for soloing over Maj7 chords. As a general rule, if something sounds good when soloing, there's probably a way to apply it to harmony, and vice versa.

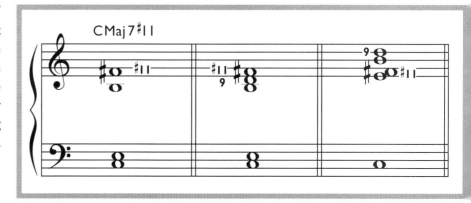

For a CMaj13, we can use just a 13th extension, or we can use the 13th in conjunction with the 9th and/or ♯11th. Another variation is the C6/9 chord, which adds a 9th extension to a C6. The way to distinguish this from a CMaj13 with a 9th is by looking for a 7th. If the chord has a major 7th, then it's a 13th extension. If there's no 7th, the 13th is actually a 6th and a fundamental part of the chord.

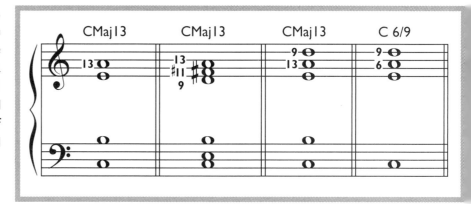

Try adding these colors wherever you see a Maj7 chord. By trial and error you will find which sounds work for your ears in any given situation.

Playing through *Groove for Groove* will give you some hands-on experience playing major chords with extensions. The tune is dedicated to the great jazz organist Richard "Groove" Holmes, whose recording of Erroll Garner's *Misty* is one of the all-time swinginest moments in jazz history.

GROOVE FOR GROOVE

There are two categories of minor chords that we will look at here: ii chords and tonic minor chords. A minor chord that is a ii chord leading to the V chord behaves differently than a minor chord acting as a i (tonic) chord in a minor key.

With ii chords, the 9th and 11th are the typical extensions. The 13th is generally not used since it is the same note as the 3rd of the V chord that is likely to follow. These extensions apply to both min7 and min7♭5 chords, and the natural 9th is generally used on the min7♭5, regardless of what key you're in (even if a ♭9 would seem more logical).

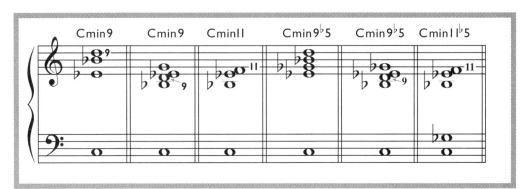

With tonic minor chords, the 9th and 11th are still useful colors but there are also two new chord types that are particularly useful. The first is the min6/9 chord in which a 9th extension is added to a min6 chord. The second is the min/Maj7 chord which is a minor triad with a major 7th (you could think of it as a minor 7th chord with a raised 7th). 9ths and 11ths can be added to the min/Maj7. The min7 chord is also fine as a i chord, and now we also have the min6/9 and min/Maj7 (with or without the optional extensions) to establish a minor home key.

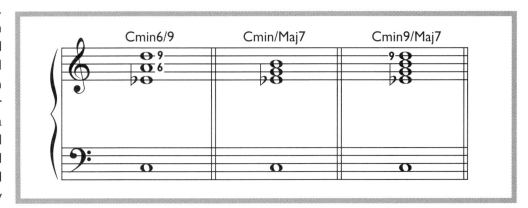

With diminished 7th chords, the method behind using extensions is very simple: a whole step above any chord tone will give you an effective color tone. Thus your options are the 9th, 11th, ♭13th and major 7th. The major 7th can be used instead of or in addition to the 6th (diminished 7th).

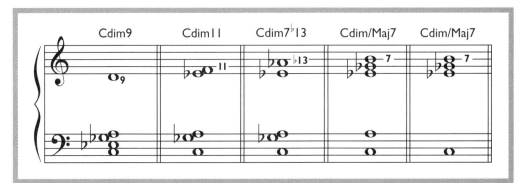

Many of the minor and diminished colors just discussed pop up in *Bello Scrofani*. Also, notice the $\frac{3}{4}$ time signature.

Track 18

BELLO SCROFANI

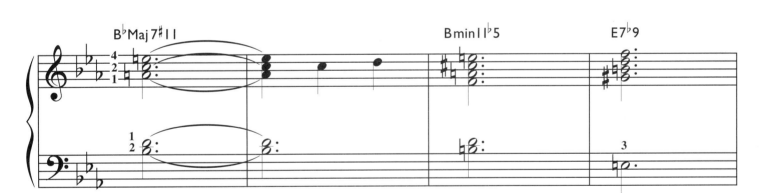

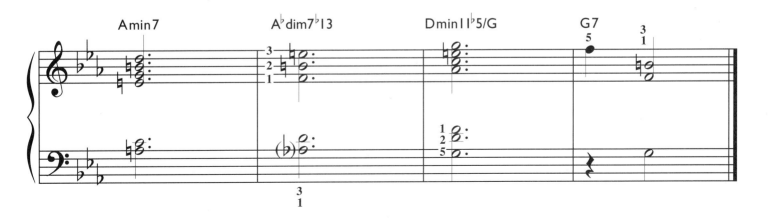

There are two typical ways of voicing a ii-V-I with extensions using rootless left-hand voicings. Let's look at the first way.

Whatever key you're in, the chords are built the same way:

ii min7	V 7	I Maj7
9	13	9
7	3	7
5	9	5
3	7	3

This is the second typical way to voice a ii-V-I with rootless left-hand voicings.

With these voicings, the chords are built this way:

ii min7	V 7	I Maj7
5	9	5
3	7	3
9	5	9
7	3	7

In a minor key, the voicing technique is the same, but be aware of notes that may need to be altered to fit the key. The ii chord is typically a min7♭5 with a 9th extension, and on the V chords, the 9ths (and 13ths, if you're using the first technique) are flatted.

The choice of which voicing technique to use usually comes down to range. You want to be low enough that you don't get in the way of the right hand, but high enough that the sound doesn't get muddy (remember from the *Beginning* section that the D below middle C is the lowest non-root note you can play that won't sound muddy).

The Squirrel and the Dog uses both of these voicing patterns. The left hand switches from one pattern to the other whenever the range makes it necessary. The changes modulate in a pattern of minor 3rds and the four keys (F, D, B and A♭) outline a diminished 7th chord, a technique used in such modern jazz tunes as *Fly, Little Bird, Fly* by Donald Byrd and *Hey, It's Me You're Talking To* by Victor Lewis.

THE SQUIRREL AND THE DOG

Track 19

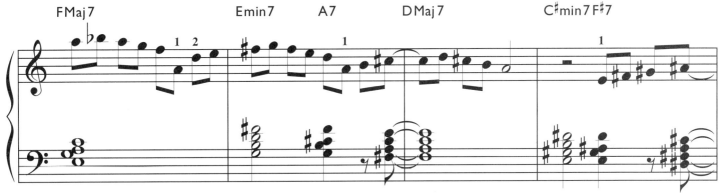

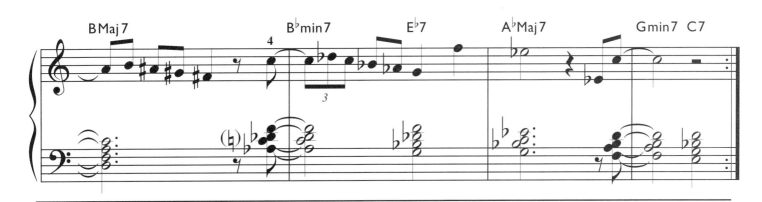

Another way to voice chords with extensions is to use other 7th chords without extensions and superimpose them over the desired root. See for yourself.

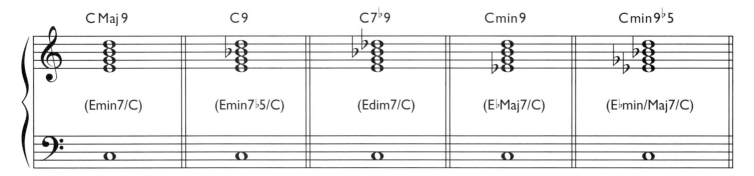

This is a good shortcut for playing chord extensions. This chart lays down what you have to do to play an extended 7th chord with this technique.

To get	play	this far above root	example
Maj9	min7	Major 3rd	Bmin7/G = GMaj9
9 (dominant)	min7♭5	Major 3rd	Bmin7♭5/G = G9
7♭9	dim7	Major 3rd	Bdim7/G = G7♭9
min9	Maj7	minor 3rd	B♭Maj7/G = Gmin9
min9♭5	min/Maj7	minor 3rd	B♭min/Maj7/G= Gmin9♭5

You can use this technique for rootless voicings as well, simply playing the superimposed chord and leaving the root to the bassist.

Keep in mind that each choice listed here actually gives you four voicing possibilities since there are four inversions of each 7th chord.

C Maj 9

(Emin7-root position)   (Emin7-1st inversion)   (Emin7-2nd inversion)   (Emin7-3rd inversion)

As we dig deeper into harmony, we will see a lot of this sort of thing. Chords, voicings, and colors are often interchangeable in this way. Work to develop your ear and it will be easy to keep on top of it. As long as you hear the sound of the notes E, G, B and D (an Emin7 chord or the top of a CMaj9 voicing) and where that sound fits in with the music, it doesn't much matter what you call the chord.

All the chords in *Remember Your Principles* are voiced with 7th chords superimposed over roots.
This is a ballad so play it slowly and get into the sound of each voicing.

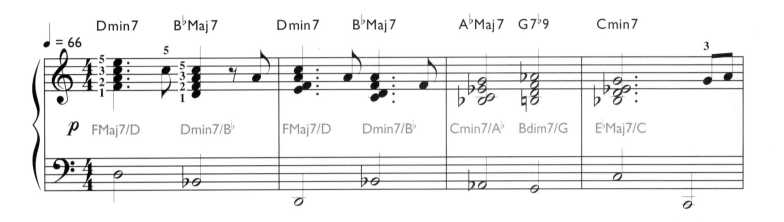

REMEMBER YOUR PRINCIPLES
Track 20

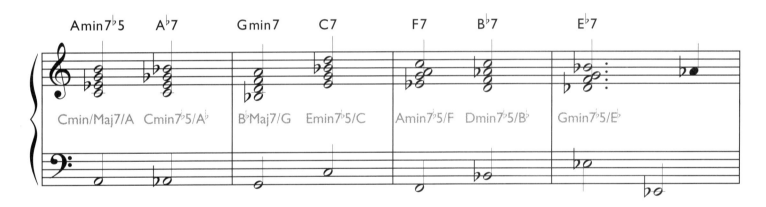

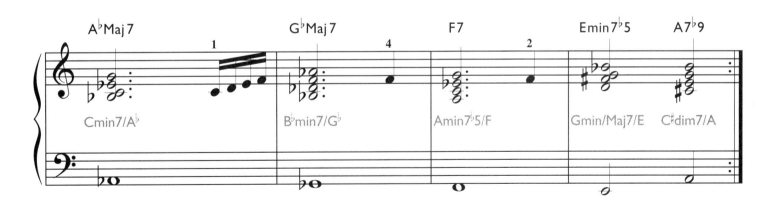

CHAPTER 4

Making the Changes

Dr. Billy Taylor was a uniquely qualified scholar of the history of jazz piano. Not only did he study, teach and write about this history, but for over 60 years, he was a part of it.

Dr. Billy Taylor, legendary jazz pianist and educator, had a really cool technique that he sometimes pulled out in performance. While he was soloing, the rest of the group stopped playing and he played an up-tempo single note solo, alternating between his right and left hand. The technical feat of soloing at a fast tempo with each hand equally well was impressive, but perhaps even more impressive was the fact that the song form and changes remained clear, even though nobody was explicitly playing them.

Dr. Taylor could pull this off because of his remarkable ability to *make the changes*. "Making the changes" is jazz lingo for soloing in a way that outlines the chord progression. If you can do this well, then no chordal accompaniment (bass, guitar, left hand piano chords) should be needed to bring out the sound of the changes and if there is chordal accompaniment, that's just gravy.

When we are soloing (or playing a written melody), each note we play has a role in relation to the chords. There are *chord tones*, which are notes from the chord that is occurring at that moment, and *non-chord tones*. Useful non-chord tones include *passing tones*, notes that come between two chord tones, and *approach tones*, notes that lead to a chord tone.

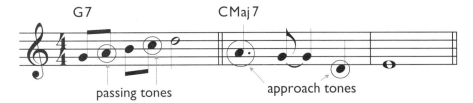

Essentially, making the changes is about bringing out the sound of the chord tones and using non-chord tones to spice up the overall sound. You don't need to cling to the chord tones at all times but being able to emphasize them well is a vital skill for any jazz soloist.

The hierarchy of rhythm is important to understand. When you have a bar of $\frac{4}{4}$, the first beat stands out as the most important beat.

When you divide the bar in half, the third beat also stands out. It is not as important as the first, but still very significant.

When we divide each half in half, each beat has some importance. The first beat still reigns and the third beat is still very important, but we now have two more beats of lesser importance, the second and fourth.

When we divide each beat in half, the same hierarchy applies, only now we have fractions of the beat, which have even less impact than the least substantial of the beats. Each "&" is weaker than the beat, and "&" of a weak beat is weaker than the "&" of a strong beat. If we kept dividing, we would see more of the same.

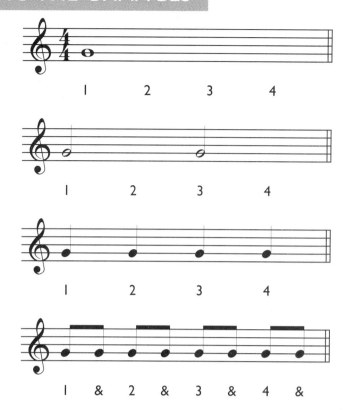

As rigid and basic as all this may sound, it is crucial for an understanding of making the changes. Our ears have been conditioned to organize sound in this way. Even though the second and fourth beat are fundamental to a jazz swing feeling, and even though syncopated phrases that often don't land on the beat are key to jazz phrasing, our ears will usually hear the note on the downbeat of the measure as the most important one.

Therefore, we need to be aware of which notes land on the strongest beats. We can lay down all the chord tones and still not sound like we're making the changes if the majority fall on weak beats or upbeats (circled notes below are chord tones).

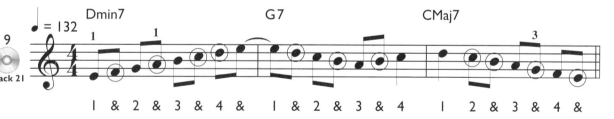

On the other hand, if the chord tones tend to happen on the strong beats, it will invariably sound like we are making the changes.

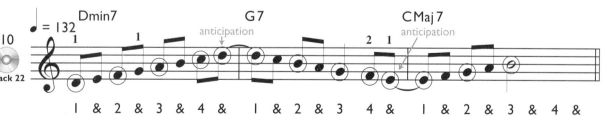

Notice that in this example some notes are anticipated, or played early. If a note is played on the "and" of the fourth beat and then tied over to the first beat of the next bar (or if there is a rest on the first beat of the next bar), then that is the note you'll hear on the downbeat even though the note wasn't actually played there. Anticipations allow us to use more varied and more exciting rhythms and still account for the proper placement of the notes.

As we discussed in Chapter 2, the modes of the major scale give us a way of addressing each individual chord in a progression. The first thought of many newcomers to modes is often, "Yeah, so what? It's all the same eight notes anyway." In case you might have this thought in the back of your mind, let's take a peek at the difference it makes to use modes. If we run the C major scale up and down over a iii-vi-ii-V-I in C major, this is what we get.

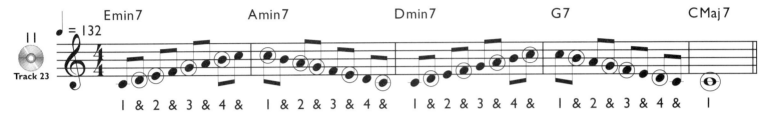

Sometimes the chord tones fall on strong beats, sometimes not. Over anything but a CMaj7 chord, it is a bit of a crapshoot. Now look at what happens if we use the appropriate mode for each chord.

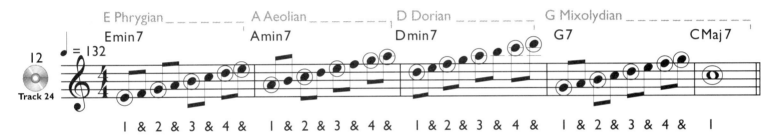

Here we consistently hit chord tones on downbeats and passing tones on offbeats. Admittedly, running straight up each mode doesn't exactly make for the smoothest sound. So let's try using each mode but taking some liberties with rhythm and line contour.

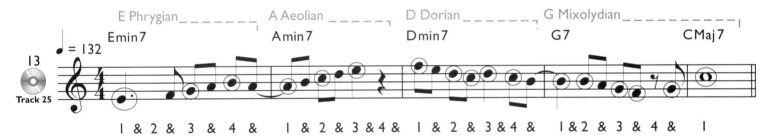

That's much better. Using modes in this way (once you take liberties like this) won't guarantee that you'll land on the "right" notes in the "right" places. It will, however, give your solo lines a focus that directly relates to the chord at hand and that makes you all the more likely to make the changes. If you're playing a ii-V in F, for example, and thinking about the F major scale, all your ideas are likely to pivot around F (see the first example below). If, on the other hand you're thinking of G Dorian over the Gmin7 and C Mixolydian over the C7, then your ideas will probably relate better to the individual chords (see the second example below).

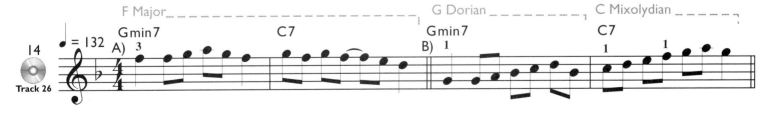

The melody of *All Them Thangs* uses the modes relating to each chord in the progression. Do the same when you improvise. The changes are in the style of the harmony found at the beginning of the Jerome Kern standard *All The Things You Are.* Use the comping method you are most comfortable with to fill in the left hand.

ALL THEM THANGS

Chromatic means not of the scale or key (the opposite of diatonic). In C Major, D♭, E♭, G♭, A♭ and B♭ are all chromatic notes. Chromatic notes are inherently dissonant but there are ways to use them to emphasize chord tones in a way that makes the overall effect pleasing to the ear once the chromatic tension is released by the sounding of the chord tone.

A *chromatic passing tone* is a chromatic note that comes between two "correct" notes. This is particularly effective when those two notes are chord tones, like the ♭7 and root of a dominant 7th or minor 7th chord.

A *chromatic approach tone* is a chromatic note that leads to a particular tone, in this case a chord tone. Generally, chromatic approach tones should fall on upbeats so it is clear that the subsequent chord tone (which would therefore be on a downbeat) is the more important note.

A *chromatic enclosure* is the surrounding of a note (here, a chord tone) with the two notes a half step away on each side. Almost certainly one or both of these notes will be chromatic.

THE BEBOP SCALE

The *bebop scale* is a helpful change-making tool with a bebop sound. Actually, there are two bebop scales, one for dominant chords, one for minor 7th chords. Check them both out in C.

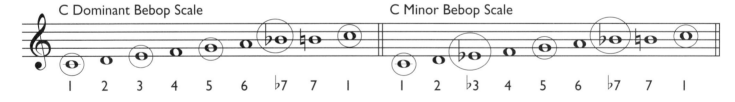

The dominant bebop scale resembles the Mixolydian mode and the minor bebop scale resembles the Dorian mode. In both cases, the difference is an added chromatic passing tone between the ♭7 and the tonic. This gives us eight note scales, and in each case, every other note is a chord tone. Therefore, if you play eighth notes and you start with any chord tone on a downbeat, you can play the scale indefinitely (or at least until the chord changes) and hit a chord tone on every downbeat.

Da Light at Tadd's House is dedicated to the great bebop composer and pianist, Tadd Dameron. The melody uses lots of chromatic notes, mostly chromatic passing tones. The chromatic notes are often found within the bebop scale. These chromatic notes fall in different places rhythmically, but are always followed by a diatonic note with a stronger rhythmic placement. When you practice soloing over this tune, focus separately on each type of chromatic tone we looked at, as well as the bebop scale.

DA LIGHT AT TADD'S HOUSE

Track 28

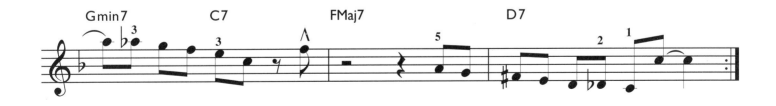

We call chord progressions "changes" because the key to their use is not so much the sound of the individual chords, but rather the sound of each chord changing to the next. It has been said that the legendary jazz pianist Bill Evans used to practice tunes two chords at a time to really dig into the sound of each change in chords.

Exploring this concept can have a deep impact on your ability to make the changes. As important as it is to play the right stuff over each chord, it is at least as important to know what to play at the moment that one chord changes to another.

From studying shell voicings, we know that the 3rd and 7th of a 7th chord define the chord's sound. Furthermore, we know that in a progression where the roots move downward in 5ths, the 3rd of one chord voice-leads smoothly to the 7th of the next, and vice versa.

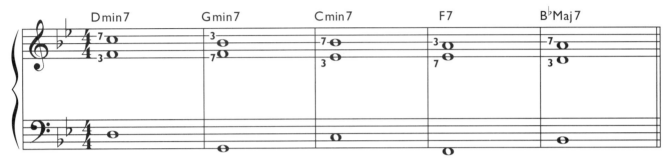

In the example above (as with all diatonic progressions with roots moving downward in 5ths), the 3rd of each chord becomes the 7th of the next chord, without the note changing. Therefore, the only note that changes in these voicings (aside from the root) is the 7th of each chord moving to the 3rd of the next. If we lay that out in single notes, it sounds like this (you can play the roots underneath):

This is an example of a *guidetone line* (sometimes called a 7-3 guidetone line). Guidetones are the core notes that define the sound of the changes, and a guidetone line is a simple line that lays out the sound of the changes with the fewest notes possible. Since the 7th of each chord in this progression leading to the 3rd of the next chord sums up the sound of the changes, that's all that is needed for a guidetone line.

Guidetones can also be used as the underlying structure to a solo line. If we start with the example below, we have a sort of skeleton, where the guidetones are laid out at the moment of each change.

We can then build upon the skeleton with other notes knowing that whatever we play, the guidetones will help show the changes at the right moments. The circled notes in the example below are the guidetones.

The Modern Jazz Quartet, featuring pianist John Lewis, was formed in the 1950s as an outgrowth of Dizzy Gillespie's rhythm section.

REVIEW: LINKING ARPEGGIOS

Having a handle on guidetones is key to making the changes. However, it isn't everything; there are other notes that can help outline the changes and when the root movement is less predictable, the guidetones often become less useful. Therefore, a review of arpeggios is in order.

Arpeggios are broken chords, that is chords played one note at a time.

They don't have to start on the root and you can vary the rhythm. The main goal is that when the chords change, you want to make a smooth transition from whatever note you're on to a nearby chord tone from the next chord.

Now that we've checked out chord extensions, we can use them sparingly, too.

Don't get carried away with extended arpeggios, though. Once you've added the extensions to a chord, you've got at least five notes, sometimes more; at that point you basically have an entire scale!

The changes for *At Least Fifty Feet* are in the style of the standard tune *How High the Moon*. The melody uses lines that are mostly built around guidetones. In your improvisations, try to create new solo lines that refer to the same guidetones. Also, try using arpeggios to smoothly link the changes. As usual, it's up to you comp creatively with your left hand. Start with something that feels comfortable and then experiment.

AT LEAST FIFTY FEET

Track 32

The melody to *1, 2, 3 . . .* uses the various change-making devices we've looked at in this chapter – modes, chromatic tones, the bebop scale, guidetones and arpeggios. Practice soloing with each of these techniques, and then try to combine them all the way this melody does. The changes are in the style of Eddie "Cleanhead" Vinson's *Four*, a tune popularized by Miles Davis.

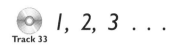

1, 2, 3 . . .

Track 33

CHAPTER 5

Substitutions

Now you know how to make the changes, you've practiced all the techniques until the neighbors made you quiet down, and you can instantly shred any chord progression you encounter like a beboppin' machine. You thought that would be the answer to your prayers but you find yourself getting bored instead. Since you no longer have a problem negotiating the changes in the tunes you're playing, you need a new challenge.

This may sound funny, but that is essentially what happened to Charlie Parker, Dizzy Gillespie and the other pioneers of the bebop era in the 1940s. To add more color to tunes and to avoid boredom playing over changes they'd already mastered, they began to use *substitution*. Substitution is the act of altering a chord progression, generally by adding new chords to it or by using new chords to replace existing ones.

The key to the concept of substitution is tension and resolution. If we build up a lot of tension in a chord progression then the resolution becomes more powerful. Just like the movies — the more mean things the bad guy does, the more happy and relieved we are when he is finally caught by the lovable detective. Substitution tends to add more excitement and bite to the changes so when we eventually release the built up tension by going "home," there is more power in the relief.

There are two common ways that substitution takes place:

1) An arranger will write the alternate changes into a tune, or the players will confer beforehand and decide on an alternate set of changes. This was often done in the early days of bebop, when the musicians would hang out and talk about substitutions they could use on a tune.

2) Spontaneously. A player (either a soloist or someone laying down the changes on a chordal instrument) spontaneously decides to substitute different changes. Experienced jazz players are often familiar with certain common substitutions and will instantly hear what is being done and adapt to it. For example, the trumpet soloist may hear the keyboardist's substitutions and change his solo lines accordingly, or the trumpet soloist may decide he wants to solo over substitute changes and the keyboardist then hears the implied substitutions and plays them. Either way, the pressure is not nearly as great as it may sound. As hip as it sounds when everybody is playing a substitution together, it often sounds fine if only one person is doing it. And we, as keyboardists, have a special advantage when we solo: we're accompanying ourselves. If we decide to use a substitution when we solo, our left hand is there to reinforce the sound of the alternate changes. Just make sure your left hand knows what your right hand is doing!

Some of the substitution techniques we'll look at involve some new concepts, but mostly we'll be taking concepts we've already been using and putting them in other places. For example, if we see this little progression in a tune,

| | F7 | | (F7) | | B♭Maj7 | || |

that IS a long time to play an F7 chord. We know that F7 is the V chord in B♭ Major and often when we see the V chord, it is preceded by the ii chord. So we throw the ii chord in there.

| | Cmin7 | | F7 | | B♭Maj7 | || |

Perhaps we're really feeling like tearing up some changes so we want to have even more harmonic activity going on. Try this substitution instead.

| | Cmin7 | F7 | | Cmin7 | F7 | | B♭Maj7 | || |

In each case, make sure not to replace the chord that we're resolving to. We don't want to uproot our home, but instead make the trip there more exciting. Later on, we encounter a couple more dominant chords that aren't acting as V chords since they don't resolve to I chords.

| | F7 | | (F7) | | G7 | | (G7) | || |

Even so, since we've established that adding the ii chord before a V chord sounds good, we throw ii chords in here as well even though the dominant chords aren't really V chords.

| | Cmin7 | | F7 | | Dmin7 | | G7 | || |

Then we notice that we're not crazy about the sound of the F7 going to the Dmin7. We wonder what chord would sound best leading us to Dmin7. Well, if Dmin7 was the i chord in a minor key, its V chord, A7, would strongly pull us to Dmin7, and so would the vii chord, C♯dim7. Even though the Dmin7 isn't really a i chord there, we treat it that way for the moment and fiddle around with the changes.

| | Cmin7 | F7 | | Cmin7 | C♯dim7 | | Dmin7 | G7 | | Dmin7 | G7 | || |

This can go on endlessly if you want it to. In general, substitution uses this sort of mix and match logic. If something sounds good, then experiment with using it somewhere else. By mixing and matching techniques like this, you can wind up with some exciting changes.

Note:

Substitutions, especially when done spontaneously, are most commonly used on solos. Substitution is valid and useful with written melodies as well, but you need to take special care that the new changes don't clash with the notes in the melody. Nothing cancels out the hipness of substitution faster than using it overzealously on the "head" and making the melody sound wrong.

In the Middle Ages, you could be punished for playing a tritone (diminished 5th/augmented 4th). They called it *Intervalis Diabolis*, which can be loosely translated from Latin as "*whoa Nelly that's a funky interval.*" A more traditional translation would be "*the Devil's Interval.*" In jazz, the tritone is one of the most useful and important intervals in our arsenal. Perhaps that is why they didn't have jazz in the Middle Ages.

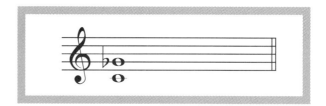

Let's say we've got a ii-V-I in G major. We voice the chords with shell voicings, since the 3rd and 7th of the chords are the key to the sound. Then we are hit by a wave of tritone awareness. The 3rd and 7th of the D7 chord make up a tritone, and that tritone is what pulls us so nicely into the GMaj7 voicing.

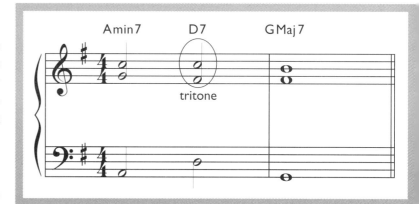

Overcome with joy, our left hand slips before we get to the GMaj7 and lands a tritone away, on A♭. Miraculously, we see that we are playing an A♭7 chord. The same tritone we were using on top fits the A♭7 as well. This is no fluke. On dominant 7th chords, we can substitute the chord a tritone away because the tritone shell made up of the 3rd and 7th of the chords will be the same. The resulting chord resolves down a half step to the I (or i) chord, as opposed to resolving down a 5th. We've already established that root motion in 5ths is very natural to the ear, and root motion in half steps is also very effective.

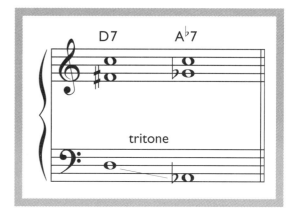

If we want to take the substitution a step farther, we can use the idea brought up on the previous page, and use the ii chord that relates to our new dominant 7th chord (rather than the ii chord in the key we're going to).

Tritone substitution, especially using the relative ii chord (as shown above) is most effective on dominant chords that resolve to the I chord. The added tension of using substitute chords can be powerful when you resolve it. If you don't resolve, it will just sound dissonant.

You can refer to this chart to find the tritone sub for any dominant chord.

chord	tritone sub	chord	tritone sub	chord	tritone sub	chord	tritone sub
C7	G♭7 or F♯7	E♭7	A7	G♭7 or F♯7	C7	A7	E♭7
D♭7 or C♯7	G7	E7	B♭7	G7	D♭7 or C♯7	B♭7	E7
D7	A♭7	F7	B7	A♭7	D7	B7	F7

The changes to *Tritone Madness* are full of tritone subs. The ii chords that precede them sometimes relate to the key we're resolving to, and sometimes they relate to the dominant chord being substituted. Try soloing over the changes, using arpeggios and matching up the appropriate modes with each chord (you won't be able to stay in just one parent scale). This chart leaves plenty of space for creative comping with the left hand.

TRITONE MADNESS

Track 34

In the changes that jazz players often use on Cole Porter's standard *Night and Day,* the progression begins like this.

| | Fmin7♭5 | | B♭7 | | E♭Maj7 | |

Now wait a minute. Fmin7♭5 to B♭7 is a ii-V in the key of E♭ minor, yet it resolves to E♭ Major. This, like tritone substitution, can add more bite to the progression. On top of that, we have the element of surprise. Let's look at a few bars of changes that you might hear players using on the standard ballad *What's New.*

| Cmin7 | Dmin7♭5 G7 | CMaj7 |

Here we begin the excerpt in C minor, play a ii-V that implies C minor, and then we resolve instead to C major. That surprising moment helps to spice up the mood of the tune.

We can do the same in reverse, using major harmony to sneak us into a minor key.

| B♭Maj7 | Gmin7 | Cmin7 | F7 | B♭min6/9 ‖

Here, what looks at first like an ordinary I-vi-ii-V-I in B♭ major changes at the last second and resolves to B♭ minor instead. There is no hard and fast rule about how to use this sort of substitution. Simply experiment with substituting minor harmony in a major key, and vice versa. If you use basic harmonic devices like ii-V's, it is hard to go wrong.

Another benefit of this sort of substitution is that it can make your improvised lines more interesting. If we play an ordinary ii-V-I in C, we can wind up with this.

| | **D Dorian**
(parent scale: C)
Dmin7 | | **G Mixolydian**
(parent scale: C)
G7 | | **C Ionian**
(parent scale: C)
CMaj7 | |

This sounds just fine, but notice that all the modes that apply to the chords are from the same parent scale. On the other hand, if we substitute a minor ii-V (and use Lydian for the I chord), we have more variety in our sound.

| | **D Locrian**
(parent scale: E♭)
Dmin7♭5 | | **G Mixolydian**
(parent scale: C)
G7 | | **C Lydian**
(parent scale: G)
CMaj7 | |

Mambo Para Eddie Y Chucho is a 32 bar tune in AABA form. It uses a Latin groove, so don't swing the eighth notes. The changes use many minor ii-V's resolving to major chords and major ii-V's resolving to minor chords. Be slow and meticulous when you practice soloing so you can find the right sound for each chord. Once you're comfortable, feel free to throw in some tritone subs, as well. This tune is dedicated to the great Latin jazz pianists Eddie Palmieri and Chucho Valdez (of Irakere).

MAMBO PARA EDDIE Y CHUCHO

As we've seen by now, one of the most dramatic sources of tension and release in a chord progression is a dominant chord resolving down a 5th to a Maj7 or min7 chord (or down a half step, if it is a tritone sub). In diatonic harmony there is only one dominant chord in any given key, which means only one chord can be used this way. Since it is such an effective sound, we should use it more often. Thanks to substitution, we can.

One of the most effective places to add a dominant chord is in a *cycle*. A cycle is a repetitive succession of chords. For example, a progression whose roots consistently move down in 5ths or half steps is a cycle. The progression in *The Squirrel and the Dog* (pg. 131) is a cycle, since it repeatedly modulates to the key a minor 3rd below. Let's take one of the most tried and true cycles in jazz, iii-vi-ii-V-I, this time in E♭.

E♭: iii	vi	ii	V	I
| Gmin7	| Cmin7	| Fmin7	| B♭7	| E♭Maj7 ||

This is a nice sounding functional cycle that gets us where we need to go. There is only one dominant chord. The first three chords are all min7's, which only builds up so much excitement. So, let's break it up a little bit and make the middle min7 chord into a dominant chord.

| Gmin7	| C7	| Fmin7	| B♭7	| E♭Maj7 ||

We can justify this theoretically (as if we needed to!) by thinking of the ii chord (Fmin7) as a pivot chord. It is the ii chord in E♭, but at the same time it is temporarily acting as a minor i chord, thus making the C7 a V chord in the key of F minor. The C7 is a *secondary dominant,* a dominant 7th chord that is the V of a chord other than the I in the home key.

Meanwhile, there's nothing to say you can't have a dominant chord resolve to another dominant chord. The resolution isn't much of a resolution but if you're in a cycle, it creates a sort of domino effect where the anticipation builds and builds until you finally resolve dramatically. Let's look at the same iii-vi-ii-V-I using all dominant chords until we resolve.

| G7	| C7	| F7	| B♭7	| E♭Maj7 ||

Wow. That's a much more intense sound than what we started with. But let's not stop there. Since we're using dominant chords, we can throw in a couple tritone subs to change the contour of the progression. Instead of root motion in 5ths, we can use root motion in half steps. Then, we can add the relative ii chords to each dominant chord. Play through the two examples below and go back to the progression we started with to see how dramatically we've intensified the progression. The bottom example is an extreme one, showing how dramatic this stuff can be.

| D♭7	| C7	| B7	| B♭7	| E♭Maj7 ||

| A♭min7 D♭7	| Gmin7 C7 | F#min7 B7 | Fmin7 B♭7 | E♭Maj7 ||

Boppin With J-Mac is dedicated to the highly esteemed jazz saxophonist and educator, Jackie McLean. These changes, which first appeared in the standard *Sweet Georgia Brown*, use cycles of dominant chords almost exclusively. These changes have been reused for such tunes as Clifford Brown's *Sweet Clifford*, Thelonious Monk's *Bright Mississippi* and Mr. McLean's *Donna* (a.k.a. *Dig*). Use some chord extensions to voice the changes. The melody uses the Mixolydian mode on the dominant chords. When you solo, use the Mixolydian as well as the dominant bebop scale and other soloing devices we've learned.

BOPPIN' WITH J-MAC

Track 36

Rhythm Changes are the second most common set of chord changes in jazz, second only to the blues. They get their name from the tune that introduced them, George Gershwin's *I Got Rhythm*. Classic jazz tunes that use these changes include Lester Young's *Lester Leaps In*, Charlie Parker's *Anthropology*, Sonny Rollins' *Oleo*, Miles Davis's *The Theme* and Thelonious Monk's *Rhythm-A-Ning*, just to name a few.

It is a 32 bar AABA form and it revolves around I-vi-ii-V-I's. The bridge shows some visionary hipness by using dominant substitution on the iii-vi-ii-V cycle. Practice these changes thoroughly before you move on to the next few pages. In addition to being a common and important chord progression, Rhythm Changes are often used as the basis for substitution. If you're already comfortable with the basic changes, you will be better able to absorb the substitution techniques used in *Golden Silver* (page 153), *Pac-Man* (page 154) and *Sample Rhythm Changes Solo* (page 155).

RHYTHM CHANGES

Track 37

A

B♭:	I	vi		ii	V		I	vi		ii	V
‖	B♭Maj7	Gmin7	|	Cmin7	F7	|	B♭Maj7	Gmin7	|	Cmin7	F7 |

E♭:	ii	V		I	B♭:	ii		V	|1.	I		V	‖2.	I
|	Fmin7	B♭7	|	E♭Maj7	|	Cmin7		F7	|	B♭Maj7		F7	:‖	B♭Maj7 ‖

B

	III 7				VI7			
|	D7		|	(D7) |	G7		| (G7)	|

	II 7				V7			
|	C7		|	(C7) |	F7		| (F7)	‖

D.C. al 2nd ending

Golden Silver is a Rhythm Changes tune dedicated to the great pianist, composer, and bandleader, Horace Silver. Significant substitutions include changing the vi (Gmin7) chord in the A-section's I-vi-ii-V to a dominant chord (G7), and preceding each dominant chord in the bridge with its relative ii chord. As you solo, make sure to account for the substitutions, and fill the rests with some brilliant comping in the left hand.

GOLDEN SILVER
Track 38

D.C. al Fine
(2nd ending only)

Pac-Man is another Rhythm Changes tune with even more substitutions than *Golden Silver*. In the first two bars, diminished chords are used (vii chords in the keys of the minor chords that follow them), and then the next two bars use tritone subs to get back down to B♭. The bridge uses tritone subs for the III and II chords (D7 and C7), creating half step motion.

PAC-MAN

Track 39

Here is a sample *Rhythm Changes* solo chorus. If somebody said, "Let's play some Rhythm Changes" and gave no further guidelines, this is some of the stuff you could spontaneously throw in. Note that since the substitutions are supposed to be improvised, the A-sections are all a bit different. The written chords are the changes that the soloist would be thinking of (and possibly playing with the left hand) while soloing.

SAMPLE RHYTHM CHANGES SOLO

Track 40

CHAPTER 6

The Blues

Before we look at the blues, try this little quiz.

The blues are:

A) A style of music developed by African Americans, often characterized by a great depth and expression of raw emotion.

B) One of the important roots of jazz.

C) A common twelve-bar chord progression, structured around the I, IV and V chords.

D) A scale that adds a $^\flat 5$ to the pentatonic minor scale, thus giving you all three of the "blue notes" ($^\flat 3$, $^\flat 5$ and $^\flat 7$) in one scale.

E) A mournful, melancholy feeling.

F) The category of colors that lie between the reds and the yellows on the color wheel.

G) All of the above.

The answer is, of course, G, all of the above (although if you thought too seriously about F you might want to spend a weekend with some Muddy Waters records). Here is a brief explanation of the other responses.

A) The blues have been a crucial, vibrant style of American music since the early part of the 20th century. Like jazz, there are many sub-styles within the blues, but they are all unified by an intangible yet powerful feeling . . .

B) . . . which is at the core of jazz. Jazz largely sprung from the blues; at one time there was a fine line between the two, with pianists like Meade Lux Lewis and Albert Ammons gaining equal respect in the blues and jazz worlds. Many influential modern keyboardists, like pianists Horace Silver and Bobby Timmons and organists Jimmy Smith and Shirley Scott, have built their styles largely from the blues.

C) Way back on page 29, we took a first look at the twelve bar blues progression. The tunes in this chapter take you from the basic form to more advanced, modern jazz blues progressions that use some substitutions. This progression (with all its variations) is far and away the most common chord progression in jazz.

D) We looked at the blues scale back on page 39. This scale is often used in blues (and jazz) and helps impart a blues feeling.

E) When someone says, "I got the blues," that is what they're talking about.

BASIC BLUES PROGRESSION

The basic twelve bar blues progression is all dominant chords, using dominant chords built off the I, IV and V. The circled chords below are the most fundamental chords in the structure of the changes; these are the chords that will consistently remain as the changes become more filled with substitutions. These changes are written out in B♭, as are the changes to the rest of the variations you'll see on the next few pages. Try transposing each progression to as many different keys as you can; jazz-style blues are very common in G, C, F, B♭ and E♭, and you're likely to periodically encounter them in all the other keys, as well.

19

Track 41

B♭:	I7		IV7		I7		
|	(B♭7)	|	E♭7	|	B♭7	| (B♭7)	|
	IV7				I7		
|	(E♭7)	|	(E♭7)	|	B♭7	| (B♭7)	|
	V7		IV7		I7		
|	F7	|	E♭7	|	(B♭7)	| (B♭7)	||

Bu's Blues is a twelve bar blues in C with these changes, dedicated to the great drummer and bandleader, Art Blakey. His Jazz Messengers included many superb pianists through the years, such as Horace Silver, Bobby Timmons, Cedar Walton, Joanne Brackeen, Mulgrew Miller and James Williams. When you solo on this tune, try mixing it up using the Mixolydian mode on each dominant chord and ignoring the changes to use the C Blues scale. When playing a blues, the blues feeling is often much more important than making the changes.

> *Remember, when you are given only a lead sheet, as in Bu's Blues below, it is expected that you will comp with your left-hand. Try something easy at first and then stretch yourself a bit.*

BU'S BLUES

Track 42

BEBOP-STYLE PROGRESSION

As with other kinds of substitution, these blues changes stemmed from beboppers having a common chord progression and wanting to expand the soloing possibilities. Tunes with these changes include Thelonious Monk's *Straight, No Chaser* and Charlie Parker's *Billie's Bounce*.

20
Track 43

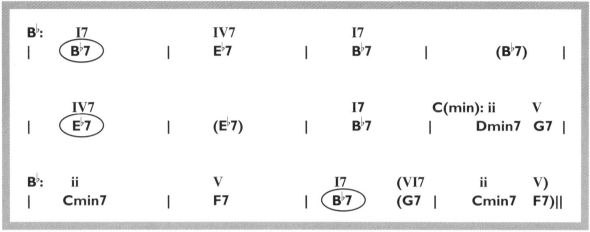

This progression is the same as the basic one until the eighth bar.

At this point, a ii-V (Cmin7-F7) is used to get us back to the I chord at the eleventh bar, and another ii-V (Dmin7-G7) is used to lead up to that ii-V. Then a I-VI7-ii-V turnaround is used at the end to bring us back to the top of the form. When you solo over this type of blues progression, adjust your thinking to acknowledge these ii-V's.

GUH-ZAP
Track 44

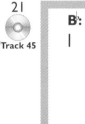

"BIRD" BLUES

Some people got used to the bebop-style blues changes and wanted to challenge themselves (and their listeners and fellow musicians) still more, so they busted out more substitutions. We call these particular changes *Bird Blues* in honor of Charlie "Bird" Parker, whose *Blues For Alice* is the best-known example of this type of progression.

These changes take the ones from the previous page to another level. The first four bars use a cycle of ii-V's to lead us dramatically to the IV chord. Then things really get funky, using some of the substitutions we checked out at the end of page 150. With tritone substitution, dominant chords lead us in half steps back to the V chord (A♭7-G7-G♭7-F7), and then each of those chords is preceded by its relative ii chord. The arrows in the example show how the resolutions of tritone subs are delayed by the relative ii chords.

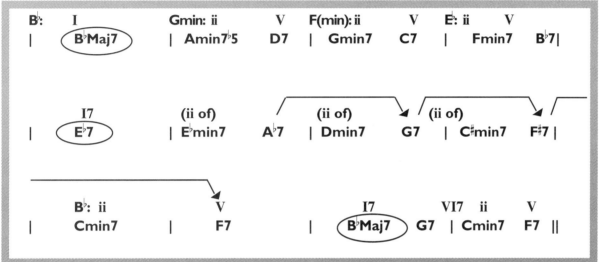

When soloing over these changes, it is usually necessary to stay in "making the changes" mode, as you're being bombarded by ii-V's. These changes can be very exciting to play or hear, since there is so much action building up to the I and IV chords.

 ## BLUES FOR BIRD

The blues progressions we've looked at so far have centered around mostly dominant chords, or in the case of "Bird" blues, major chords. Here we have a blues progression in a minor key. Frequently played minor blues tunes include Dizzy Gillespie's *Birks' Works* and John Coltrane's *Mr. P.C.*.

22
Track 47

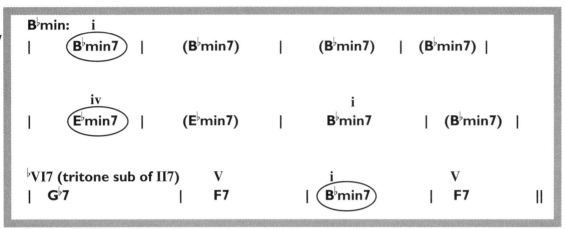

A nice feature of this progression is the ♭VI7 chord on the ninth bar. The ♭7 of the chord corresponds with the ♭5 of the key of the tune, giving you an extra built-in blue note (the ♭3 and ♭7 are implied by the i chord). Soloing over these changes, you can use various change-making techniques, or you can just groove on the minor pentatonic and blues scales.

Mr. Dee Gee, dedicated to the great trumpeter, composer, and bandleader Dizzy Gillespie, is a blues in F Minor. The melody alternates between modes (Dorian on the min7 chords, Mixolydian on the dominant) and the F Blues scale. When you solo, move freely between them.

MR. DEE GEE
Track 48

There is often a fine line between what is a blues tune and what isn't. Check out the changes that Miles Davis used on *Solar*, a tune he popularized.

23
Track 49

	Cmin7		(Cmin7)		(Cmin7)	Gmin7 C7	
	FMaj7		(FMaj7)		Fmin7	B♭7	
	E♭Maj7	E♭min7 A♭7		D♭Maj7	Dmin7♭5 G7 ‖

So is it a blues or isn't it? Well, there is no clear answer. It is twelve bars long and goes to the IV chord on the fifth bar. Beyond that, the changes aren't that blues-like. So whether or not this is a blues really depends on who you ask. Some tunes like Ornette Coleman's *Ramblin'* and Charles Mingus' *Better Get Hit in Your Soul* clearly sound like blues tunes but have atypical forms and changes. Your best bet is to listen for the feeling without getting caught up in categorizations. If it feels bluesy, go for it and don't worry about what kind of tune it is.

Newk's Kinda Blues is dedicated to tenor saxophone great Sonny Rollins, who used these changes on his tune *Doxy*. It has the feeling and character of the blues, although in this case it is a sixteen bar form. Play it like you would play any other blues.

NEWK'S KINDA BLUES
Track 50

The primary way to develop a good blues feeling is by listening, just like developing your swing feel. Listen to great blues artists like keyboardists Pete Johnson, Otis Spann, Sunnyland Slim and Professor Longhair, and don't limit yourself to keyboardists. Check out the suggestions at the end of this book for jazz records that make dramatic use of the blues and keep your eyes and ears open for good blues stuff. Some living legends of the blues just might be coming to your town this summer.

These two pages offer a few suggestions for devices that help bring out a blues feeling. Coupled with a little bit of listening to the blues, it should come together very quickly.

One good way to bring out a blues feeling is by emphasizing the blue notes (♭3, ♭5, ♭7) in the key you're in, whether or not they match up with the changes at that moment. In fact, the tension of hearing a blue note against another "incompatible" chord tone can be quite intense and bluesy.

As we've said before, the blues scale (which has all three blue notes) can be very helpful in bringing out a blues feeling. As with the individual use of the blue notes, you needn't worry about whether the individual notes match up with the chords. Just go with the feeling of the scale.

Grace notes (notes played very briefly before other notes) can be very effective, too. Since, as keyboardists, we can't bend and smear notes like a guitarist, singer or horn player (unless we use the pitch bend wheel on a synthesizer), we need to use other means to simulate that effect. Thelonious Monk proved that grace notes can come close to implying a bent-note feeling.

Tremolos (alternating between two or more notes as quickly as possible) are a common device used in blues keyboard playing and they're sometimes used to help give a blues sound in jazz.

Crushed notes (a series of notes played quickly enough to sound like a collective blur) and *double-stops* (two notes played simultaneously in the midst of a single note line) are also common blues devices that project a blues feeling when we use them in a jazz context.

WHEN TO USE BLUES DEVICES AND FEEL

Look at the first couple bars of changes used in the standard *Willow Weep For Me*: dominant chords on the I and IV, very much like a blues. Now check out this solo line over the same two bars.

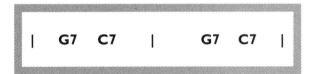

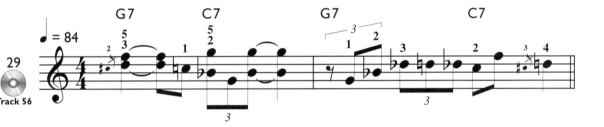

We can use a blues feeling and blues devices here and it sounds perfectly appropriate, even though the tune as a whole is not a blues tune. Other standards like *Gee Baby, Ain't I Good To You, Love For Sale* and *You Don't Know What Love Is* lend themselves well to funky blues interpretations. Look out for minor keys or changes with lots of dominant chords. If you're playing with other people, the main test is how they're interpreting the tune so keep your ears open.

By the same token, be aware of situations in blues tunes where overt use of blues devices may not be the wisest choice. If you're playing a ii-V, you often have more responsibility to make the changes. Blues licks might be out of context. On a "Bird" blues (page 159), for example, playing just blues licks and devices defeats the purpose of using all those nifty substitutions. Ideally, you want to deeply absorb the blues so that they come out naturally wherever they may belong.

The Phinest Blues, dedicated to Phineas Newborn, Jr., is an example of the balance between using blues devices and holding back from them. The melody uses mainly blues feeling and devices, except on the ii-V's in the eighth, ninth and tenth bars, where more of an attempt is made to make the changes. Experiment with the same concept when you solo.

THE PHINEST BLUES

Phineas Newborn, Jr. spent some time in B.B. King's band before his jazz career took off in the 1950s. He could inject a blues feeling into any kind of tune at any tempo.

Commercial Ave. & Suydam St. shows the same concept in the context of a standard. The changes are inspired by the A-section of Cole Porter's *Love For Sale*. Notice how the melody is blues-based for the first eight bars, more beboppish and changes-oriented over the harmonic cycle that follows and then blues-based again over the minor chord in the last two bars. When you solo, experiment with different ways of balancing the two approaches. Try playing the whole thing bluesy, try making the changes all the way through, and then use your instincts to combine the two.

COMMERCIAL AVE. & SUYDAM ST.

Track 58

CHAPTER 7

Altering Dominant 7th Chords

Since the 1950s, **Cecil Taylor** *has forged a unique path at the piano. Always a controversial figure, he has nevertheless received much high acclaim.*

Seems like there are two kinds of people: people who stay put and people who go places. The first kind is perfectly content to relax wherever he or she may be, with no particular drive to go anywhere and no desire for anything wild to happen. The second kind is constantly on the go, always looking out for the next destination and ready for whatever excitement may come along.

Well, there's a striking parallel in the world of harmony. There are two kinds of dominant 7th chords — dominant 7th chords that stay put and dominant 7th chords that go places: *unresolving dominant chords* and *resolving dominant chords.*

— **Resolving dominant chords** are, predictably, dominant 7th chords that resolve to another chord, usually down a 5th or (if there is tritone substitution) down a half step.

— **Unresolving dominant chords** are dominant 7th chords that stay put for a while and don't resolve in a predictable way like resolving dominants do. An example is the IV chord on the second bar of a blues which doesn't resolve anywhere, but simply goes back to the I chord where it came from.

In this chapter, we're not concerned with unresolving dominants. The chord extensions we learned in Chapter 3 are plenty to make an unresolving dominant as fancy as it needs to be. We're concerned about resolving dominants. Once again, as with substitution, we're dealing with tension and resolution. The more tension, the more powerful the resolution. Since a resolving dominant chord is inherently a chord that will lead to something that releases the tension, we can pile that tension on to make the resolution really spectacular.

The technique we're going to look at is the use of *chord alteration.* Whereas chord extension generally involves adding notes that are logically implied, chord alteration involves changing some of the typical notes. This is usually done on dominant chords, and the four alterations that are commonly used are the ♭5, ♯5, ♭9 and ♯9. Using one (or more) of these notes in a resolving dominant chord greatly increases the bite in the chord and therefore the power of the resolution.

THE ♭9 CHORD

Back on the middle of page 124, when looking at dominant extensions, we noted that in a minor key the 9th of the V chord would actually be a ♭9. Here we re-examine the ♭9 as an altered note. Whether or not we're in a minor key, we can add a ♭9 extension to our resolving dominant chords. As shown in the two voicings on the right, you can use the 5th in the voicing (1st example) or not (2nd example); it is more common not to.

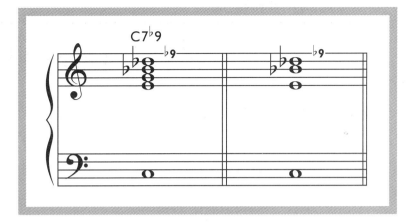

This alteration can be particularly useful when the dominant chord in question is part of a cycle and leads to a minor chord, as in the VI7 chord (circled in example below) that can be put into a I-vi-ii-V or iii-vi-ii-V.

30
Track 59

| B♭Maj7 | (G7♭9) | Cmin7 | F7 | Dmin7 | (G7♭9) | Cmin7 | F7 | |
| I | VI7 | ii | V7 | iii | VI7 | ii | V7 | |

THE ♯9 CHORD

The dominant 7th ♯9 is best known to rock 'n' rollers as the *Purple Haze* chord or the *Foxy Lady* chord, based on Jimi Hendrix's liberal use of it. The ♯9 adds perhaps even more bite to a dominant chord than the ♭9. As with the ♭9, you can go with or without the 5th when voicing a 7♯9 chord. In this case, it is much more common to omit the 5th. Enharmonic equivalents are often used to notate extensions for the sake of ease. For example, the ♯9 of a C7♯9 chord would technically be D♯ but it is written above as E♭. Since we're most concerned with the sound, there is no need to fixate on those things if notating something a different way makes life easier.

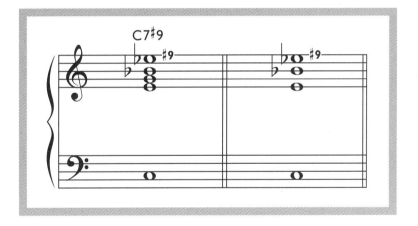

Notice that the ♯9 is the enharmonic equivalent of the ♭3. Therefore, a dominant 7th chord with a ♯9 has the sound of the natural 3rd from the basic chord and the ♭3 blue note in the same chord. In addition to all its other applications with resolving dominants, the blue note makes this chord very effective in the blues.

31
Track 60

| | F7♯9 | | B♭7 | | F7 | | F7♯9 | | B♭7 etc. |

THE ♭5 CHORD

In Chapter 3, we looked at a couple instances where the ♯11 was used. To give us a Lydian sound we can use it in a Maj7 chord. It is an optional color in a dominant 13th chord, since it doesn't clash with the 5th like the natural 11 would. The ♭5 is enharmonically equivalent to the ♯11 but the connotations are different; whereas a ♯11 implies that a natural 5th could also be included, ♭5 implies that the natural 5th has been replaced by the note a half step lower. The two notes obviously sound the same but the ♭5 is inherently an altered note since it replaces a regular chord tone.

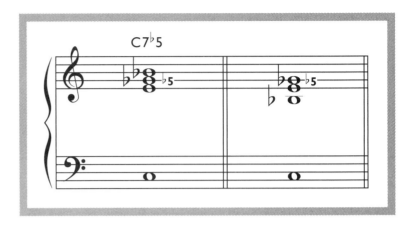

THE ♯5 CHORD

Like the ♭9, the ♭13 is a note we looked at back on page 124 as an extension for a V chord in a minor key. The ♯5 is enharmonically equivalent to the ♭13 but, as with the ♯11 and ♭5, the connotations are different. ♭13 implies that there could be a natural 5th in the voicing; ♯5 makes it clear that the 5th has been replaced by the note a half step higher. In fact, the ♯5 is by far more common, since having a natural 5th and a ♭13th in the same chord would create a very strong clash.

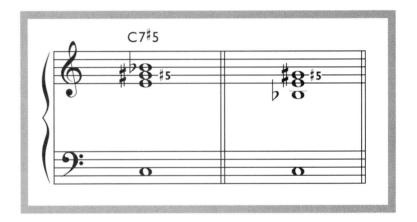

Among their many uses, dominant chords with ♭5's or ♯5's resolve very nicely to chords with natural 9ths. Whether the chords of resolution are major, minor or dominant chords, the ♭5 and ♯5 both voice lead very smoothly to the natural 9.

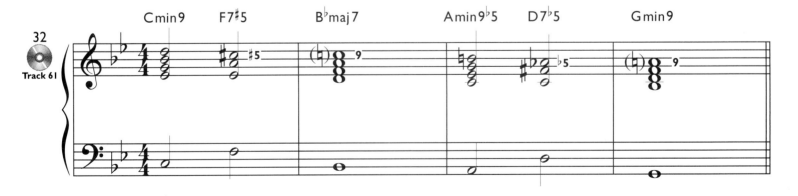

Here you'll have the opportunity to use all four alterations: ♭9, #9, ♭5 and #5. If you feel like soloing over the changes, use the same techniques you normally would and try sticking in the altered notes when they come up.

24 HOURS, BUT NOT IN A ROW

Track 62

If the point of having an altered note in a dominant chord is to build more tension (leading to a resolution), then it stands to reason that two altered notes in the same chord will create even more tension than one. Dominant chords with two altered notes are sometimes called *double tension chords*. Since we have four altered notes to work with, we have four possibilities for double tension chords. Remember that by simply omitting the root at the bottom, you can play these as rootless voicings.

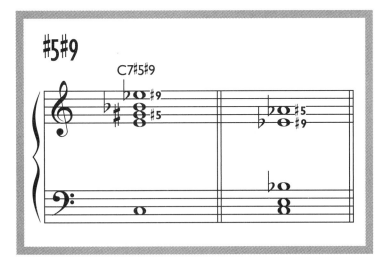

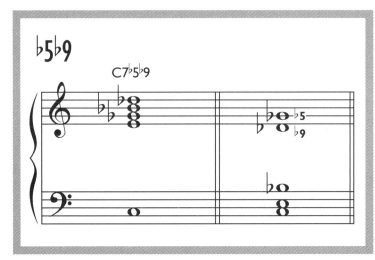

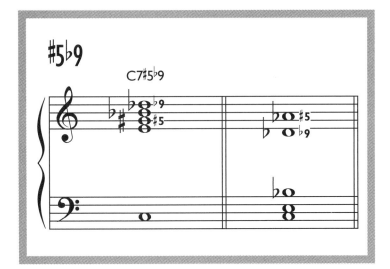

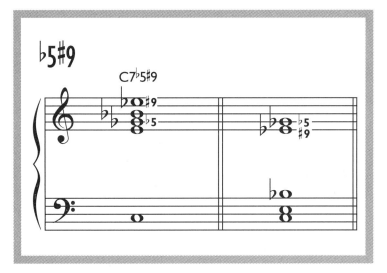

Notice that the first voicing for each type of double tension chord is voiced straight up: root, 3rd, (♭ or ♯) 5th, 7th and (♭ or ♯) 9th. The second voicing for each chord type has a shell on the bottom (root, 3rd and 7th) with the 9th and 5th stacked on top of that. What voicing you use depends on both voice leading and whether you want the 5th or the 9th to be on top.

Although certain situations suggest certain voicings, these chords are basically interchangeable in function. Any double tension chord will have the effect of building a tremendous amount of tension. They are often jointly referred to as *altered dominant chords* or simply *altered chords* (sometimes the abbreviation "alt." is used). If you're told simply to play an altered chord, that means to play a double tension chord of your choice.

Rowles with the Changes is a tribute to pianist Jimmy Rowles, who was known for his chord voicings. All the dominant chords here are played as double tension chords and voiced as rootless voicings requiring both hands. The tempo should be brightly swinging, but also slow it down to hear the sound of each double tension chord by itself and as it resolves to the next chord.

ROWLES WITH THE CHANGES

Track 63

If we take a dominant chord with a shell voicing, we've looked at six colorful extensions and/or alterations that we can add on top.

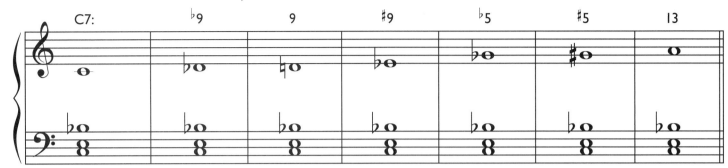

We've already combined the unaltered extensions (9 and 13) with one another and we've combined alterations (♭9, #9, ♭5, #5). What's left to do is to mix and match. There are four common combinations: 13♭9, 13#9, 9#5 and 9♭5.

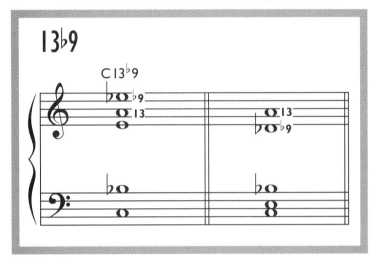

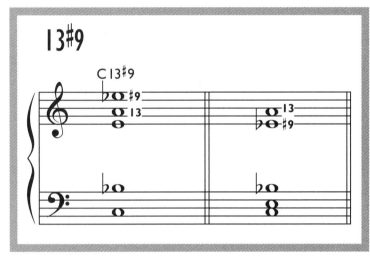

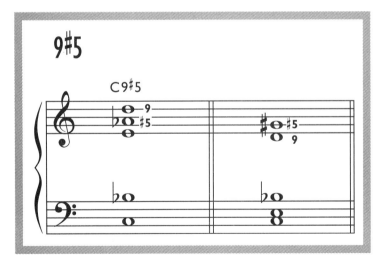

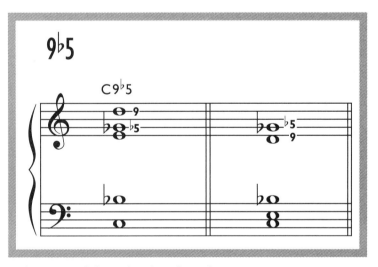

This category of chords has a very interesting sound; the combination of altered and unaltered color makes the chords sound like they want to resolve but want to stay put. One common use, then, is on dominant chords where you want to build tension but not a tremendous amount (for example, the first dominant chord in a cycle where there are many more to follow). Another very helpful use is on resolving dominant chords with a natural 5th, 9th or 13th in the melody; using one of these chords allows you to give an edge to the voicing without clashing with the melody. For example, an A7 with an F# (13th) in the melody might be a good place to use a 13♭9.

Long Point is a ballad using dominant chords with both altered and unaltered extensions. Savor the rich sounds of these dominant chords.

LONG POINT

Track 64

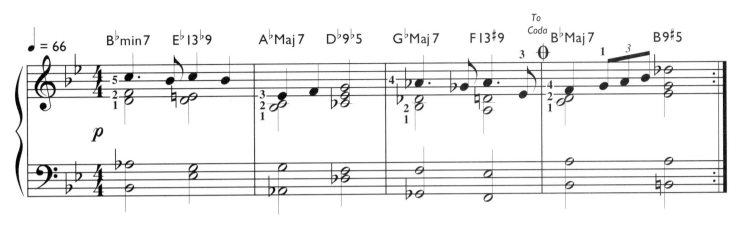

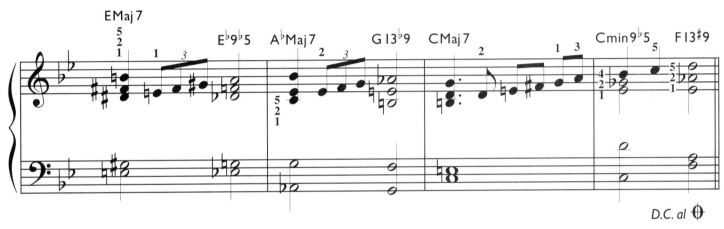

D.C. al ⊕

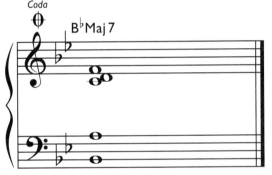

*The tirelessly inventive pianist and composer **Mary Lou Williams** was a driving force in the jazz community for seven decades. Born in 1910, she was the first widely influential female instrumentalist and composer in jazz.*

Having explored all these possibilities for alterations, let's review by looking at all of them in one place. This chart has all the altered chord types we've looked at as well as the unaltered extensions we learned in Chapter 3, all relating to C7. The net result is fifteen different ways of building onto any dominant chord.

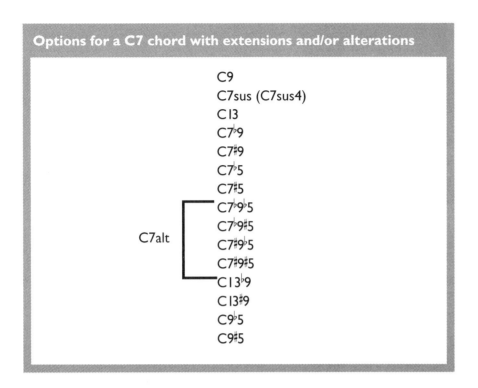

Using all the voicing concepts you know, try all of these colors on each of the twelve dominant 7th chords. We've discussed the functions of these different kinds of dominant chords and we will look at that subject more in the next chapter, but let your ears take over some of that work from your brain. By knowing the sound of each of these chords and how they differ from one another, your ears will be a great help in telling you which sound you need to use at any moment.

Try this drill. Take each of the twelve dominant chords one by one (either chromatically or around the circle of 5ths), and voice a shell (root, 3rd and 7th) in your left hand. Then, with your right hand, try all the different color possibilities. Notice the differences in sound, sometimes subtle and sometimes dramatic.

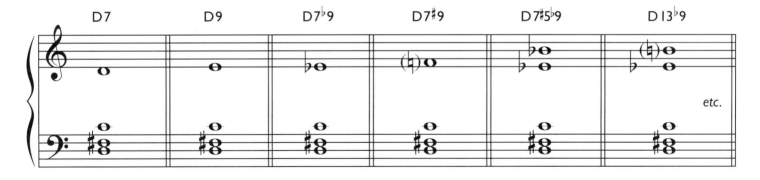

This tune uses changes in the style of Rodgers and Hart's *Lover*. A wide variety of dominant chord colors are used and they are voiced as left hand rootless voicings in the style we learned on page 130.

SPRINT THE 400

Track 65

D.C. al Fine

CHAPTER 8

Comping

We first looked at comping on pages 63–66. The same concepts still apply, only now we have a lot more skills to bring to our comping. Our voicings are more sophisticated and varied and we're more experienced playing and listening to different kinds of tunes. Comping (short for "accompanying" and/or "complementing") is what we do when we're improvising accompaniment for a soloist. The soloist could be a horn player, guitarist or bassist, or it could be ourselves, with our left hand comping for our right hand. Tuning in with the soloist and giving him or her your support is the most obvious element of comping and a substantial one. Equally important is functioning well within the rhythm section.

WORKING WITHIN THE RHYTHM SECTION

When jazz musicians and fans talk about the swinginest bands of all time, they're usually bands that were anchored by exceptional rhythm sections. Here are some examples:

— Count Basie (piano), Freddie Green (guitar), Walter Page (bass) and "Papa" Jo Jones (drums) in the Count Basie Orchestra.

— Red Garland (p), Paul Chambers (b), and Philly Joe Jones (d) in the Miles Davis Quintet.

— Jimmy Smith (organ), Kenny Burrell (gtr), and Donald Bailey (d) in the Jimmy Smith Quartet.

— McCoy Tyner (p), Jimmy Garrison (b), and Elvin Jones (d) in the John Coltrane Quartet.

The rhythm section is the heart and soul of any jazz ensemble. If they sound good, the band will inevitably sound good. If they're not swingin', the band will most likely struggle. Typically a rhythm section has a chordal instrument, a bass instrument and a percussion instrument. The most common lineup is keyboard, bass and drum set but there are variations. Guitar or vibraphone can replace (or join) the keyboard. An organ can cover bass lines and in recordings of the 1920's, it is common to hear tuba playing the bass parts. Auxiliary percussion can be added to the drum set, especially in Latin jazz. Sometimes there are even more surprising variations. The classic Ornette Coleman quartet of the late 1950's used no chordal instrument at all, just bass and drums. On the other hand, Miles Davis had three keyboardists playing at the same time (Chick Corea, Herbie Hancock and Joe Zawinul, later of Weather Report) on his pioneering fusion album *In A Silent Way*.

These are some ideas that will help your comping. Don't bog yourself down trying to memorize them, just click your heels three times and say "I LOVE SWING!"

Intent

Often it is as important to project the feeling that you know what you're doing as it is to actually know what you're doing. When you comp, be sincere and confident in what you play, even if it is not perfect. Playing with authority helps the rhythm section gel.

Listening

The most important rule in comping is listen. Dumbo the elephant is a good role model because you want to have the biggest ears you can. Listening constantly to the other players in the group requires a lot of focus but that is what gives meaning to everything else you do.

Oneness of the Rhythm Section

A great rhythm section sounds telepathic. For example, the section of Kenny Barron, Buster Williams and Ben Riley from the group SPHERE, often sound like they've planned every note when they're improvising together, because they're so tuned in to one another that everything locks up. Strive for this kind of tightness, whoever your section-mates may be.

Voicings

If you're the only player laying out the chords at any given moment, voicings are important because that will be the sound of the harmony and one of the main sources of stimulation for the soloist. If you're not the only comper, your voicings are important for the sake of compatibility as well. You and the guitarist (or vibraphonist or whoever) need to make sure your voicings don't clash. If you play a D9 while he plays a D7♭9, that's bad news.

Energy

You will be a valuable asset to any band if you bring lots of energy. Being able to push the music and inspire the other players with energy and intensity can help bring the music to another level. Don't be afraid to sweat, the soloists will greatly appreciate it.

Sensitivity

Many potentially good rhythm sections have been ruined by having a guitarist and a pianist who are both unwilling to simply stop playing and let the other comp. Enthusiasm is crucial, of course, but don't step on any of the other players' toes.

Waiting

Dizzy Gillespie once said, "It has taken me my whole life to learn what not to play." Just because you have something cool to play doesn't mean now is the time to play it. Save it for the appropriate time and if that time doesn't come, that's o.k., just let it go.

Intensity Curve

The heart rate monitor is the same for a person as for a jazz tune — a flat line is bad news. Ups and downs are crucial to give a feeling of life. Don't get stuck doing the same thing for three choruses in a row. Take it somewhere.

New Directions

Never mind what sounded good last week, yesterday or fifteen minutes ago. In the words of Charlie Parker, "Now's the Time." Be on the lookout for new things to play.

Groove

Second only to listening in importance. If you put a rhythm section of Horace Silver, Doug Watkins and Art Blakey of the Jazz Messengers on the stand, they would swing so hard that the soloist could be your Aunt Gertie playing tin whistle and it would sound great. A good groove is the key to a good sounding ensemble and that groove lies in the hands (and feet) of the rhythm section.

The next few pages deal specifically with how to support the soloist when you comp. We'll take a few solo choruses from a B♭ blues, each with a different mood. The choruses become progressively more intense. Then we'll take a look at an appropriate comping approach to that chorus. We won't try to make every last rhythm and chord color match up, since in an actual performance situation you would not hear the whole solo before you chose your comping ideas. The basis is a bebop style blues. Chord symbols in the solo are those implied by the solo and the chord symbols in the comping examples show what changes are being used by the comper.

Here we are at the beginning of a horn solo. The horn player is starting by laying out fairly simple ideas with a lot of space in between.

FIRST CHORUS

Even if the solo were not beginning so simply, we'd probably want to lay back at first. This way we have somewhere to go later on with the intensity curve. Also, by playing sparsely in the beginning we are able to take a step back and listen to the soloist. What is their rhythm like? What kinds of colors are they playing? How loud are they? We can only find these things out by listening and that way we can better judge what to do as we get more daring down the line.

This chorus of comping, therefore, is a bit of a skeleton. The rhythms include some anticipations and other syncopation to push the swing a bit, but overall they're pretty simple. The chords are largely shells, with some three note voicings to add a bit more color. They, too, like the solo, are deliberately simple. Note that all the voicings are rootless as well, based on the assumption that there's a bassist in the rhythm section.

FIRST CHORUS, COMPING

Track 66

Let's skip ahead in time a bit. By now, we've spent a couple choruses laying back and it is time to bring it somewhere. As the third chorus begins, we decide to beef up the chords a bit. The horn player has begun to play more notes and is now beboppin' instead of just playing simple melodies.

THIRD CHORUS

It is appropriate for us to have a greater density of notes to match the increase in intensity. The chorus begins with unaltered extensions in the chords and a couple simple substitutions to add color and motion. When the ii-V's start to come in on the eighth bar, some alterations are added to the dominant chords to intensify the resolutions. The rhythm is still reserved enough for there to be somewhere to go, but there is a definite increase in the rhythmic activity and syncopation.

Notice that even when these chords in the comping and the chords used by the soloist don't match exactly, it still sounds fine. Since the moments of tension and release are occurring at the same time, it is safe to throw in some substitutions like this as a soloist or a comper (you will, after all, be resolving the tension in sync with one another). In fact, it helps build the intensity. This is not to say that you should begin comping a Bird blues without any indication that the soloist is going to do the same, but it does mean that you needn't be scared to take some calculated risks when you comp.

THIRD CHORUS, COMPING

Track 67

Solo

The solo has been going on for a while and it is time for another significant leap in the intensity. The soloist is now playing quite a few notes, far removed from the reserved pace of the first chorus and noticeably more intense than the bebop statements of the third chorus. Not only is the soloist playing more notes but the note choices have changed, as well. He is throwing in a lot of altered notes on dominant chords and implying some substitutions in his lines.

SIXTH CHORUS

It is time for us to respond similarly. Altered dominant chords are now appropriate, as are substitutions. More rhythmic density (and intensity) is called for and we make use of that. Essentially, it is time to throw caution to the wind and give the soloist some fire to support the energy he is giving.

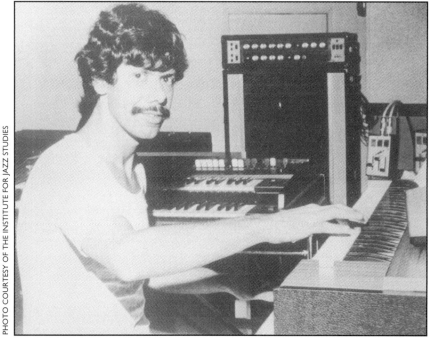

Chick Corea *emerged in the 1960s as a sideman with the likes of Blue Mitchell, Stan Getz and Miles Davis before striking out as a leader in the 70s. Chick is an exciting and daring comper who brings energy and fire to any situation.*

SIXTH CHORUS, COMPING

Track 68

Chapter 8—Comping   **183**

In a straight ahead jazz context, "Latin" has taken on a generalized meaning. It could refer to Latin American styles and grooves, like salsa and merengue, or to Brazilian styles, like Bossa Nova and Samba. Some jazz musicians, such as the Latin American pianists Hilton Ruiz and Danilo Perez, are experts at both straight ahead jazz and authentic Latin music. The Latin grooves typically played by jazz players, however, are sort of combinations of all these grooves.

At its most generic level, the word "Latin" in jazz simply means "straight eighth notes." Bud Powell's *Un Poco Loco*, Duke Ellington's *African Flower*, Joe Henderson's *Recordame* and James Williams' *Alter Ego* are examples of Latin modern-jazz tunes. Also, Brazilian composer Antonio Carlos Jobim wrote many Bossa Nova or Samba tunes that have since become jazz standards, including *The Girl From Ipanema, Desifinado, How Insensitive, Corcovado* and *Wave*. The next two pages give some examples of Latin rhythms and rhythmic patterns that you can draw from when playing Latin tunes. For further study, listen to some Latin and Brazilian music and spend some time with musicians who play it. Most straight-ahead players can get away with not being well versed in the authentic stuff but the more you know, the better off you are.

SALSA

In *salsa* (a generic term for a number of Afro-Cuban styles), the keyboard parts usually revolve around *montunos*. A montuno is a repetitive, exciting, highly rhythmic figure that drives the band. In a jazz context, montunos run the risk of being overbearing so save them for moments of high excitement. You can hear some great montunos by listening to keyboardists like Eddie Palmieri and Pappo Lucca (of La Sonora Ponceña). Below are a couple montunos over a pattern of ii-V's to give you an idea.

BOSSA NOVA

Ever since Stan Getz popularized the fusion of jazz and Brazilian music in the 1960's, the Bossa Nova has been the most common "Latin" groove among jazz musicians. In Brazilian music, the chords and rhythms are typically played on acoustic guitar. The examples below approximate some of those rhythms and show what kinds of rhythms a keyboardist could play on a Bossa Nova.

SAMBA

Samba rhythms are similar to those of the Bossa Nova but faster and more aggressive. The rhythm is felt "in two." Rather than focusing on every beat in a bar of $\frac{4}{4}$, you focus only on the first and third beats, as though it were $\frac{2}{2}$ time. Here are some examples of Samba comping.

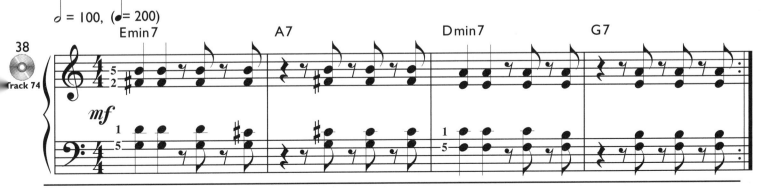

CHAPTER 9

Afterwords

To begin our wrap-up, here is *Carob Powder*, a tune for you to dig into. The changes are based on the chords from the Ray Noble standard *Cherokee*. These changes have served as a testing ground for jazz players for many years, evidenced by *Koko*, Charlie Parker's demolition of the changes. The beboppish melody incorporates some of the soloing techniques from this book and many of the voicings we examined are in there, too. Have fun with this, you've earned it!

CAROB POWDER
Track 75

D. C. al Fine

Imagine reading a manual entitled *How to Walk*. It would probably read something like this:

"Stand upright. Lift your right leg up with your knee bent slightly. Move it forward and place the heel on the ground. Pivot forward and lift your left leg, repeating the process as your right foot rolls forward to the toe and lifts up. In order to do this faster, a greater amount of muscular exertion is needed…"

The information is thorough and accurate. However, if you'd spent your whole life sitting in a chair, the manual probably wouldn't do you much good. Kids learn to walk not by reading about it, but by watching other people do it and endlessly trying it themselves. There is no real learning without actual doing.

Jazz is no different. You can read these books cover to cover and you'll absorb a ton of important information. That information alone, however, won't substitute for the experience of getting out and playing with other people. It is a similar case of trial and error where sometimes you make it from point A to point B on two feet and other times you fall down. That is how you really learn jazz.

There's a famous jazz legend about Charlie "Bird" Parker. He wasn't yet at the level of stature he eventually reached and he was on the bandstand, playing. Legend has it, drummer "Papa" Jo Jones was so unimpressed by his playing that he threw a cymbal at Bird. If that happened to Charlie Parker, we can expect that we'll probably mess up occasionally, too. On the other hand, things will also go great when you play with other people, regardless of your level. People don't devote their lives to jazz because they dream of fame, fortune and their face on the cover of *Time* magazine. They do it because playing jazz can be one of the most exhilarating experiences a human being can have. Equip yourself with some tunes (see the list later in this chapter) and get yourself out there to play–gigs, jam sessions, sitting in with other groups, whatever. Playing with and in front of other people will solidify your skills much faster and more thoroughly than anything else could. If something doesn't work, that can give you clarity about what to practice.

Then there is the issue of simply hanging out with other musicians. It may sound odd to endorse hanging out, as opposed to using that time to practice or memorize theoretical concepts. In fact, there is some validity to the stereotype of people with berets hanging out in smoky clubs at 3 a.m., talking about the relative merits of the different baritone saxophonists on the scene. The beret, smoky club and 3 a.m. time frame are all highly unnecessary. The hang, on the other hand, is an important part of a jazz musician's life and development. It is a great opportunity to exchange ideas.

First of all, there are some things that you only learn in that kind of setting. A book can share a lot of information but it can't sit down and talk to you. Musicians talk about changes on tunes, records to check out, who is on the scene now, gig experiences and so on. Even if every piece of information you get isn't enlightening or even wholly accurate, the information you get is dynamic and personal, just like jazz itself.

Second of all, jazz is an inherently social form of music. The playing we do in a jazz group revolves around group interactions and relationships. Hanging out with musicians can help strengthen the bonds that are so crucial when you get on the bandstand. Likewise, being a familiar and likeable presence can lead to a lot more opportunities. When someone is looking for a keyboardist for a gig or a jam session, they'll obviously want someone who can play. In addition, though, they'll want someone who's reliable, serious, and pleasant to hang out with. Simply being present and not being a jerk can get you more gigs than you might think.

PACING

We've all probably been to hear an uninspiring band and thought, "All these songs sound the same." That danger exists as much in jazz as in any other form of music. Luckily, we've explored enough different concepts to have a variety of tune types we can play on a gig or at a session. Standards, ballads, bebop tunes and Latin tunes are among the choices we have and we should make the most of those choices. There are also other considerations like tempo, feel, key and overall mood. These, too, can greatly impact the way that tunes should logically follow one another. If you play three medium swing standards in E♭ all in a row, even you might forget what tune you're playing by the third one. Mix up the different styles and feels. Throw in a slow tune between two faster ones. Make sure that you're going through a variety of keys. Adapt your solos to the changing needs of the tunes so that the different moods are that much more distinct. The listeners will greatly appreciate the variety.

PRACTICING

Not much needs to be said about practicing here – if you've made it this far, you clearly have an effective work ethic and can make good use of your practice time. The main issue that needs to be brought up is a question that is often asked by keyboard students of all levels. That question is this: "What do I need to practice?" The answer is "whatever you need to practice." In other words, we all have different strengths and weaknesses. One player might have no problems with soloing but still can't comfortably play left hand voicings. Another player might have great chord voicings but can't handle anything faster than a ballad. Only you can judge your strengths and weaknesses. If you're playing with other people (see the previous page), it should be clear what they are.

When you practice, pinpoint the things you need to work on and practice them. If we can handle an F blues with no problems, our instinct is to play that, since it is fun to play things that sound good. Catch yourself when you do this and make it harder. Use an F blues to practice scales, voicings or substitutions that you haven't yet mastered. Or play the same thing in A♭ instead. At the same time, don't stretch so far that you can't absorb the things you are practicing. Strive to find the place just beyond your comfort zone and spend most of your practice time in that place. In any case, keep using the things you practice on actual tunes. That way they'll be useful in real-life situations. Also, by doing this you can tell whether you've really learned the things you've practiced.

DEALING WITH DIFFERENT KEYBOARDS

For better or worse, the keyboardist is the one person in a jazz group who often doesn't bring their own instrument to the gig or session. When you do bring a keyboard, even if yours isn't top of the line, you know what to expect. If you're using the house instrument, it is anybody's guess. Some venues have gorgeous Steinway grand pianos, always kept immaculately in tune, and of course we all love playing at such places. At many clubs, however, you may encounter a beat-up upright with missing strings and when you mention to the club owner that it is out of tune, he says, "But I just dusted it this morning." When you encounter the latter situation, try this approach. Take a deep breath, look at the instrument and say, "I'm not going to let you hurt me. Let's be friends." If the instrument isn't great, there is nothing you can do except relax and play your stuff anyway. Trying to make the instrument sound in tune will make your hands sore. Just be aware of broken strings or particularly out-of-tune notes and beyond that, just let it go.

Much of the vocabulary that we use as jazz musicians comes from the vast body of tunes that jazz players have played through the years. The best training any jazz musician can get is from playing with other people. And you can't play with other people if you don't know any tunes. If you want to take your jazz playing to the next level, devote some time to learning tunes. You can learn tunes from lead sheets, from records or directly from other musicians. The best way to learn any tune is by combining a couple of these methods. Use a lead sheet but then check it against a famous record. Do all the changes match? Are they in the same key? Cross referencing like this will give you a more thorough understanding of a tune. It also might save you the embarrassment of starting a tune in the wrong key on the job. Often, there is no "correct" key or set of changes, so it is up to you to adjust to the situation you're in and be aware. For example, a popular fake book has Autumn Leaves written in E Minor, whereas most players do it in G Minor. E Minor isn't wrong but you should be aware of these sorts of things and be ready to adapt.

Standards

All The Things You Are
Autumn Leaves
Body and Soul
Caravan
Cherokee
Girl From Ipanema
Green Dolphin St.
Have You Met Miss Jones
How High The Moon
I Can't Get Started
I'll Remember April
Misty
My Funny Valentine
Night and Day
Take the "A" Train
Satin Doll
Softly as in a Morning Sunrise
Stella by Starlight
Summertime
There Is No Greater Love
There Will Never Be Another You
What Is This Thing Called Love?

Modern Jazz Tunes

All Blues
A Night in Tunisia
Blue Bossa
Blue Monk
Footprints
Four
Joy Spring
Lady Bird
Maiden Voyage
Mr. P.C.
Oleo
'Round Midnight
So What/Impressions (same harmony)
Straight, No Chaser
Tune Up
Woody 'N You

The tunes listed are some basic tunes that you'll probably encounter at gigs or jam sessions. Start by learning some of these as well as any other tunes that you hear folks playing and suspect that you might need to know.

RECORDINGS

The recordings listed here are classic albums that help to drive home points made in this book. Particularly emphasized are voicings and comping, making the changes and the direct and indirect use of the blues. Get your hands on any of these records you can. Study them, but also enjoy them. The common thread of all these albums is that they all sound great.

— Louis Armstrong and Oscar Peterson: *Louis Armstrong meets Oscar Peterson* (some of the tastiest comping you'll ever hear)
— Kenny Barron: *Canta Brasil*
— Count Basie: *April in Paris*
— Art Blakey and the Jazz Messengers: *Moanin'* (with Bobby Timmons on piano)
— Clifford Brown and Max Roach: *Clifford Brown and Max Roach* (with Richie Powell on piano)
— Sonny Clark Trio: *Sonny Clark Trio*
— Chick Corea and Return to Forever: *Light as a Feather*
— Miles Davis: *Kind of Blue* (four tracks with Bill Evans on piano and one with Wynton Kelly. This is the album that popularized the use of modes.)
— Miles Davis: *Someday My Prince Will Come* (with Wynton Kelly on piano – amazing comping)
— Eddie "Lockjaw" Davis: *Smokin'* (with Shirley Scott on organ)
— Duke Ellington and John Coltrane: *Duke Ellington and John Coltrane*
— Bill Evans: *Sunday at the Village Vanguard*
— Stan Getz with Joao Gilberto: *Getz-Gilberto* (with Antonio Carlos Jobim on piano)
— Herbie Hancock: *Maiden Voyage*
— Eddie Harris: *The In Sound* (with Cedar Walton on piano)
— Roy Haynes Trio: *We Three* (with Phineas Newborn, Jr. on piano)
— Freddie Hubbard: *Ready for Freddie* (with McCoy Tyner on piano)
— *Jazz at Massey Hall* (with Bud Powell on piano and featuring Charlie Parker and Dizzy Gillespie)
— Jack McDuff: *Live*
— Jackie McLean: *Bluesnik* (with Kenny Drew on piano. Every cut is a variation on the blues.)
— Charles Mingus: *Mingus Ah Um* (with Horace Parlan on piano)
— Charles Mingus: *Oh Yeah!* (with Mingus on piano)
— Thelonious Monk: *Brilliant Corners*
— Oliver Nelson: *Blues And The Abstract Truth* (with Bill Evans on piano. Every cut on the album is a variation on either the blues or Rhythm Changes.)
— Eddie Palmieri: *Sun of Latin Music*
— Sonora Ponceña: *Algo De Locura* (with Pappo Lucca on piano)
— Bud Powell: *Amazing Bud Powell, Vol. I*
— Sonny Rollins: *A Night at the Village Vanguard, Vol. I and 2* (There is no keyboard or guitar on these tracks and Sonny gives us a special lesson in making the changes.)
— Horace Silver: *The Jody Grind*
— Jimmy Smith: *Back at the Chicken Shack*
— Art Tatum: *Best of the Pablo Solo Masterpieces*
— Mickey Tucker: *Blues in Five Dimensions*

Have fun practicing, playing and listening. See you in *Mastering Jazz Keyboard*, where we will cover advanced jazz concepts such as symmetrical scales, the modes of the Lydian diminished scale and the harmonic and melodic minor scales, advanced substitutions, 4th voicings, building intensity, lyricism and lots more.

MASTERING JAZZ KEYBOARD

This book was acquired, edited, and produced
by Workshop Arts, Inc., the publishing arm of
the National Keyboard Workshop.
Nathaniel Gunod, acquisitions, editor
Amy Rosser, editor
ProScore, Novato, CA, music typesetter
Cathy Bolduc, interior design
Audio tracks recorded by Collin Tilton at Bar None Studio, Northford, CT

CONTENTS

INTRODUCTION

Welcome to the *Mastering* section. By now, you understand the importance of swing. You've listened to a lot of great jazz. You have some facility with voicings and soloing. You've probably played some gigs and had some hands-on experience and training. Now you want to take it to the next level. This section is designed to help take you there. By now you realize that no method book can turn you into a successful jazz musician unless you get out there and integrate what you have learned by playing. With that in mind, *Mastering Jazz Keyboard* lays out a lot of advanced information to put to use in the real world. By being introduced to concepts like modal playing, advanced substitution and non-diatonic harmony, the door will be opened to new and more challenging kinds of tunes. By learning 4th voicings and upper structures, you will have more options for your voicings. By learning about superimposed pentatonic scales and the many scales in Chapter 4, you will have a broader palate of colors to use when you solo. What you do with all this information is up to you.

By now you surely realize that learning to play jazz is an ongoing process, so learn this information at your own pace. Nobody masters Coltrane changes or the modes of the Lydian diminished scale in a week or a month. Just keep moving forward, learning the things you need to learn to do what you have to do. If you've got a solo gig coming up, work on solo playing. If you're gigging with a Wayne Shorter fan, work on non-diatonic harmony. By now you've got the foundation, and you'll spend the rest of your musical life refining and adding things. It is a glorious journey and I am sure you will continue to enjoy it.

ACKNOWLEDGMENTS

Thank you to everyone who made this project possible (including many people who didn't make it onto this list): to Nat Gunod, Dave Smolover, Burgess Speed and everyone else at NGW and Workshop Arts; to Alfred Music Publishing; to Collin Tilton at Bar None Studios; to Dan Morgenstern, Esther Smith, and the rest of the people at the Institute of Jazz Studies; to Steve Bennett, Karl Mueller, Wynne Mun, Jeff Grace, Amanda Monaco, Damion Poirier, Jimmy Greene, Noah Richardson, Jeff Bartolotta, Roberto Scrofani, Rachel Green, the Ten Eyck family and all the rest of the friends who directly or indirectly helped me to put these books together; to all my students who taught me how to teach; to ECA and the Artists' Collective for getting me started with jazz; to the Music Department at Rutgers for all their support and training; to Eva Pierrou, Clara Shen and Wanda Maximilien for their expert piano teaching; to Mike Mossman, Sumi Tonooka, Joanne Brackeen, Larry Ridley, Phil Schaap, Ralph Bowen, and especially Ted Dunbar, George Raccio and Kenny Barron for selflessly sharing their jazz knowledge; to my dear friends and inspiring colleagues from Positive Rhythmic Force, Jason Berg, Ben Tedoff and Sunny Jain; to my family, Mom, Dad, Alison, Jennifer, Matthew and Annie for their boundless support and patience; and to Kate for everything.

00

Track I

An MP3 CD is included with this book to make learning easier and more enjoyable. The symbol shown at bottom left appears next to every example in the book that features an MP3 track. Use the MP3s to ensure you're capturing the feel of the examples and interpreting the rhythms correctly. The track number below the symbol corresponds directly to the example you want to hear (example numbers are above the icon). All the track numbers are unique to each "book" within this volume, meaning every book has its own Track 1, Track 2, and so on. (For example, *Beginning Jazz Keyboard* starts with Track 1, as does *Intermediate Jazz Keyboard* and *Mastering Jazz Keyboard*.) Track 1 for each book will help you tune to the CD.

The disc is playable on any CD player equipped to play MP3 CDs. To access the MP3s on your computer, place the CD in your CD-ROM drive. In Windows, double-click on My Computer, then right-click on the CD icon labeled "MP3 Files" and select Explore to view the files and copy them to your hard drive. For Mac, double-click on the CD icon on your desktop labeled "MP3 Files" to view the files and copy them to your hard drive.

CHAPTER 1

Review

To get the most out of the *Mastering* section, you should have made it comfortably through the material in the *Intermediate* section or have the equivalent knowledge and skills. This review will quickly go over the basics. If anything doesn't ring a bell, go back and look over the topic before moving on. Likewise, if you're still shaky on any of the topics from the *Beginning* section like basic 7th chord voicings, harmonic analysis or soloing in a major or minor key, take a little time to review. If all those things are cool, then you're good to go!

MODES OF THE MAJOR SCALE

A mode of a scale is what you get when you play that scale beginning from a note other than the usual tonic. The relative minor (or the *Aeolian mode*) is an example of a mode of the major scale.

In jazz, we make much use of the seven modes of the major scale. To the right are the seven modes of the C Major scale. The harmony implied by each mode is named in parentheses, next to the name of the mode, and shown by circling the notes of the mode.

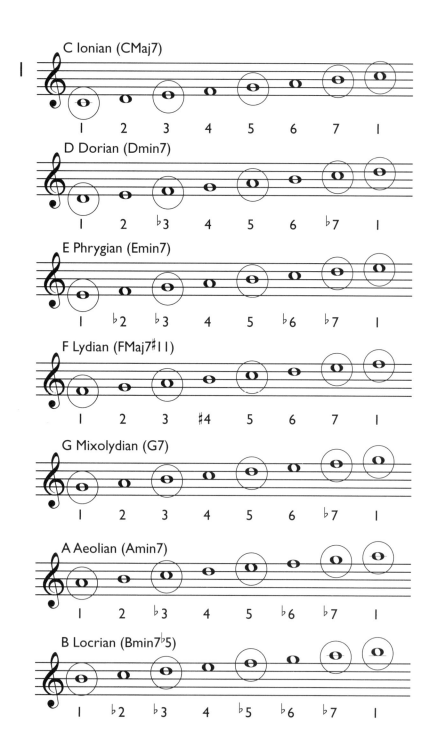

There are a couple of ways that we typically use the modes when we solo. The first way is to match them up with the diatonic chords in a key.

Chord	Mode	Formula
I	Ionian	1, 2, 3, 4, 5, 6, 7
ii	Dorian	1, 2, ♭3, 4, 5, 6, ♭7
iii	Phrygian	1, ♭2, ♭3, 4, 5, ♭6, ♭7
IV	Lydian	1, 2, 3, ♯4, 5, 6, 7
V	Mixolydian	1, 2, 3, 4, 5, 6, ♭7
vi	Aeolian	1, 2, ♭3, 4, 5, ♭6, ♭7
vii	Locrian	1, ♭2, ♭3, 4, ♭5, ♭6, ♭7

For example, on the diatonic progression iii-vi-ii-V-I in E♭ Major, you might do this:

2

iii	vi	ii	V	I
G Phrygian	C Aeolian	F Dorian	B♭ Mixolydian	E♭ Ionian
Gmin7	Cmin7	Fmin7	B♭7	E♭Maj7

The other typical use for modes is to insert the modes that match up well with individual chord types within a progression. When using the modes this way, you generally have to use a variety of modes, rather than simply using one major scale and beginning it from different notes. In this case, it is important to know the modes as independent scales and not just variations on a parent major scale. The list below shows the mode usually paired with each common 7th chord in a modern jazz setting. Other, less common mode options are also shown.

Chord	Most Common Mode	Other Mode(s)
Maj7	Lydian	Ionian
7	Mixolydian	—
min7	Dorian	Aeolian, Phrygian
min7♭5	Locrian	—

The example below shows how we might use this concept over a set of changes:

3

Parent Major Scale:	B♭	D	E♭	C	G
Mode:	C Dorian	A Mixolydian	D Locrian	G Mixolydian	C Lydian
Chord Progression:	Cmin7	A7	Dmin7♭5	G7	CMaj7
	i	VI7	ii	VI7	I7

Here's an example of how that might sound:

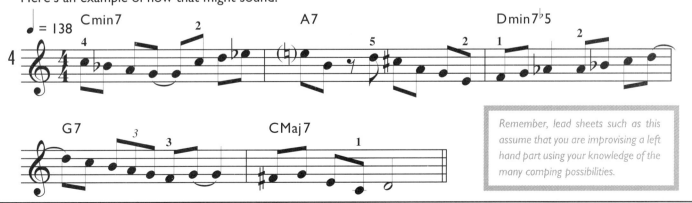

Remember, lead sheets such as this assume that you are improvising a left hand part using your knowledge of the many comping possibilities.

Way back in the beginning of our jazz studies, we learned that we could form a triad by stacking 3rds. Later on, we learned that we could form a 7th chord by stacking another 3rd on top of a triad. With extensions, we simply continue to stack 3rds thereby bringing 9ths, 11ths and 13ths into the picture.

On major 7th (Maj7) chords, the common extensions are the 9th, ♯11th and 13th. The 13 is enharmonically equivalent to 6, which is sometimes used in place of the 7th in the chord. If the 7th is present, that note is considered a 13th. If there is no 7th, it is the 6th of a 6th chord. Also, the 5th in the chord becomes an optional note that is often omitted.

On dominant 7th chords (7), the same extensions are used as on the major 7th. In addition, the natural 4 (enharmonically equivalent to the natural 11) sometimes replaces the 3rd, making the chord a 7sus. As with the Maj7, the 5th is often omitted from the voicings.

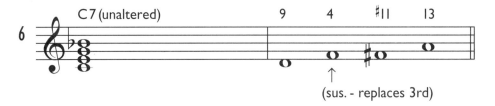

On dominant 7th chords that resolve down a 5th or a half step, altered extensions are often used. These alterations build a great deal of tension which is then released when the dominant chord resolves. The four altered notes are the ♭5, ♯5, ♭9 and ♯9. Remember, jazz players often use enharmonic respellings for readability and in favor of flats. So, it is more likely to find an E♭ written for a ♯9 than a D♯, and an A♭ written for ♯5 than a G♯.

With dominant chords we have many possibilities for colors and color combinations:

Options for a C7 chord with extensions and/or alterations		
C9		C13♭9
C7sus		C13♯9
C13		C9♭5
C7♭9		C9♯5
C7♯9		C7♭9♭5
C7♭5	C7alt*	C7♭9♯5
C7♯5		C7♯9♭5
		C7♯9♯5

* Remember, when "alt" appears in a chord symbol, it means you can play any dominant chord with an altered 5 and 9 (♭5 or ♯5 and ♭9 or ♯9).

On minor chords that participate in cycles (particularly as *ii* chords), the common extensions are the 9 and 11. The same is true for minor 7 ♭5 chords (min7♭5).

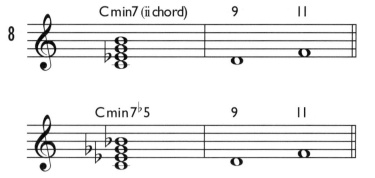

On tonic minor chords (minor chords functioning as *i* in minor keys), there are more options. First of all, there are three options for turning the minor triad into a four note chord. The usual min7 is an option as are the minor 6 (min6) and the minor/major 7 (min/Maj7). Once that choice has been made, the 9 and 11 are again options for extensions.

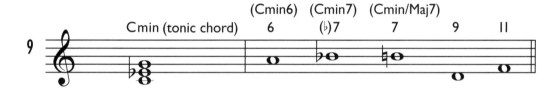

On diminished 7th chords, any note a whole step above a chord tone works well as a color tone. That means the 9, 11, ♭13 and major 7 all work as color tones.

Below is a quick example of some left hand voicings using these colors and some typical ways of incorporating them.

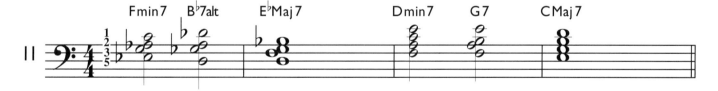

Substitution involves changing the harmony in a tune or chord progression. Musicians or composer/arrangers sometimes make substitutions in advance. Other times, the players spontaneously throw in substitute changes to add more motion and excitement to a progression. As a rule, we leave the significant points of rest and resolution intact. The chords leading us there are fair game, however. As long as we don't blindly throw in chords that clash with the written melody as it's being played, we have a lot of freedom to make the harmony more exciting. We'll dig deeper into this concept in Chapter 3, but for now let's look at some substitution techniques we checked out in the *Intermediate* section.

We'll begin with this simple (one might even say boring) five measure chord progression in B♭ Major. It begins on a B♭Maj7 chord, goes to the V chord for a while and then comes back to the B♭Maj7.

12

First, we decide to throw in another chord to give us a bit more to solo on and to create more motion in the changes. Since the ii-V is a well established diatonic device, we add the ii chord.

13

We can also play with the rhythm of the ii-V and have it repeat so that we have more motion and more chords to solo over.

14

The ii-V's improve the changes, but we still have more B♭Maj7 than we need at the beginning. So, we throw in the vi chord.

15

We're going to try a few ways to make the progression more exciting. We borrow some chords from B♭ Minor (the parallel minor) to create more suspense and uncertainty about the tonality. It's all released, of course, when we arrive on the final B♭Maj7.

16

Now we'll go back to the I-vi-ii-V-I option but instead of playing it straight, we substitute secondary dominant chords for the min7 chords. Each dominant chord resolves down a 5th to the next one, creating a sort of domino effect that culminates in the resolution to B♭Maj7.

17

B♭Maj7	G7	C7	F7	B♭Maj7

We can take that progression and spice it up further with tritone substitutions on the dominant chords. Here are two different examples of that.

18

B♭Maj7	G7	G♭7	F7	B♭Maj7

B♭Maj7	D♭7	C7	B7	B♭Maj7

Finally, we can take any of those progressions and temporarily think of each dominant chord as a V chord. Then we can add the ii chord that would relate to each one.

19

B♭Maj7	Dmin7 G7	D♭min7 G♭7	Cmin7 F7	B♭Maj7

B♭Maj7	A♭min7 D♭7	Gmin7 C7	F♯min7 B7	B♭Maj7

These are just some examples of possible substitutions.

*The legendary and innovative **Earl "Fatha" Hines**, born in 1903, spent the better part of the 20th century at the top of the jazz piano heap.*

An important soloing skill, especially in a bebop-derived style, is the ability to *make the changes*. Making the changes is soloing in such a way that the sound of the changes is clearly brought out by the line. Soloing in a key while thinking about a single scale is fine but you're unlikely to make the changes that way. To make the changes, more attention must be paid to the individual chords in a progression and playing the notes that will bring out the sound of those chords.

The other key to making the changes is rhythm. Not only is it important to play the notes of the chords in your solo lines, but they need to be emphasized rhythmically, as well. A chord tone played on a downbeat (or anticipating a downbeat) will sound much stronger than a chord tone played on an offbeat.

Here are a few techniques that we examined in the *Intermediate* section:

Modes. Using modes in the way we discussed on page 199 will help you to make the changes.

Arpeggios and Guidetones. In both of the first two books in this series, we discussed soloing with arpeggios, chords played one note at a time. By this point, the definition has become looser, since we now have extended chords that have as many notes as an entire scale. To use arpeggios to solo, just think about playing the notes in the chords. Using some extensions and/or passing tones is fine, just make chord tones your primary focus. Within the realm of arpeggios, we also looked at guidetones—though you can use guidetones in any context. Guidetones are the 3rd and 7th of a chord, the same notes as in a shell voicing. When one note in a shell voice leads to another, it helps define the sound of the change. You can emphasize those notes in your solo and it will have a similar effect. The example below uses mostly chord tones and when the chords change, guidetones (circled) are used.

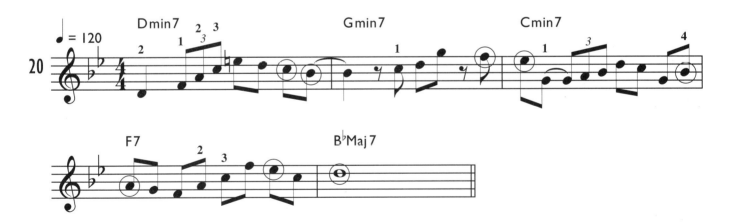

Chromatic Notes. We can use *chromatic notes*, notes not in the key, to help bring out the sound of the changes. Chromatic approach tones are chromatic notes that lead to non-chromatic tones. Chromatic passing tones are chromatic notes that fall between two non-chromatic notes. Hitting these notes and then resolving them to chord tones can help emphasize those chord tones.

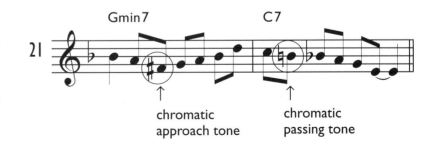

chromatic approach tone

chromatic passing tone

We also have the bebop scale, a scale that includes strategically placed chromatic passing tones. There are actually two bebop scales, one for dominant chords and one for minor chords. Each one puts a chromatic passing tone between the ♭7 and the tonic, making an eight-note scale where every other note is a chord tone.

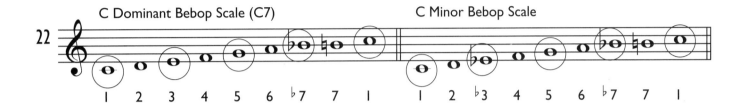

This example uses chromatic passing tones. The bebop scale is used on the Gmin7 and F7 chords.

Loafin' Blues is a blues melody in F. Play it as you normally would, but also play it without chords in the left hand to hear how the line itself brings out the sound of the changes.

LOAFIN' BLUES

Track 2

CHAPTER 2

Modal Playing and 4th Voicings

*The **John Coltrane** quartet of the 1960s, featuring pianist **McCoy Tyner**, were groundbreakers in the modal jazz movement going on at that time.*

We first looked at modes on page 112 and we've come to see that the modes are very useful for playing over individual chords in a progression. In the mid 1950s, George Russell published the *Lydian Chromatic Concept of Tonal Organization*. One of the things this monumental book did was re-introduce modes to the music world in a contemporary context. As the '50s went on, artists like trumpeter Miles Davis and pianist Bill Evans experimented with the modes. This culminated in the 1959 recording of the landmark Miles Davis album *Kind of Blue*, featuring Evans and saxophonists John Coltrane and Cannonball Adderley. Tunes like *So What* showed that modes were not only useful over individual chords, but could actually be used instead of individual chords. At this point people like Coltrane had stretched chord progressions and substitutions to a point of great harmonic complexity (see Chapter 3). Some players felt that all those chords and the obligation to make the changes made their solos too predictable and restricted. Miles and his cohorts tried to break down these limitations. *So What*, for example, used the following harmony:

24

D Dorian	D Dorian	E♭ Dorian	D Dorian
— 8 bars —	— 8 bars —	— 8 bars —	— 8 bars —

Imagine that—a whole tune with just these two modes and no individual chords. Dmin7 and E♭min7 would obviously be the implied chords but by referring to the modes, there was no obligation to be bogged down by chords. The soloists could just focus on creating melodies within the seven notes of each mode and Evans could comp freely within each mode.

Since the 1950s, modal playing has become much more common, and it's now an integral part of the jazz musician's vocabulary. Modal tunes like John Coltrane's *Impressions*, Freddie Hubbard's *Little Sunflower*, Eddie Harris' *Freedom Jazz Dance*, McCoy Tyner's *Passion Dance* and Herbie Hancock's *Maiden Voyage* are commonly played in modern jazz. In addition, old standards like *Caravan* and *Softly As In A Morning Sunrise* are now often played in a modal style.

4th VOICINGS

Tertian harmony refers to harmony based on 3rds. When we stack two 3rds, we get a triad. Add another 3rd on top and we get a 7th chord. Keep stacking 3rds for 7th chord extensions. Most of our chords and voicings so far have come from tertian harmony. In the 1960s, musicians like McCoy Tyner, Eric Dolphy and Eddie Harris popularized the use of *quartal harmony* (harmony based on 4ths). Since our concept of chords is so firmly entrenched in tertian harmony, we tend not to use quartal harmony as a whole new harmonic concept. Instead, we often use 4ths as the basis for voicing chords we already know.

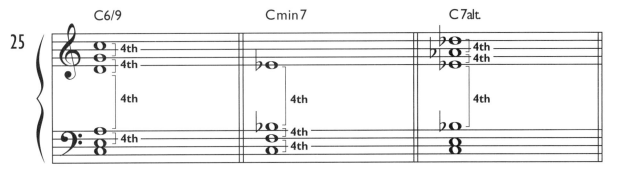

A chord voicing that makes significant use of perfect 4ths is a *4th voicing*. As long as the 4ths are central to the sound of the voicing, it's fine to use other intervals as well, if that makes it easier to form the desired chord.

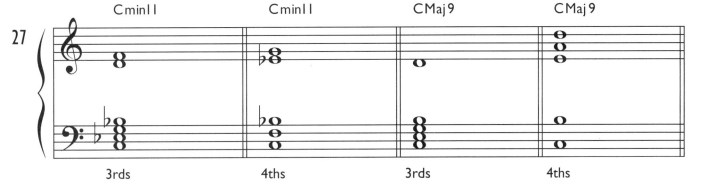

Compared with the tight sound of chords built from 3rds, 4th voicings are much more open sounding. It stands to reason that they fit perfectly into the sound of modal jazz, where a freer sound is part of the whole concept.

Experiment with different chord types, seeing what 4th voicings you can come up with. Some, like min7♭5 and dim7 chords, are less adaptable to 4th voicings. Others, like Maj7 and min7 chords, often seem like they were made for 4th voicings. In any case, this experimentation will greatly increase your comfort level with quartal harmony.

The voicing to your right was the basis of the harmony in the Miles Davis recording of *So What*, and we can therefore refer to it (or any other chord voiced this way) as a *So What* voicing. The structure of the voicing is this: three perfect 4ths stacked on top of one another, with a major 3rd added on top.

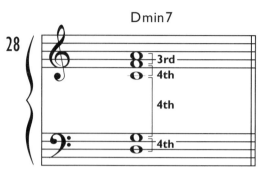

In a modal context, we're not limited to simply plunking this voicing down over the appropriate minor chord, even though it sounds good. We can use the voicing to move diatonically (remember, diatonic means "of the scale") through the mode we're in, D Dorian in this case. To do this, we simply start from any note in the mode and stack three 4ths and a 3rd. With *So What* voicings, one of the 4ths may be an augmented 4th and the 3rd may be major or minor. Whichever type fits the mode is the one to use.

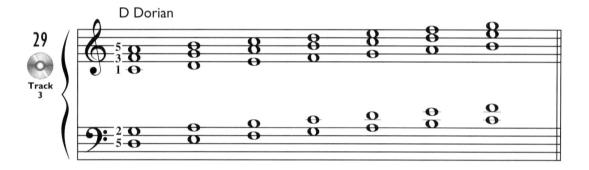

When playing modally, you needn't worry about whether the voicing of the moment spells out the main chord of the mode. For example, the second voicing above doesn't sound much like a Dmin7 chord but that's fine because the overall sound of the mode is what matters, not individual chords within it.

Try this 4th, 4th, 4th, 3rd structure to play through other modes in other keys. When you're in a mode that's not all white keys, it takes a little more thought. As an example, let's look at E♭ Dorian, the mode used on the bridge of *So What*.

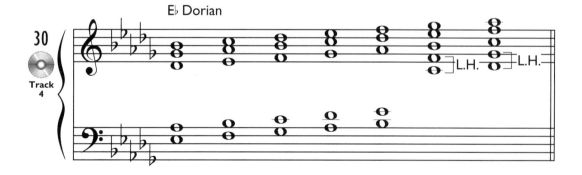

George's Concept is dedicated to George Russell, the granddaddy of modal jazz. The melody here is voiced in the way just described – diatonically with *So What* voicings. If you don't feel grounded as you hear the voicings, reach down and play the roots to hear the context more clearly.

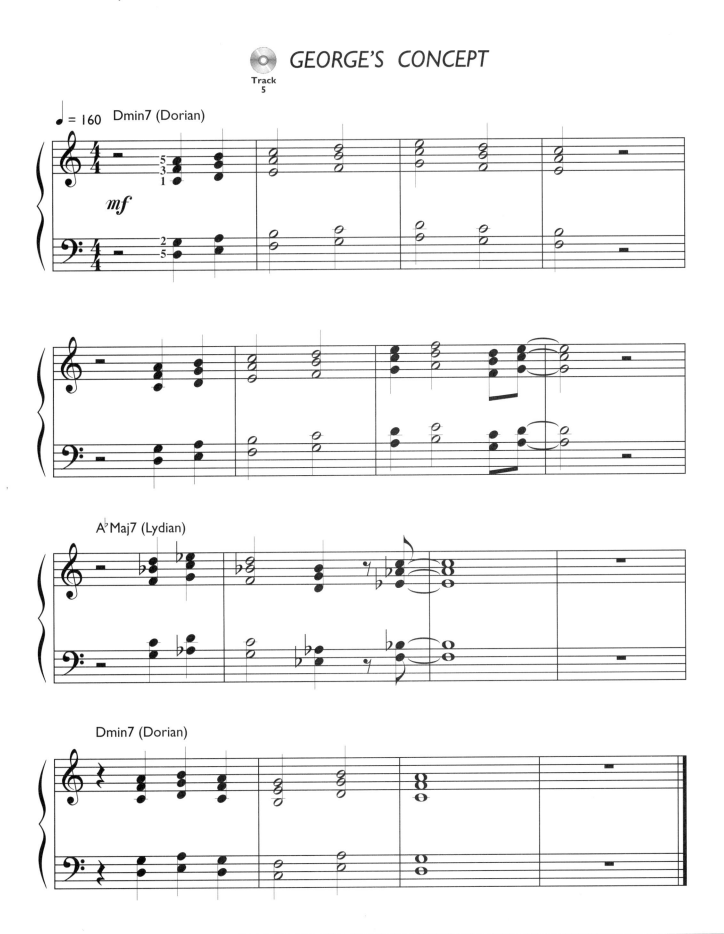

GEORGE'S CONCEPT

Track 5

Another way that keyboardists sometimes use *So What* voicings is in the form of *parallel voicings*. Whereas diatonic voicing implies that you adjust the size of the intervals to fit the mode, parallel voicing implies that you use exactly the same voicing every time, in this case perfect 4th, perfect 4th, perfect 4th, major 3rd. In the example below, parallel *So What* voicings are used to move up the D Dorian mode with the notes from the bottom of each voicing.

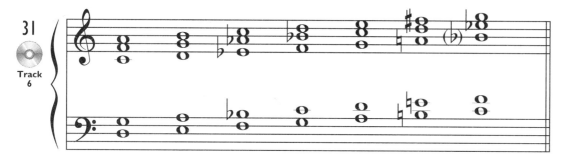

You'll see that the voicing built from B has an F♯ as the melody note. Another way to use these parallel voicings is voicing from the melody note down. Instead of going up the D Dorian mode with the bottom note in each voicing and building the voicings upwards, we can pay attention to the top note, making sure that it matches up with the mode and going down from there to find each voicing.

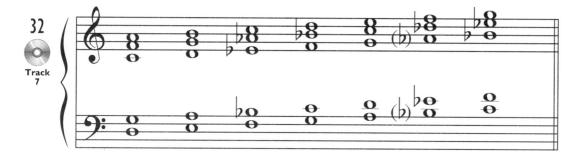

It's clear that some of these voicings are far removed from the sound of the D Dorian mode, but it still sounds good. The idea is that by setting the ear up with the sound of the voicing type, you can move that voicing type elsewhere and even if all the notes don't match up, the ear has something to latch on to. To make it clear what the mode of origin is, keyboardists often use this technique popularized by McCoy Tyner: bash out a 5th with the tonic and 5th degree of the mode (the root and 5th of the main chord of the mode) in the lower register of the keyboard with your left hand to establish the tonality before you play the voicings.

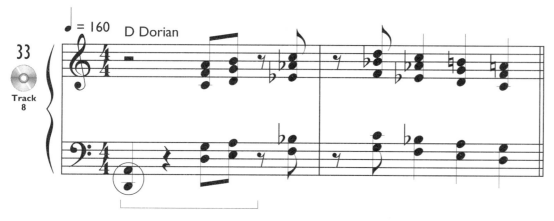

George's Concept is presented here with parallel *So What* voicings. Pay attention to the 5ths in the lower register and how much they help ground the sound of the voicing in the mode.

GEORGE'S CONCEPT: Parallel *So What* Voicings

MODAL SOLOING

When we deal with tunes that have lots of chords, we have plenty to keep our minds occupied without thinking about much else besides making the changes. All the ways of making the changes, all the different sounds that could be applied to this chord, then the next one...

In modal jazz, not having changes to be concerned with (except perhaps the change from one mode to another every so often), our minds are freed to think about other things. Not what we're going to have for a snack on the set break, but important musical things. The absence of changes also means that if you don't make your solo "say something" melodically, there will be less going on to counteract the boredom.

LYRICISM AND PACING

Between the absence of fast-moving changes and the openness of modes and 4th voicings, you have a lot of room to breathe when you solo on a modal tune. Use it! Miles Davis is not considered a master of modal jazz because he could shred modes at lightning-fast tempos. He's considered a master because the melodies he created in his improvisations were always lyrical and beautiful with just the right rhythm. Strive to be lyrical and economical in your soloing. Since you don't have to worry about wrong notes, focus on creating a memorable melody. Here is an example of a simple Dorian melody:

And then there's the issue of pacing. A good, simple melody hardly needs extra justification but here it is anyhow: a simple melody gives you somewhere to go with the intensity. When you're into the latter stages of a solo and the intensity of the music is rising, you'll be happy that you didn't blow all your chops in the first chorus. Plus, it just sounds better when the music develops and grows over time instead of staying at one level (more on this in Chapter 7).

CHORDS

When soloing, we obviously don't have enough fingers left over to play spread-out five note voicings, so we generally use three-note 4th voicings with the left hand. Just play two diatonic 4ths within the mode.

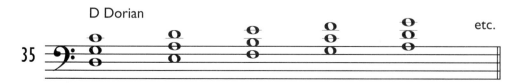

Of course, nobody says you can't use full five-note chords as part of your solo. Here's the beginning of the melody from the previous page, harmonized with diatonic *So What* voicings.

If the melody sounds good, it stands to reason that it will sound as good but more dramatic when you flesh it out like this with chords.

SIDESTEPPING AND RESOLVING

You're walking along a sidewalk, minding your own business. There's an open manhole ahead, so you have to change your path for a moment and wander into the edge of the street which makes you feel a bit tense. You pass the manhole, get back on the sidewalk and go on your merry way, relieved to be back in a comfortable place to walk. *Sidestepping* (sometimes called *side-slipping*) in a jazz solo is very much like this. You step outside the normal path for a moment and then go back to it. By resolving (going back to the normal path), you ensure that the sidestepping ends up as a detour but not a complete change in your route.

Sidestepping can be very useful in modal soloing. Although good melodies and a great swing feel can take you far, you can only do so much with seven notes, especially if you're playing a long solo. Sidestepping breaks things up a bit, adding other notes into the picture and giving a greater impact to the notes in the original mode once you return to it.

All you need to do to sidestep is play notes not associated with the mode you're in. Going to the mode a half step up or down ensures you'll have many altered notes. Your left hand should generally do the same, playing 4th voicings from outside of the mode to make it clear that you're purposefully going elsewhere and not simply hitting wrong notes. Laying down McCoy Tyner-style 5ths with the left hand is a good way to punctuate your return to the mode of origin.

Here is a two-chorus sample solo over *George's Concept* using the techniques discussed in this chapter. Observe what each hand is doing and how they work together. Then work on playing your own solos over the tune. Have fun!

Track 13

GEORGE'S CONCEPT: *Sample Solo*

CHAPTER 3

Advanced Substitution & Reharmonization

*Legendary pianist **Art Tatum** had the ability to boggle the mind with his harmonically daring and complex reharmonizations of standard tunes. This is most apparent in his extraordinary solo recordings. Since the 1930s, jazz musicians of all styles have long been in awe of his technique.*

In Chapter 5 of the *Intermediate* section we studied substitution. In the bebop era, players began to change the chords in familiar progressions and/or add chords to them. This provided them with a greater challenge and more harmonic stimulation.

This was taken to the extreme in the late 1950s. People had been experimenting with more complicated substitutions throughout the '40s and '50s. Then saxophonist John Coltrane began taking substitution to another level. It began with his 1959 composition *Giant Steps*, whose changes were among the most harmonically advanced that anybody had seen up to that point. He took the concept behind *Giant Steps* (to be discussed later in this chapter) and used it to create mind-blowing substitutions over standard changes. The changes to the standard *How High the Moon* became *Satellite*, the changes to Eddie "Cleanhead" Vinson's *Tune Up* became *Countdown* and the changes to Charlie Parker's *Confirmation* became *26-2*. A new precedent for substitution was set by using what some people called "Coltrane changes" or "*Giant Steps* changes."

These substitutions often reach the point where they can be considered *reharmonizations*. A reharmonization (or "reharm") is a comprehensive overhaul of the changes in a tune. Substitution is a tool used to reharmonize a tune (although there's often a fine line between a reharmonization and a lot of substitutions). Whereas Coltrane wrote a lot of original tunes based on standard changes saturated with substitutions (including those listed above), he was also famous for playing reharmonized standards. On these, he retained the original melody to the standard and thoroughly altered its harmony. *Out Of This World*, *My Favorite Things* and *But Not For Me* are among the well known tunes he recorded in this style.

This chapter will begin with some of the substitutions that people began using once those discussed in the last book became more common. Then we will move on to "Coltrane changes."

CYCLES

Let's begin our discussion of cycles with the old warhorse, the I-vi-ii-V, here in C Major.

39

I	vi	ii	V	I	vi	ii	V	I
CMaj7	Amin7	Dmin7	G7	CMaj7	Amin7	Dmin7	G7	CMaj7

We know that the chords in the cycle resolving down a 5th can be changed into dominant 7th chords to create more momentum in the cycle.

40

CMaj7 (A7)	(D7) G7	CMaj7 (A7)	(D7) G7	CMaj7

Other substitutions can be used to increase the buildup in a cycle. For example, we can throw in some tritone subs.

41

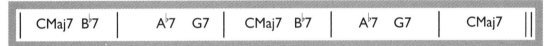

CMaj7 (E♭7)	(A♭7) (D♭7)	CMaj7 (E♭7)	(A♭7) (D♭7)	CMaj7

We can also use this common progression used by Jimmy Heath in *C.T.A.* and Ray Charles in *Hit The Road, Jack*. It is just another tried-and-true method for cycling back to the tonic.

42

CMaj7 B♭7	A♭7 G7	CMaj7 B♭7	A♭7 G7	CMaj7

We can stretch the progression so it covers the whole five bars and use some tritone subs...

43

E7	E♭7	D7	D♭7	CMaj7

...and spice it up by adding the relative ii chords to the Dominant 7th chords, giving us a series of ii-V's moving down chromatically (in half steps).

44

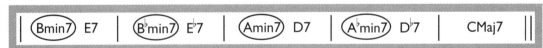

(Bmin7) E7	(B♭min7) E♭7	(Amin7) D7	(A♭min7) D♭7	CMaj7

Here's a slick progression that was popularized by Thelonious Monk, who used it in *Humph*. Simply extend the cycle by working backwards from the point of resolution (in this case, CMaj7) and keep adding the chord a 5th higher. You'll wind up with a progression that resolves downward in 5ths every two beats for four bars, creating an explosive resolution once you get to the I chord.

45

A♭7 D♭7	G♭7 B7	E7 A7	D7 G7	CMaj7

RHYTHM CHANGES

In *Riffin' in Rhythm* you will find the fingering indication: "4—." This indicates that your 4th finger slides down a half step off of the black key and on to the white. This is a typical jazz fingering.

When we looked at *Rhythm Changes* (the changes from Gershwin's *I Got Rhythm*) in the *Intermediate* section, we noticed that they were great changes for using substitution. Since the changes revolve around cycles (I-vi-ii-V's on the A-section and the Dominant 7th chords moving downward in 5ths on the bridge), they are ready-made for the insertion of cycles like those we looked at on the previous page.

Riffin' in Rhythm is a simple Rhythm Changes tune that we can use to review the progression and song form. This way we'll be well prepared for the altered versions that follow.

RIFFIN' IN RHYTHM

Track 14

D. C. al Fine
(Take the 2nd Ending)

Our next Rhythm Changes tune is *Talk To Me, Brownie*. This tune is dedicated to the remarkable trumpet player Clifford Brown, who used these substitute changes on *Brownie Speaks*.

TALK TO ME, BROWNIE

In the 1970s, a sort of jazz supergroup was formed with such luminaries as trumpeter Dizzy Gillespie, drummer Art Blakey, saxophonist Sonny Stitt and pianist Thelonious Monk. The group was called the Giants of Jazz. This Rhythm Changes tune is dedicated to Monk, who popularized the substitution used on the A-section and Stitt, who used changes like those you see in the bridge in his classic composition, *The Eternal Triangle*.

REMEMBERING TWO GIANTS

Track 16

Below we have a sample solo over Rhythm Changes. This is an example of what substitutions a player might use (and how that would impact the subsequent solo line) in the latter, more intense stages of a solo over an ordinary Rhythm Changes tune.

SAMPLE RHYTHM CHANGES SOLO

"*Giant Steps* changes" or "Coltrane Changes" can be intimidating at first glance but they're quite logical. The changes pass through three different keys, each a major 3rd apart from the other two. In the case of *Giant Steps* itself, the three keys are B, G and E♭.

This series of three key centers is sometimes called an *augmented matrix* because it outlines an augmented triad (in this case, G-B-D♯/E♭. All the chords you see in the progression relate back to this matrix; any chord in the tune is either a ii, V or I chord in one of these three keys.

It Takes Big Feet is based on the changes to *Giant Steps*. When you solo, practice very slowly at first so you can keep track of which key you're in at any moment.

IT TAKES BIG FEET

Remember these changes? They're from the first sixteen bars of the progression that gave us *All The Things You Are* by Jerome Kern and *All Them Thangs* (page 137).

47

Fmin7	B♭min7	E♭7	A♭Maj7	D♭Maj7	G7	CMaj7	(CMaj7)

Cmin7	Fmin7	B♭7	E♭Maj7	A♭Maj7	D7	GMaj7	(GMaj7)

Below, in *All Them Thangs Trane Was*, an augmented matrix is inserted into each eight bar section. The first eight bars use E, A♭ and C and the second eight bars use B, E♭ and G. In each case, the reharmonization is logical because the second and third keys in each matrix (A♭ and C & E♭ and G) are part of the original harmony. When you practice this tune, keep track of which keys you're passing through and notice the intense, modern flavor that this reharmonization adds to these familiar changes.

 ALL THEM THANGS TRANE WAS

Track 19

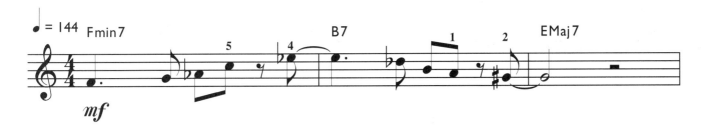

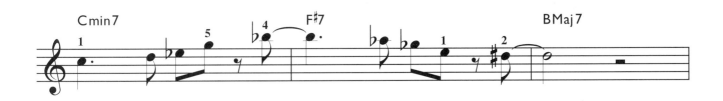

Here we reach a ridiculous level of harmonic sophistication as we use a Coltrane-type reharmonization over Rhythm Changes. In fact, the A-section uses a diminished matrix in which the keys B♭, G, E and D♭ outline a diminished 7th chord. The bridge is reharmonized with the augmented matrix that includes the keys of B♭, G♭ and D. This tune is dedicated to the highly respected guitarist, composer and educator Ted Dunbar, who wrote several books on harmony, substitution and the use of matrices.

TED, CAN YOU DIG IT?

Track 20

D.C. al Fine
(Take the 2nd Ending)

PUTTING THESE SUBSTITUTIONS TO WORK

Now that we have these great substitutions under our fingers and in our ears, we need to consider how we're going to use them. For starters, we have the tools to comprehend tunes like Coltrane's *Countdown* and *26-2* should we need to play them. But what about adding our own substitutions? Let's say we want to throw in some of our own funky substitutions. Well, there's a time and a place for everything. Some appropriate situations to do this include:

1) You've conferred with the other musicians beforehand and agreed upon a set of substitute changes.

2) You feel confident that the other musicians playing at that time (the bassist, the soloist if you're comping, etc.) will hear and appropriately respond to the substitutions you throw in. This could be because you play with them often and they know your stuff or because they simply have great ears and can naturally hear these things.

3) The tune is at a high enough level of intensity that even if you're the only one playing the alternate changes, the tension will sound good and will be resolved at an appropriate moment.

Here are some less appropriate moments to use your slickest substitutions:

1) You're accompanying a singer on I Got Rhythm and haven't given any thought to whether or not your substitutions are compatible with the melody.

2) It's the beginning of a solo and the music hasn't yet built up to that level of intensity.

3) When you called the tune, the bassist said, "What's rhythm changes?"

4) You're playing the cocktail hour of a black-tie corporate party where you got the gig by assuring the event coordinator that you knew all the tunes from Cats.

The substitutions in this chapter are very powerful and should be used carefully. If you use them all the time, they lose the power of surprise and sometimes the intensity they bring to a tune just isn't appropriate. If you're conscious of this, however, and have the control to use them when it's the right time, you'll be very grateful to have such a sophisticated tool at your disposal.

CHAPTER 4

New Scales

One way that a jazz musician can broaden his or her palate of colors is by using different scales. So far, most of the scales we've used have been in one way or another derived from the major scale, such as the modes and the pentatonic scales. In this chapter, we're going to look at some scales that are not derived from the major scale. This will give us new and exciting sounds, some of which match with chords for which we've never had totally compatible scales.

THE JAZZ MELODIC MINOR SCALE

The *melodic minor scale* is common in classical music. Most classical pianists practice this scale that goes up as a natural minor scale with a raised 6th and 7th (or a major scale with a lowered 3rd) and comes back down as an ordinary natural minor scale.

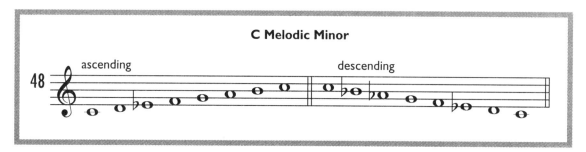

This is because the raised 6th and 7th pull upward toward the tonic, whereas the normal ♭6th and ♭7th (of the natural minor) pull downward to the 5th. The scale reflects this gravity.

In jazz, we can use the ascending form (the version with the raised 6th and 7th) going up and down, giving us one consistent scale to work with. We sometimes call it the *jazz melodic minor scale*.

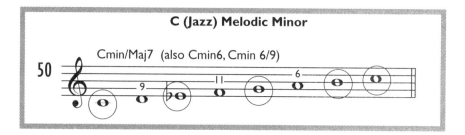

The jazz melodic minor is a wonderful scale to use on tonic minor chords like min/Maj7, min6 and min6/9. Not only that, but by starting this scale from different notes, we can derive modes in the same way that we did with the major scale. The modes of the melodic minor are among the most useful scales in the jazz musician's vocabulary.

MODES OF THE MELODIC MINOR

The modes of the melodic minor scale each have names of their own that reflect their similarities to other scales. Like the modes of the major scale, each of these modes should be thought of as a scale in itself and practiced accordingly. They are shown below (as modes of the C Melodic Minor scale) with their compatible harmonies.

SECOND MODE: DORIAN ♭2

The second mode of the melodic minor gives us a Dorian mode with a lowered 2nd.

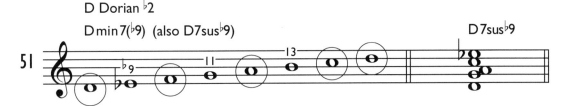

This scale implies a min7 chord with a ♭9. Since that's not a commonly found chord, an even more practical use for this scale comes up when you have a Dominant 7th sus chord (where the 4th replaces the 3rd) with a ♭9. Here is an ideal scale for that situation.

THIRD MODE: LYDIAN AUGMENTED

The third mode of the melodic minor gives us a Lydian mode with a raised (augmented) 5th.

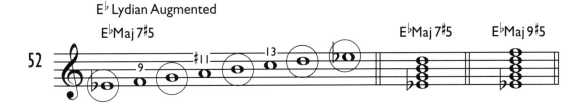

The Lydian augmented scale is perfect for another chord that is new to us, the Maj7♯5 chord. The Maj7♯5 is what the name implies, a Maj7 chord with a ♯5 replacing the natural 5th. All other Lydian-type colors that you would add to a Maj7 chord (9, ♯11, 13) sound fine on a Maj7♯5.

FOURTH MODE: LYDIAN DOMINANT (LYDIAN ♭7)

The fourth mode of the melodic minor gives us a Lydian mode with a lowered 7th.

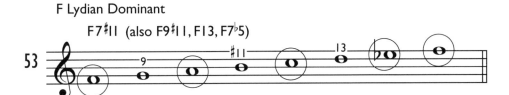

The Lydian dominant scale matches with the sound of a dominant 7th chord with a 9, ♯11 (♭5) and 13. Any combination of these colors is suited by this indispensable scale, which is a colorful alternative to Mixolydian on unresolving and/or unaltered dominant chords.

FIFTH MODE: MIXOLYDIAN ♭6

The fifth mode of the melodic minor gives us a Mixolydian mode with a lowered 6th.

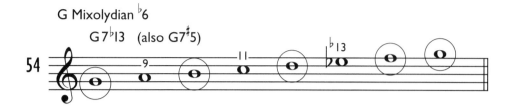

The Mixolydian ♭6 implies a dominant chord with both a natural 5th and a ♯5 (♭13), making it useful in situations where both notes are desired, and somewhat useful on ordinary dominant 7th ♯5 chords (though the natural 5th makes this a bit less useful for those). Like the Lydian Dominant, it has more bite than a Mixolydian mode, but still works on unresolving dominant chords.

SIXTH MODE: LOCRIAN ♯2

The sixth mode of the melodic minor gives us a Locrian mode with a raised 2nd.

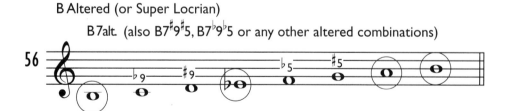

At long last, a scale to use with min7♭5 chords that accommodates the natural 9th! Up until now, we've only had the Locrian mode which has a ♭2 that clashes with the 9th commonly used as an extension on a min7♭5. Here we have the min7♭5 compatibility, and with the natural 9th.

SEVENTH MODE: ALTERED SCALE ("SUPER LOCRIAN")

The seventh mode of the melodic minor gives us a Locrian mode with a lowered 4th.

B Altered (or Super Locrian)

B7alt. (also B7♯9♯5, B7♭9♭5 or any other altered combinations)

The lowered 4th is enharmonically equivalent to the major 3rd. Therefore, we have a scale that fits altered dominant chords flawlessly. We have the root, 3rd and ♭7th (the shell of a dominant chord) and all four altered notes: ♭9, ♯9, ♭5 and ♯5. This makes the scale ideal for altered dominant chords. It is perhaps the most powerful scale in jazz for building up tension on a dominant chord that's going to resolve.

Take your time learning this tune, as it uses every mode of the jazz melodic minor scale at least once. For soloing especially, make sure you have each mode under control as you play.

 THE MELODIC MINERS

Track 22

Symmetrical scales are scales built from the symmetrical repetition of an interval or a short intervallic pattern. This makes them very easy to play and remember, since all you have to know is one or two intervals and you've got the whole scale down.

WHOLE TONE SCALE

The *whole tone scale* is a six note scale that consists entirely of whole steps. There are really only two whole tone scales, C and D♭. Once you get to D, you're just repeating the C scale from another note and the concept of modes doesn't apply since the scale sounds the same regardless of which note you start on.

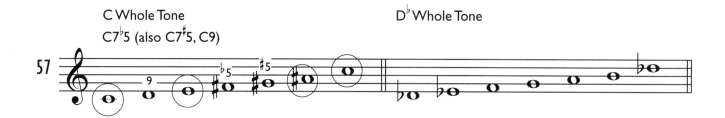

This scale implies a dominant 7th chord with a natural 9th, a ♭5 and a ♯5, and the scale sounds great with a chord that has any combination of those colors. The whole tone scale is a common scale in modern jazz. Its most famous proponent, Thelonious Monk, used it often.

HALF/WHOLE AND WHOLE/HALF DIMINISHED SCALES

The half/whole diminished scale is a scale that begins with a half step followed by a whole step. That pattern is repeated until we get an eight note symmetrical scale.

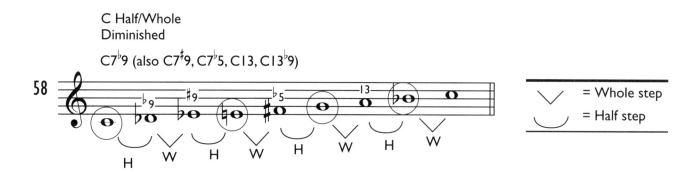

This scale implies a dominant chord with a ♭9, ♯9, ♭5 (♯11) and a 13th, and works with any of these colors (or combinations thereof). It's the first scale we've found that fits the 13♭9 and 13♯9.

The whole/half diminished scale uses the same pattern, only it begins with the whole step.

C Whole/Half Diminished

Cdim7

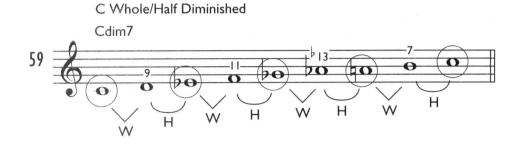

This is the first scale we've found that works over dim7 chords. Not only that, but the colors in the scale match with the extensions that we use on dim7 chords (9th, 11th, ♭13th, major 7th).

Condiment Man uses the whole tone scale and the two types of diminished scales (half/whole and whole/half). Dig into these scales when you solo. Feel free to experiment with mixing and matching between the whole tone and half/whole diminished scales on the dominant 7th chords.

CONDIMENT MAN

Track 23

Surely we remember the harmonic minor scale that we've been playing since the early days of our piano training. Now, in the context of what we've learned since, we can use the scale on min/Maj7 chords. Not only that, but it gives us another scale from which to derive modes that can be used in other harmonic situations.

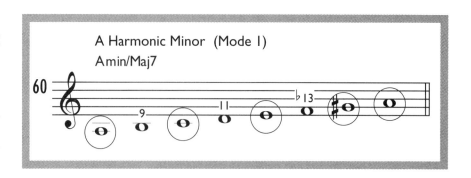

A Harmonic Minor (Mode 1)
Amin/Maj7

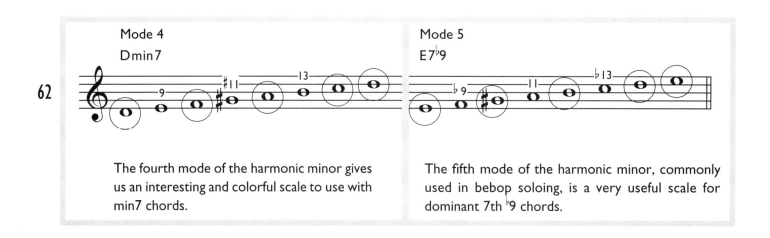

Mode 2
Bmin7♭5

The second mode of the harmonic minor gives us another scale to use with min7♭5 chords.

Mode 3
CMaj7♯5

The third mode of the harmonic minor gives us another scale to use with Maj7♯5 chords.

Mode 4
Dmin7

The fourth mode of the harmonic minor gives us an interesting and colorful scale to use with min7 chords.

Mode 5
E7♭9

The fifth mode of the harmonic minor, commonly used in bebop soloing, is a very useful scale for dominant 7th ♭9 chords.

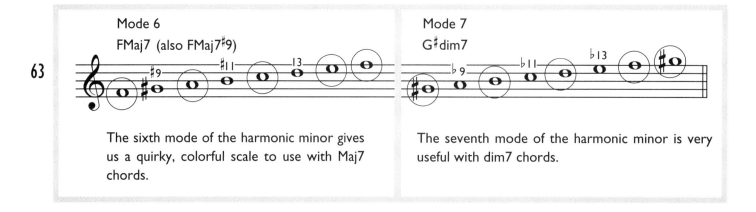

Mode 6
FMaj7 (also FMaj7♯9)

The sixth mode of the harmonic minor gives us a quirky, colorful scale to use with Maj7 chords.

Mode 7
G♯dim7

The seventh mode of the harmonic minor is very useful with dim7 chords.

Greene Machine is a tune that uses all seven modes of the harmonic minor scale. The changes are in G Major and its relative minor, E Minor. Notice that the scale choices relate to the individual chords and not always to the E Harmonic Minor scale.

GREENE MACHINE

Track 24

*As the leader of the Solar Arkestra, keyboardist **Sun Ra** (born Herman Blount in 1914) carved a special niche for himself during his 79-year visit to Earth.*

PHOTO COURTESY OF THE INSTITUTE OF JAZZ STUDIES

Our search for scale colors and mode-deriving possibilities brings us to the *Lydian diminished scale*, so named because it is a Lydian scale with a lowered 3rd. This modern-sounding scale works over min6/9 and min/Maj7 chords. Since it has a ♭5 (♯11) as well as a natural 5th, it also works with dim7 chords. The modes are also colorful and versatile.

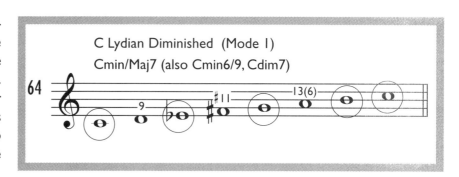

C Lydian Diminished (Mode 1)
Cmin/Maj7 (also Cmin6/9, Cdim7)

Mode 2
D7♭9 (also D13♭9, D7sus♭9)

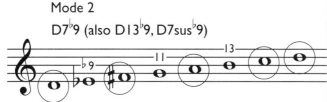

The second mode of the Lydian diminished sounds great with a variety of dominant 7th ♭9 chords including the 13♭9 and the sus♭9.

Mode 3
E♭Maj7♯5 (also E♭dim7)

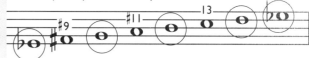

The third mode of the Lydian diminished gives us another Maj7♯5 possibility. Since there is a ♭3 (♯9) as well as the major 3rd, it will also work with a dim7.

Mode 4
F♯dim7

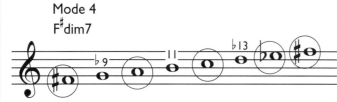

The fourth mode of the Lydian diminished is yet another that works quite well with dim7 chords.

Mode 5
GMaj7 (also GMaj7♯5)

The fifth mode of the Lydian diminished, having both a natural 5th and a ♯5 (♭13), can be used over both Maj7 and Maj7♯5. This scale is sometimes called the *harmonic major*.

Mode 6
Amin7♭5

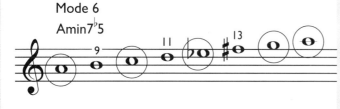

The sixth mode of the Lydian diminished is another great scale choice for min7♭5 chords, as it includes the natural 9th.

Mode 7
B7♭9 (also B7♯9, B7♯5, Bmin7)

The seventh mode of the Lydian diminished sounds great with dominant 7th chords with a ♭9, ♯9, or ♯5 (or any combination thereof). It works over min7 chords since it has a minor 3rd (♯9).

Lennieage is dedicated to the influential pianist and composer, Lennie Tristano. We get the opportunity to use all seven modes of the Lydian diminished scale here. Take your time as you practice this (especially as you solo) so that you can find each mode comfortably.

LENNIEAGE

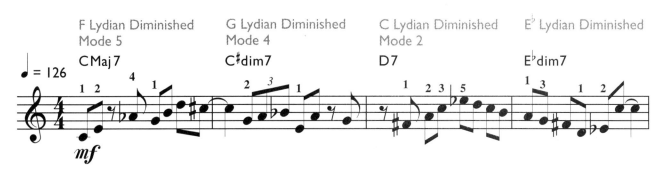

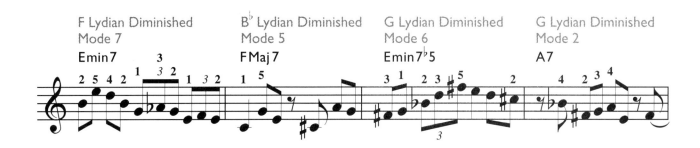

This modern-sounding tune, dedicated to the extraordinary French jazz pianist, Michel Petrucciani, uses a variety of scales and modes chosen from those we've looked at in this chapter. Practice each scale slowly until you can play the whole tune at tempo.

UN PORTRAIT DE MICHEL

Blues for Yusef was written for multi-reed player Yusef Lateef, a musician with a great legacy of sharing his encyclopedic knowledge of scales with the world. The tune uses scales from this chapter in the familiar context of a B♭ blues.

BLUES FOR YUSEF

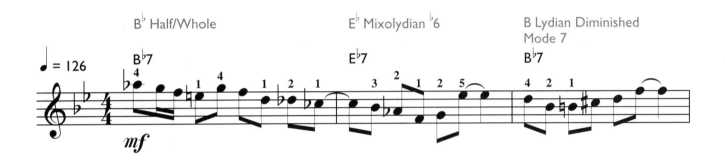

CHAPTER 5

Triads & Pentatonic Scales Revisited

Keith Jarrett (born in 1945) has helped to prove how useful triads can be in a sophisticated modern jazz context. This is particularly evident in his 1970s solo performances, such as the Köln Concert, of which there is a live recording.

TRIADS REVISITED

Now it's time to take another look at triads.

"What's that, you say?
Triads?
Kid stuff!
I'm a sophisticated 7th chord-using jazz musician now. I haven't had to deal with triads since I was playing Louie, Louie *and* Wild Thing."

Well, whether or not that's what you're thinking, we're about to take a step back so we can take many steps forward, by looking at what triads can do for us now. We used triads to get our feet wet with harmony, and we know that most forms of Western music (pop, rock, R&B, classical, early jazz, etc.) rely heavily on triads. In modern jazz keyboard, rather than dismissing triads as not "hip" enough, we have some uses for them that are very hip indeed. In fact, the earthy, accessible sound of triads often helps bridge the gap between the simple and the complicated. Triads within an otherwise complex structure can give the ears something to latch on to.

Probably the most significant use of triads in modern jazz keyboard is in *upper structures*. Upper structures are 7th chord voicings with triads superimposed on top. Before saying more about this, let's look at some examples of the most common upper structures on dominant chords.

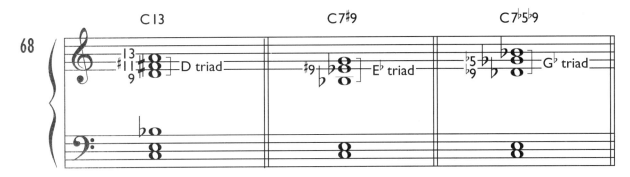

Notice how in several of these voicings, not only does the triad give you some useful chord colors, but it takes care of one of the fundamental chord tones as well. The upper structure voicings above sound great and are easy to remember. And they work on other chords as well as dominant 7th chords. Look at these examples:

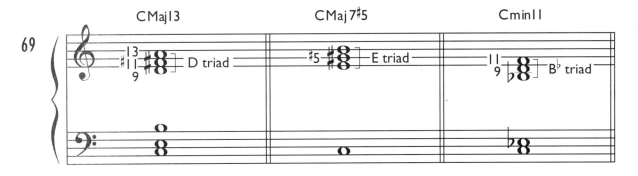

Likewise, the triads you use for upper structures don't have to be major triads:

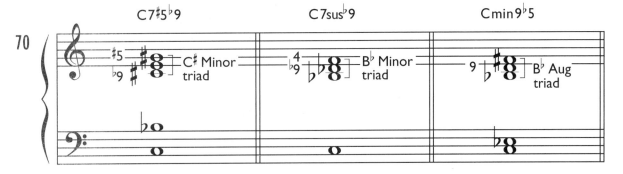

TRIAD POSSIBILITIES FOR 7th CHORD VOICINGS & THE EXTENDED COLORS THEY IMPLY

To explore every possible upper structure would take a book all its own, but the chart below should keep you going for quite a while. It lays out most of the upper structures that are practical for day to day use and shows which additional colors are implied by using those triads. Some of them don't add much (or anything) to the original chords but some are exceptionally colorful.

Maj7 chords

Major Triads

I	(none)
II	9, $^\sharp$11, 13
III	$^\sharp$5
V	9

Minor Triads

iii	(none)
vi	13 (6)
vii	9, $^\sharp$11

min7 chords

Major Triads

III	(none)
IV	6, 11 (use with tonic minor chords)
VII	9, 11

Minor Triads

i	(none)
ii	9, 11, 6 (use with tonic minor chords)
V	9

Dominant 7th chords

Major Triads

I	(none)
II	9, $^\sharp$11, 13
$^\flat$III	$^\sharp$9
IV	(sus)4, 13
$^\flat$V	$^\flat$9, $^\flat$5
$^\flat$VI	$^\sharp$9, $^\sharp$5
VI	13, $^\flat$9
$^\flat$7	(sus)4, 9

Minor Triads

i	$^\sharp$9
$^\flat$ii	$^\flat$9, $^\sharp$5
ii	13sus (with 9)
$^\flat$iii	$^\sharp$9, $^\flat$5
$^\sharp$iv	13, $^\flat$9, $^\flat$5 ($^\sharp$11)
v	9
vi	13
$^\flat$vii	(sus)4, $^\flat$9

min7$^\flat$5 chords

Augmented Triads

II+	9
$^\flat$V+	9
$^\flat$VII+	9

Major Triad

$^\flat$VII	9, 11

Minor Triad

$^\flat$iii	(none)

dim7 chords

Major Triads

II	9
IV	11
$^\flat$VI	$^\flat$13
VII	(major) 7

Minor Triads

ii	9, 11
iv	11, $^\flat$13
$^\flat$vi	$^\flat$13, (major) 7
vii	(major) 7, 9

USING THESE CHARTS

For now, assume any triad listed in these charts is played above a C Major harmony, and we are thinking in the key of C. Refer to the Maj7 chords chart on the upper left. If you play II (a D Major triad in the key of C) above a C Major chord, the notes of the D Major triad are the 9, $^\sharp$11 and 13 of the C chord:

D = 9 above C
F$^\sharp$ = $^\sharp$11 above C
A = 13 above C

This kind of thinking will work in any key with any triad on this chart.

Before we get bogged down exploring charts, let's put some of these to use. Most of the useful upper structures on the chart can be found in this exercise. Here we use these voicings to go through a version of the tune *You Neeque* from page 77. These changes are also very similar to those you find in the standards *There Will Never Be Another You* and *You're a Weaver of Dreams*. Play it slowly to get used to the sound and physical layout of each voicing. Try varying the rhythm to make this into something you could use to comp. The gray chord symbols are the triads being played in the right hand providing upper structures over the basic harmonies played in the left hand.

YOU NEEQUE: Chord Study with Upper Structures

Track 28

A *bi-tonal triad* is simply a triad played over a different bass note. Sometimes a bi-tonal triad will actually spell out a 7th chord. Sometimes it will evoke a 7th chord but leave out key notes. Sometimes it will not resemble any known 7th chord—it will simply have its own quirky sound. This is another way to think about upper structures. In any case, bi-tonal triads have an open sound that is very useful in more impressionistic modern tunes.

Keith's Inspiration is dedicated to Keith Jarrett, who has made ample use of bi-tonal triads throughout his career. All the chords in the tune are bi-tonal triads. Listed above each chord is the 7th chord it most closely resembles (if any). For instance, when you see a bi-tonal chord such as C/G♭ in a modern jazz chart, thinking of it as G♭7♭5♭9 will allow you to solo over it using the same techniques you would ordinarily use to solo over an altered dominant chord. The chart on page 240 will help you to see how these bi-tonal chords have been interpreted as 7th chords. Dig into these sounds.

KEITH'S INSPIRATION

This tune uses both bi-tonal triads and upper structures. In the case of the upper structures, the upper triads used are noted in gray. As with the last couple tunes, you should really dig into the sound of each voicing. Soloing over these changes will give you a nice opportunity to use some of the new scales we learned in the last chapter. The chords are loosely based on the changes from Wayne Shorter's beautiful *Fee-Fi-Fo-Fum*.

CLIMB THAT BEANSTALK

Track 30

When we first encountered pentatonic scales, they were an easy and earthy-sounding way to start soloing. In the context we're about to study, they're still easy and earthy but also immensely hip. Very much like the triads we just explored, pentatonics can give us the freedom to take our solos into more ambiguous waters without totally disorienting the ear. The 1960s were a very fertile time for pentatonic experimentation, with keyboardists like McCoy Tyner, Chick Corea, Herbie Hancock and Larry Young all exploring the different possibilities. From that point on, the versatility of pentatonics was established and they have become a common tool in modern jazz.

Note:

In this section, we will be using only the major pentatonic scale for the sake of narrowing down the subject a bit. Minor pentatonic scales (containing the same notes, but beginning from the 6th degree of the major pentatonic) can also be used.

SUPERIMPOSING PENTATONICS

To superimpose something in music is to place it somewhere other than the expected place. Upper structures are an example of this, putting triads in a different place than you'd normally expect. *Superimposed pentatonics* are pentatonic scales other than the most predictable ones in a given situation.

When we first learned to solo, we thought about what key we were in and used scales that began from the same note as that key.

71

C Major scale...				
Emin7	A7	Dmin7	G7	CMaj7

Then, as we learned more scales and modes and became more comfortable with changes, we added the option of using scales that began from the same note as each chord in a progression.

72

E Dorian	A Half-Whole Diminished	D Dorian	G Altered	C Lydian
Emin7	A7	Dmin7	G7	CMaj7

With pentatonics, we can start from notes other than the roots of the chords or the tonic of the key. For example, over a CMaj7 chord, we have not one but three major pentatonic options.

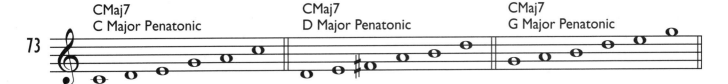

The roots of the triads from which we could form upper structure major triads over a major chord (I, II and V—the III resulting in the ♯5 can't be used in this context *[see page 240]*) are also notes from which we can begin major pentatonic scales over a major chord (1, 2 and 5). This applies as a general rule — pentatonic scale options for soloing over a chord generally coincide with upper structure triad options for that chord. Some caution should be used, since a pentatonic scale has two more notes than a triad and therefore two more potential clashes. There's no need to shy away from a scale that has a clashing note in it. Just think of that note as an avoid note. An *avoid note* is a note in a scale that may clash with the chord and should be used cautiously and not emphasized.

Here's an example. We know that the triad built from the 6th of a dominant chord gives us a 13♭9 sound. The corresponding major pentatonic scale has a major 7th in it (in relation to the dominant chord). We simply de-emphasize that avoid note and reap the benefits of the rest of the scale.

avoid note

This chart lays out some of the most common major pentatonic superimpositions:

Where to begin major pentatonic:	Implied chord/color tone (*means "avoid note").
Maj7	
2	9, 3, ♯11, 13, 7
5	5, 13, 7, 9, 3
min7	
♭3	3, 11, 5, ♭7, 1
4	11, 5, 6, 1, 9
♭7	♭7, 1, 9, 11, 5
(dominant) 7sus	
4	4, 5, 13, 1, 9
7	♭7, 1, 2, 4, 5
(dominant) 7	
2	9, 3, ♭5 (♯11), 13, 7*
♭3	♯9, 4 (11)*, 5, ♭7, 1
♭5	♭5, ♯5, ♭7, ♭9, ♯9
♯5	♯5, ♭7, 1, ♯9, 4 (11)*
6	13, 7*, ♭9, 3, ♭5

USING THIS CHART

Assume for now that the Maj7, min7, 7sus and 7 chords all have a root of C. The numbers on the left indicate which scale tone (in C) the major pentatonic scale will start from, resulting in the tones indicated on the right. For instance, if you play a CMaj7 chord and play a major pentatonic scale starting on 2 (D), the resulting tones are 9, 3, ♯11, 13 and 7 in C.

D Major Pentatonic Scale:	
Scale Tones	In C
D	9
E	3
F♯	♯11
A	13
B	7

Herbie Times Five, written for Herbie Hancock, pays tribute to both his use of pentatonics and to the incredible versatility that sometimes makes him seem like five different musicians in one. The melody is based on superimposed pentatonics. On the following page is a sample solo chorus that demonstrates how to use and smoothly link these pentatonics.

HERBIE TIMES FIVE

Track 31

Try playing this sample solo and your own solos with these superimposed pentatonics. Then try soloing over the changes using a more traditional approach and notice the difference in sound. The pentatonics have a more open sound, less tied to laying out the changes.

 HERBIE TIMES FIVE: *Sample Solo*

Pentatonic superimposition can be an effective way to add variety to your solos in a modal context. Let's say we're soloing over the D Dorian section in *George's Concept* (page 209). Obviously, we can use the Dorian mode.

This sounds perfectly fine but after a while, it can become harder to find new sounds and ideas when you always have the same seven notes to choose from. This is where pentatonics come into the picture. We can use F Major Pentatonic…

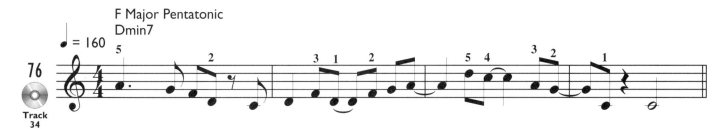

… G Major Pentatonic…

… or C Major Pentatonic.

Each of these three pentatonics, although still drawing from the same seven notes of the Dorian mode, has its own distinct sound and feel. Having all three to draw upon can bring variety to a modal solo. And best of all, you can switch and combine them as often as you want.

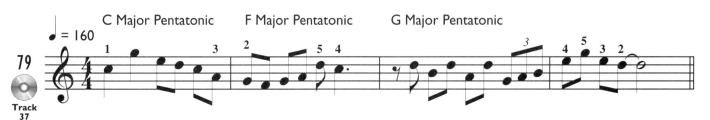

Here's a sample solo chorus on *George's Concept* using multiple pentatonics. Notice that sometimes common tones are used that overlap from one scale to the next, making for a smoother transition. In addition to learning this solo, try your own solo with the same concept of using different pentatonic scales over a single mode.

GEORGE'S CONCEPT: *Sample Solo with Multiple Pentatonics*

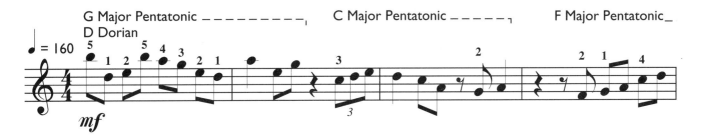

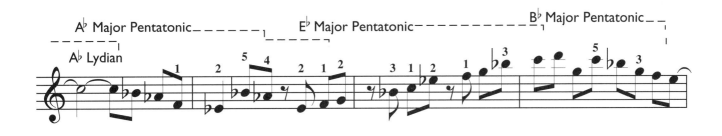

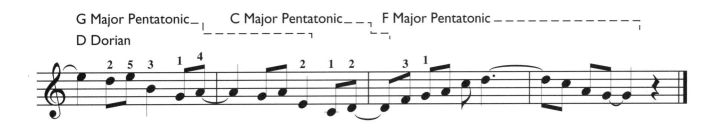

No, this doesn't mean you need to bring your Steinway out onto the patio or hook your synth up to a generator and play on the street. *Outside* (or *out*) in jazz typically means outside of the tonality of the moment. More generally, "out" refers to the more dissonant side of the music. The stereotype of "out" music involves someone hitting the strings of the piano with a hammer while somebody else screeches vacuum cleaner-like sounds on an oboe. Taking the music outside by no means has to be weird, however. In fact, being able to take the music outside can be an essential way to build and maintain intensity (we will discuss this more in Chapter 7).

In modal playing, this concept is very useful. We've already touched on this on page 213 when we discussed sidestepping and resolving. Playing multiple choruses with such limited note choices can cease to be freeing and can begin to be stifling if you don't have the means to take the music somewhere. Listen to McCoy Tyner's solo on *Passion Dance* from his album *The Real McCoy*. On it, he uses not only pentatonics that fit what should be played on an F7sus chord (the basis of the tune's harmony), but also pentatonics that don't seem to relate at all. Check out this example in that style.

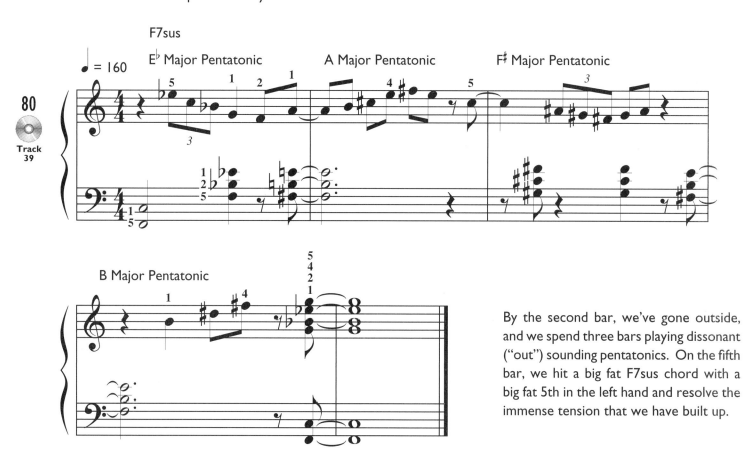

By the second bar, we've gone outside, and we spend three bars playing dissonant ("out") sounding pentatonics. On the fifth bar, we hit a big fat F7sus chord with a big fat 5th in the left hand and resolve the immense tension that we have built up.

Being able to resolve the tension is the key factor in using outside pentatonics successfully, To see this in action, play the example above, leaving out the chord at the end and notice the difference. Using a 5th in the left hand to lay down the tonality and/or returning to a more appropriate scale will generally bring you back. You may choose to do this after four bars, after eight bars or even after a full chorus, depending on how far into the tune you are and how much tension you want to build up.

Beyond this concept of tension and resolution, there are no specific rules for the use outside pentatonics. Simply try using some dissonant sounding scales (the ones that aren't on the chart) and see if you can build and resolve some tension.

This sample chorus demonstrates how a McCoy Tyner-influenced pianist might solo over *George's Concept* using outside pentatonics. Notice both the use of these outside scales and the way they're eventually resolved.

Track 40

GEORGE'S CONCEPT: *Sample Solo with Outside Pentatonics*

CHAPTER 6

Solo Playing

We keyboardists are fortunate to be able to play effectively by ourselves. You can only play trumpet or bass by yourself for so long before the listener starts wishing there was a band but a good keyboardist can play solo for hours at a time. In addition to not having to share the gig money or space on the bandstand with anybody else, there are artistic benefits to being able to play solo. Your ideas are the only ones being presented and there's nobody to lean on. This is a challenge but it's also a great opportunity to hone your playing and show the world your sound. Not to mention the fact that as a working jazz keyboardist, you will invariably be called upon to play solo gigs. Traditionally, solo playing has been most closely associated with the piano, though there are certainly examples of solo organ and/or synthesizer. A list of the all-time great solo pianists in jazz would include James P. Johnson, Fats Waller, Earl Hines, Art Tatum, Hank Jones, Thelonious Monk, Bill Evans, Keith Jarrett and Kenny Barron, just to name a few. Most top-notch pianists through the years have done at least some solo playing and quite a few (including all those just listed) have made at least a couple albums of solo playing.

A thorough study of solo keyboard playing would easily take up a whole book of its own. This chapter will serve as an overview of useful techniques with a few suggestions for research for those who are interested in pursuing this style of playing.

As you explore the world of solo keyboard, listening to and practicing the different styles and techniques, keep this in mind: a keyboard is not a full band. "*Yeah, yeah,*" you may be thinking, "*and the moon isn't made of green cheese, either.*" As obvious as this statement sounds, it's important to remember that you don't have bass, drums or another soloist when you're playing solo. You could approach this in either of two different ways (or any combination of the two) and your preference here greatly impacts your solo style:

---

1) *Play so much stuff that you don't notice that the band is missing. Techniques like stride and walking bass help to fill in the gaps left by having no band. Players from the pre-bebop era like Fats Waller and Art Tatum, and those influenced by them, tend to use this approach.*

---

2) *Accept your limitations and don't worry about what's missing. The solo playing of Bill Evans, for example, was usually marked by a looseness that left the ear to fill in gaps like not hearing the root of every chord in the bass or a constant, churning rhythm. Likewise, sparseness was a key facet of Thelonious Monk's influential solo playing.*

Big Brother Hank is dedicated to the great pianist Hank Jones, the eldest of three brothers who all became jazz legends (the other two being composer and cornet master, Thad, and drum powerhouse, Elvin).

We will use this tune to explore some solo keyboard techniques. Learn the melody and changes well before you move on. Spend some time soloing over the changes which are in the style of Tadd Dameron's *Lady Bird*.

In a career spanning more than sixty years, **Hank Jones** *(1918–2010) was the pianist on hundreds of recordings.*

BIG BROTHER HANK

Track 41

One way to fill in the space when you play solo is by taking over the bassist's job and playing a *walking bass line* in your left hand. A walking bass line is usually a line in quarter notes that lays out each beat of the rhythm and lays down the roots of the chords at key moments.

Look at the note choices in the walking bass line above. The root is always played as soon as a new chord appears. The other notes are chord tones, passing tones from a scale appropriate to the chord or chromatic passing tones on weak beats that are resolved on the next beat (like the A natural in the second bar). Notice the accent marks on the second and fourth beat of every bar. Although the first and third beats are the most significant for the harmony, the second and fourth beats are the *backbeat*, the beats that make the music swing and groove. The bassist (or keyboardist filling the bassist's shoes) is responsible for laying down the harmony on the important harmonic beats, while at the same time emphasizing the rhythm of the backbeat to push the groove.

Another way that we can push the groove in a bass line and break up the monotony of constant quarter notes is by playing *ghost notes* in between the quarter notes. *Ghost notes* are implied notes, notes that are not emphasized nearly as much as the rest but are hinted at for an effect. Notes in parentheses are ghost notes. Remember to give a little extra boost to the notes that land on the second and fourth beats.

The notes chosen for ghost notes are generally chord tones, often the root. These ghost notes give a significant boost to the forward motion of the beat.

Your right hand is free to do as it pleases. It can play chords or single lines. If the left hand groove is strong and the right hand lines are making the changes, there's no need to play chords unless the mood strikes you.

To dig deeper into bass lines, listen to what the bassists do on your favorite jazz records. Most of the times that you listen to great bass players like Paul Chambers, Ray Brown, Sam Jones, Ron Carter, Jimmy Blanton and Charles Mingus, you will hear swingin' walking bass lines. In addition, the organ often takes on bass line duties in a band, so check out some organists. Organists like Jimmy Smith and Richard "Groove" Holmes are renowned for their bass lines. Some pianists, like Dave McKenna, use walking bass lines in their solo playing. Transcribe some bass lines to see what the greats use, paying close attention to the feel. Then, practice your bass lines alone, adding right hand figures (and ultimately whole improvised solos) little by little as the bass lines get more comfortable.

Here we have the melody to *Big Brother Hank* as it might be played with a walking bass line. Once you have this down, try noodling around with each hand. Improvise a new bass line and try soloing over the walking bass.

BIG BROTHER HANK: *Walking Bass*

STRIDE

Stride piano was the solo piano technique of choice before the bebop era of the 1940s. It was also used in a group setting, especially when there was no bassist in the group. Stride is a left hand technique characterized by the "oom-pah oom-pah" sound of bass notes on the first and third beats and chords (higher up in register) on the second and fourth beats.

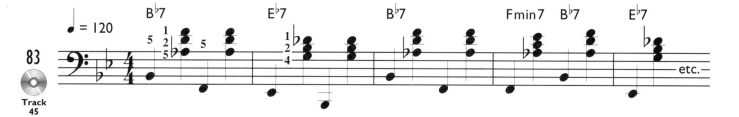

The bass note is usually the root. If the same chord is kept for a while, the bass notes usually alternate between the root on the first beat and the 5th on the third beat. The voicings of the chords can vary based on your tastes and your chops. Four note extended voicings can sound great in stride piano but as you may have gathered from playing through that first example, stride left hand parts are not the easiest things in the world to execute. Once your chops are up to the task, you can experiment with fuller and fuller voicings, but let's start simple. For the chords on the second and fourth beats, try using simple two note shell voicings. That way, as your hand is jumping all over the place, the chords will be a little easier to zero in on.

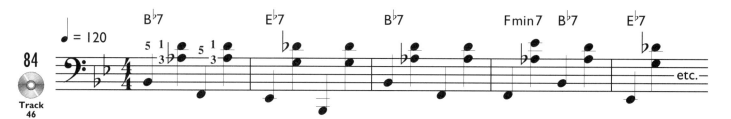

Since you're playing the chords with your left hand, your right hand is free to play single notes.

Another technique sometimes used in stride piano as an occasional change of pace from all the oom-pahs is *walking 10ths*. To play walking tenths, you skip the normal stride pattern and play 10ths in the left hand moving up stepwise to get you from one chord to the next.

If your hand isn't big enough to play 10ths comfortably, roll them by playing the bass note and then leaping up to the 10th as quickly as possible, making the bass note seem like a grace note.

Some stride pianists to check out are James P. Johnson ("the Father of Stride Piano"), Fats Waller, Willie "the Lion" Smith, Earl Hines, Teddy Wilson and the king of stride, Art Tatum, who sometimes sounds like he has three hands. Seek out their solo recordings so you can focus on the stride. For an interesting modern interpretation of stride, check out the solo piano of Thelonious Monk and Jaki Byard. To build your stride chops, practice, practice and practice. Try using stride over different tunes, gradually increasing the size of your voicings and the tempos. When you feel more comfortable, try soloing over stride left hand patterns.

Big Brother Hank is presented here with stride left hand. The voicings are varied, ranging from four note extended voicings to shells, and there are a couple bars of walking 10ths thrown in for good measure. Approach this in the same way you approached the walking bass example two pages ago, gradually experimenting more and more with each hand.

BIG BROTHER HANK: *Stride*

Track 48

Now that we have looked at ways to fill in the space with the left hand, let's work on letting that go and accepting that it's okay to have some gaps (the second approach from the beginning of this chapter). We've worked on making the changes in our solos to the point where the left hand can just hang out and clutch a tall glass of ice water while the right hand spells out the harmony. If the right hand keeps a good, solid groove going with its lines and does a good job of making the changes, the left hand can play skeletal two note voicings (see "Bebop Style Left Hand Voicings" on page 57) and the sound will be full.

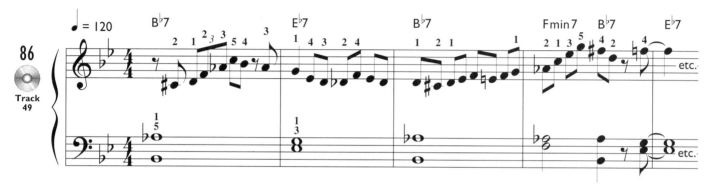

Meanwhile, if even more fullness is desired without departing from the relaxed vibe we've created, throw in some chords. Choose a few sustained notes in your solo and harmonize them.

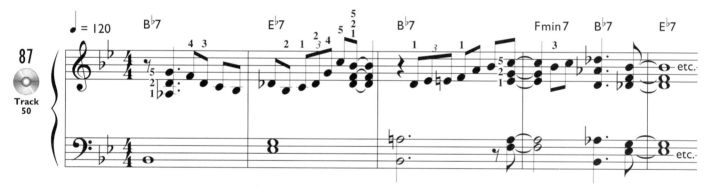

Even rootless chords are fine in moderation, as long as you throw in enough root position voicings to keep the overall sound from becoming ambiguous.

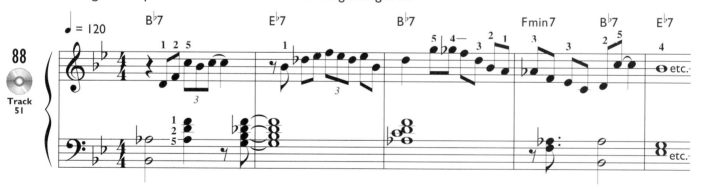

This style of solo piano can be a real litmus test of how strong your stuff is. Your solo lines, voicings, rhythm and overall conviction are in the forefront. The reason that this style works in the hands of Bill Evans, Thelonious Monk, or Kenny Barron is that they have all that stuff together. If some weakness comes out when you're playing this way, don't be discouraged. You will learn what you need to practice, which can actually be a blessing in disguise.

This is a sample solo chorus over *Big Brother Hank* in the style we just discussed. Notice how the solo is taken up by a combination of single note lines and chords. Some substitutions are thrown in too. You have nobody else that you're in danger of confusing, so why not have some fun and use some substitutions?

BIG BROTHER HANK: *Sample Solo*

The great tenor saxophonist, Lester Young, used to say that you have to tell a story when you play. Nowhere is this more apparent than in a ballad. Standard ballads like *Body and Soul, My One And Only Love, Angel Eyes* and *Here's That Rainy Day* have been testing grounds for generations of jazz players—and chops and theory aren't the key. In fact, some of the greatest ballad players of all time, like Miles Davis and Dexter Gordon, are noteworthy for how few notes they played in their solos on ballads. Being sensitive, lyrical and telling a story are the kinds of things that will give you respect as a player of ballads. Your touch and your note choices are in the forefront.

Practicing ballads can be a different sort of process than practicing more up-tempo tunes. We deal with many of the same issues, like voicings and note choices in our solos. Practicing such things as lyricism, pacing, and sensitivity is a bit more elusive. We can tell when we're making the changes, voicing the chords effectively or handling the tempo, but it can be tricky to determine whether or not we're telling a story. Think of this as an ongoing process. Even the greatest players are constantly striving to move forward. Be aware of these issues when you practice and let yourself integrate them at your own pace.

Note:

Although ballads can be played with either swing or straight eighth notes, *An Evening With Kate* is played with straight eighths.

Learn the ballad *An Evening With Kate,* loosely based on the chord changes from Horace Silver's lovely ballad *Peace.* We'll use it to check out some aspects of ballad playing so become well acquainted with the melody and changes.

 AN EVENING WITH KATE

Track 53

PLAYING THE MELODY

When playing up-tempo tunes, it's common to see players who seem like they're just hacking through the melody so they can get it over with and move on to the solo, which is what they're waiting for. This attitude is pretty self-defeating, in general, but on a ballad it's the kiss of death. The way we play the melody on a ballad usually makes or breaks the overall quality of our performance of the tune. There are some classic ballad recordings like Duke Ellington's *Melancholia* and Charles Mingus's *Self Portrait in Three Colors* on which nobody solos at all! These are first-class tracks solely on the grounds of how beautiful the melodies are and how well they're played.

Let's take the first couple of bars of *An Evening With Kate*. You should always know a ballad's melody well enough to play it precisely, but once you do, you can stretch it for expressive effect. Here are two ways of embellishing the beginning of the melody.

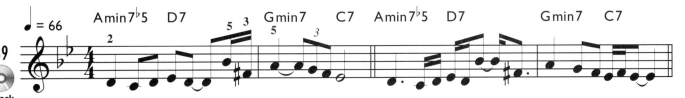

You can also throw in some *fills* (short phrases to fill space) when you come to a long rest or sustained note. Let's look at a couple examples with the third and fourth bars of the tune.

These fills are simple and melodic. It's also possible to use florid, dramatic fills like Art Tatum or Oscar Peterson, but you're better off saving that until you have their level of chops.

Then comes the issue of voicing. Let's move on to the next bar (bar five) and look at a few different ways we can voice the melody and changes there.

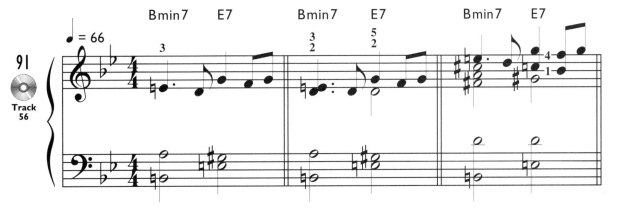

The first example is very stark and bare-boned. The second is fuller but still subtle. The third is dramatic and colorful. All three approaches are valid. The types of voicings you choose depend on your taste and the musical situation of the moment. Shell voicings are great when you want something dark and spacious, giving the melody room to breathe. When things get more dramatic, it's time to break out your richest voicings. Be flexible.

Here's an example of how we might play the melody to *An Evening With Kate* for solo keyboard. The melody is stretched around a bit, a few fills are thrown in and there are a couple of substitutions (the chord symbols of which are in parentheses). Get comfortable with this and try your own interpretations of the melody.

AN EVENING WITH KATE: *Solo Keyboard*

Track 57

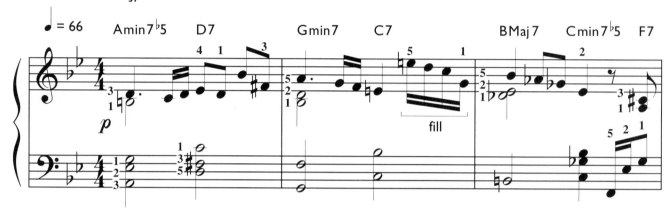

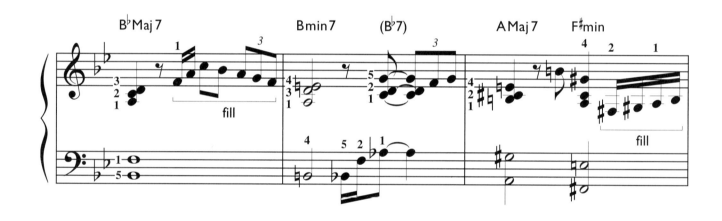

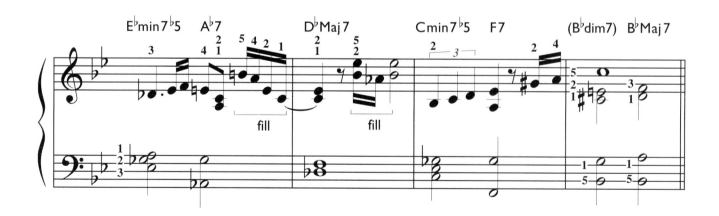

Here we have a sample one-chorus solo on *An Evening With Kate*, also for solo keyboard. The theory and technique behind soloing on a ballad is essentially the same as it is for soloing over anything else, just slower. Slower could mean that you can cram in twice as many notes but try not to think that way — it's slower for a reason. Try your own solos over this tune and don't be afraid to leave space and to let notes linger for a long time.

Track
58

AN EVENING WITH KATE: *Sample Solo*

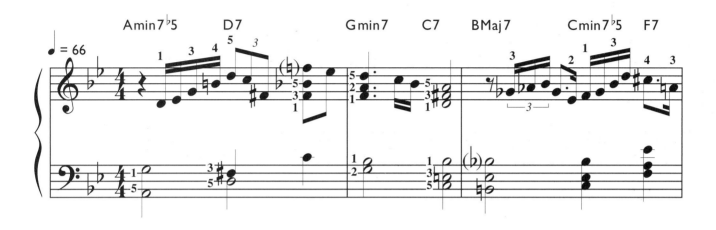

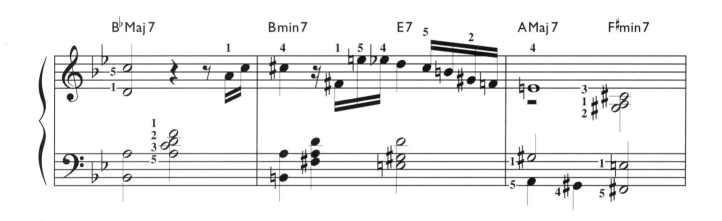

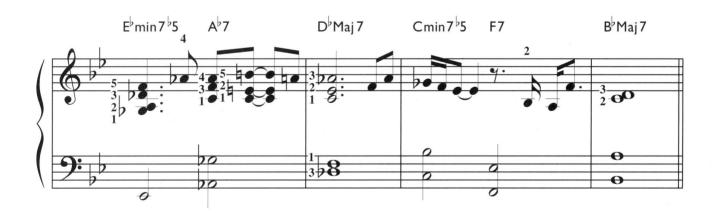

DUO PLAYING

Sometimes you'll find yourself in the in-between situation where you're not solo, but you don't have a whole band, either. Duo playing can be tremendously expressive and interactive; since you only have one other person to interact with, you can focus all your energy on that. Sensitivity is of paramount importance, as is groove (whether it be external or internal). Some modern jazz keyboardists who have had great success playing duo include Bill Evans (who recorded duos with singer Tony Bennett, guitarist Jim Hall and bassist Eddie Gomez) and Chick Corea (whose duo partners include singer Bobby McFerrin, vibraphonist Gary Burton, and fellow keyboardist Herbie Hancock).

Here are some suggestions for how to approach different duo configurations.

Keyboard/Horn (trumpet, saxophone, trombone) Duo
You become the entire rhythm section for the horn. Depending on the skills and preferences of the horn player, you can lay out a consistent rhythmic pattern with stride or walking bass, or you can play more openly and just be confident that you and the horn player will both know where you are at all times. When it comes time for you to solo, it's solo keyboard, baby.

Keyboard/Vocal Duo
This is essentially the same as playing duo with a horn but more caution is usually required. The voice is the most difficult instrument with which to keep your bearings, since you can't just press a key to get the desired note. Unless your singer is Bobby McFerrin or Betty Carter, you need to take special care to play voicings that emphasize (and never clash with) the melody. It's also helpful to keep the rhythm as steady as possible.

Keyboard/Bass Duo
This is sort of a stripped down version of the normal combo instrumentation. Play as you normally would, making sure not to let the lack of drums make you lose the beat.

Keyboard/Drums Duo
Let her rip! Organ/drum duos are fairly common, with the keyboard taking walking bass duties in the left hand and using the right hand for solos and chords. Piano/drum duets can use the same format, the piano can play stride or the piano can simply ride the rhythm of the drums and follow the groove, playing whatever feels right. If the drummer has it together, you needn't be confined by having to lay down a steady left hand pattern.

Keyboard/Guitar Duo
This can be a very rich sound, since you have two different chord-playing instruments. On the guitar solos, the keyboard can act the same way it would with a horn duo. On the keyboard solos, the guitar can play chords while the keyboardist plays a bass line or vice versa. It's also possible to simply throw bass lines and such things out the window and just feed off one another.

Keyboard/Keyboard Duo
This is probably the hardest kind of duo playing. The approach is similar to that of keyboard/guitar duos, but extra special caution must be taken so nobody steps on anyone's toes. If the keyboards are different (organ/piano, for example), that's much easier, due to the different timbres. If it's two pianos, lay back and listen, making sure you don't play anything that clashes with your duo-mate. Ways to do this include playing simple voicings and playing in a different register, either higher or lower than the other keyboardist.

CHAPTER 7

Building Intensity

You've probably met some people who don't understand the appeal of jazz. Wouldn't it be great to give them an article like this? By learning how to effectively build intensity when we play, perhaps we can make it a reality.

THE JAZZ KEYBOARD GAZETTE

JAZZ IS NOT BORING!!

by Jazz Keyboard Gazette correspondent
I.M. Swingin

In a shocking report just in from the Exciting Music Research Laboratory, it has been scientifically proven that jazz is not boring. "It's true," said EMRL spokeswoman Ima Groovehound, "some people have been missing the boat for years now, erroneously thinking that jazz only belongs in elevators, cocktail lounges and other venues where it's kept in the background. In fact, our research proves that jazz is an exciting form of music that warrants *listening to with one's full attention!*"

Shocking words, indeed. The results were compiled through years of research with such high-technology equipment as the Groove-ometer. Subjects were blindfolded and exposed to recordings by such jazz artists as Duke Ellington, Charlie Parker and John Coltrane. They were brought to hear live shows at top jazz clubs around the world. The research shows that the unsuspecting subjects saw great depth, energy, groove and melodic interest in the music. "Basically, they dug the swingin' jazz," said Ms. Groovehound.

In the wake of this news, music fans have been found roaming the streets, desperately trying to make up for lost time. "We've had over a hundred people come in looking for *Kind of Blue* by Miles Davis since lunchtime," said record store owner B. Boppin. Meanwhile, the EMRL has planned an extensive campaign to help society adjust to their findings. "There are two levels to our plan," said Ms. Groovehound, "the first level is to educate the listeners, teaching them what to listen for and where to find good jazz. The second level is to educate the musicians. Now that this knowledge has been made public, they have more responsibility to play high quality music that goes somewhere. It's imperative that the musicians be dedicated to playing music that can build intensity and thereby earn and maintain people's interest." Perhaps with this information, the young jazz artists of today might become the Beatles of tomorrow.

PHOTO COURTESY OF THE INSTITUTE OF JAZZ STUDIES

*Will **Count Basie**, whose swinging big band took the jazz world by storm in the 1930s, become the next Elvis Presley?*

OCTAVES

Guitarist Wes Montgomery had an effective formula for building the intensity in his solos. He would play a chorus or two of single note lines, then a chorus of octaves and a chorus of block chords. Each switch would build the energy level and his solos always went somewhere.

At the keyboard, there are a couple common ways of using octaves in a solo. The first way is to play your solo line in octaves with your right hand and play normal left hand voicings with the same rhythm as the solo line. Here's an example of this over the beginning of a C blues.

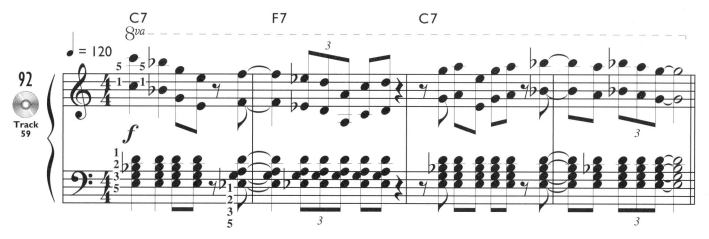

This sort of octave gives a tight, funky sound. Melodic phrases and groovy rhythms are emphasized over bebop-type solo devices, since the right hand octaves cut down your speed (unless you're Oscar Peterson). Hearing the melody doubled in this way, with the added emphasis of having both hands pounding out the same rhythm, can be very intense. These octaves are most closely associated with Bobby Timmons, who used them to great effect on his tunes like *Moanin'*, *This Here* and *Dat Dere*, as well as on standards.

The other kind of octaves are commonly associated with Phineas Newborn, Jr., although Oscar Peterson and Bud Powell are among those who used them before Phineas. For these octaves, you play the same solo line in each hand, two octaves apart. Check out this example over the first few bars of a rhythm changes in B♭.

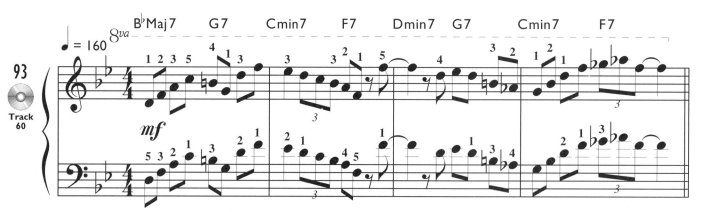

With these octaves, the lines are typically more rhythmically active and beboppish. Since there are no chords being played once you go to both hands to solo (unless you have a guitarist in the band), you're under more obligation to fill in the space. Rhythms tend to be denser and it's more important to make the changes if you want the sound of the harmony to come out. Of course, if you choose to play harmonically ambiguous lines, that's o.k. too, especially on modal tunes. In either case, if you want to use this kind of octave, do some slow practicing of lines with your left hand. If you miss some notes here and there, the sound will still come across but it's worth spending some time working out fingerings and chops issues with your left hand.

Tune for Timmons, dedicated to Bobby Timmons, uses both of the octave types we just discussed. Experiment for a chorus or more with each type when you solo. The chords are loosely based on the changes from Dizzy Gillespie's *Bebop*.

TUNE FOR TIMMONS

Fine

D.C. al Fine
(no repeat)

BLOCK CHORDS: LOCKED HANDS STYLE

The first kind of octaves we looked at on page 266 could also be thought of as *block chords*. When every note of a melody line is harmonized, you have block chords and since each octave was accompanied by a chord in the left hand, they could accurately be called block chords. When people refer to block chords for keyboard, though, they're usually referring to a style called *locked hands*. This style was developed by Milt Buckner and popularized by George Shearing, evoking the sound of a big band's saxophone section. Locked hands involves four or five note voicings for two hands in which the voicings move up and down the keyboard, closely following the melody notes—hence the name "locked hands," since the hands move up and down the keyboard together.

Typically the voicings have one note in the left hand and three or (more often) four in the right hand. The voicings we will look at are in *close position*, which means that the chosen notes in the chords are as close together as possible, usually within the space of an octave.

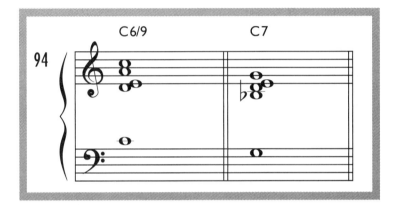

Here's where things get interesting and we're going to draw heavily upon the concept of tension and release. The way we generally use locked hands is by starting with a melody that places chord tones on the strong parts of the beat (downbeats) and passing tones on the weak parts of the beat (upbeats). We harmonize the downbeats normally and harmonize the upbeats with *diminished passing chords*. A diminished passing chord in this setting is the dim7 chord a half step below the normal chord (which could also be thought of as a rootless 7♭9 chord a 5th above the normal chord). This way, every upbeat is harmonized with a tense chord that is immediately resolved at the next downbeat. This all goes by so fast that the ear processes it as sounding like the original chord and not a barrage of changes.

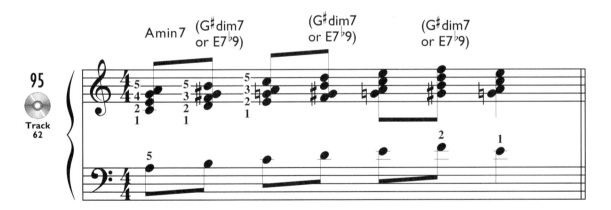

As with the Phineas Newborn-style octaves, you still get the right effect even if you don't flesh out every note with a chord. Sometimes you have a melody that's either too fast to execute this way or the notes don't work out (the chord tones fall on upbeats, for example). As long as the bulk of the notes are harmonized in locked hands, the effect will be strong.

Lock-Up is a tune voiced for locked hands. The diminished passing chords are marked where they appear. Notice that in the last three bars there are a couple places where the melody notes aren't harmonized but the overall sound remains. When you're comfortable with what's written, try your own locked hands solo over the changes.

LOCK-UP

Track 63

Another effective way to build intensity is by changing the rhythm. If you've been playing in a straight-ahead style, these two types of rhythmic oddities will take the music elsewhere. Then, if you bring back the straight ahead rhythm, the release can be cathartic. Or, if you prefer your rhythms to be ethereal, you don't necessarily need to return to hard-swinging.

HEMIOLA

No, *hemiola* is not an infectious disease. It's the superimposition of one meter on top of another, like playing phrases of $\frac{3}{4}$ when you're in $\frac{4}{4}$ time.

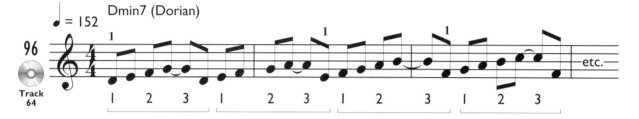

Common types of hemiola include $\frac{3}{4}$ over $\frac{4}{4}$ (what we just saw), $\frac{3}{8}$ over $\frac{4}{4}$, $\frac{2}{4}$ over $\frac{3}{4}$ and $\frac{3}{8}$ over $\frac{3}{4}$ (if you feel very adventurous down the road, you can try more adventurous things like $\frac{5}{4}$ over $\frac{4}{4}$ or $\frac{7}{4}$ over $\frac{4}{4}$). Until you're naturally comfortable with hemiola, here's a way to practice it. Record yourself (on a tape recorder or sequencer) playing some changes in one time signature and try playing or singing solo lines in another time signature, trying to keep track of where you are in the form of the tune.

RHYTHMIC DISPLACEMENT

Rhythmic displacement involves shifting where we put a line. Instead of laying out our lines and chords right where the changes and song form say we should, we deliberately play them early or late to break up the rhythm.

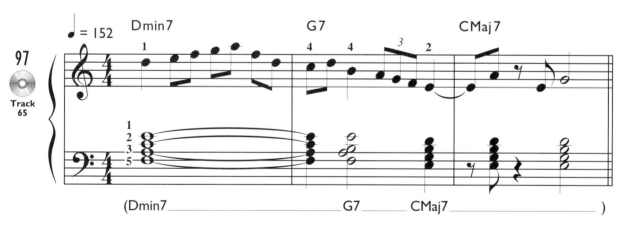

In the hands of skilled rhythmic displacers like pianists Bill Evans, Paul Bley and Keith Jarrett, this creates ambiguity in the song form and rhythm, which keeps things from getting predictable and has an explosive effect when you re-establish the underlying form. Practice this a little bit at a time, so that the ambiguity doesn't cause you to lose the form. Even once you've got it under control, be cautious. An unsuspecting rhythm section might hear your displacement, think the tune got turned around, and follow you!

Bley-zin was written for the pioneer of rhythmic sophistication Paul Bley and the changes are in the style of the Cole Porter standard *What is This Thing Called Love.* The A-section uses "three over four" ($\frac{3}{4}$ over $\frac{4}{4}$) hemiola and the bridge uses rhythmic displacement. In each case, the underlying chords are written on top and the alterations that are the basis for the melody are noted underneath. At first, play the chords above in strict $\frac{4}{4}$ time while you play the melody. Once that's comfortable, try feeling the $\frac{3}{4}$ on the A-sections and the displaced chords on the bridge without losing the basic rhythm and form of the tune.

BLEY-ZIN

Track 66

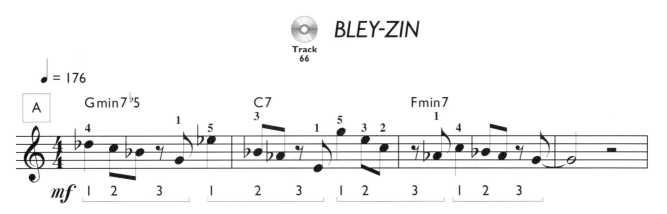

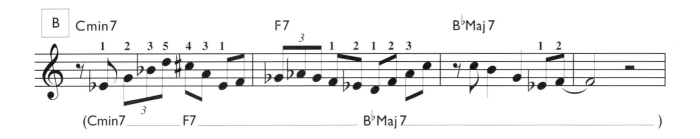

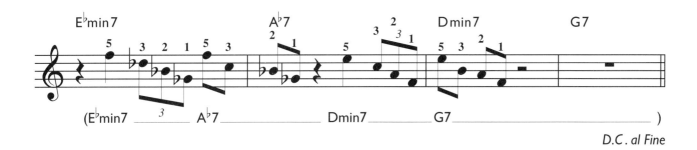

A *cluster* is a group of notes played very close together. The sound of two or more notes played right up close is inherently biting and dissonant. When drama and intensity are called for, clusters can be very useful as both soloing devices and voicings.

To begin checking out clusters, try playing harmonic 2nds. We have done this with inner voices in a chord voicing, but the impact is intensified when the cluster is more exposed. Find two notes that relate to a chord and are a whole step or a half step apart and play them at the same time. Here are some examples with whole steps . . .

. . . and here are some examples with half steps.

You can also stick one of the two notes an octave higher. The result is more spaced out but equally biting.

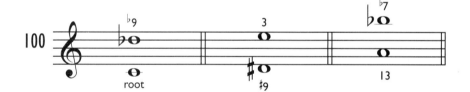

Clusters can also be played with quite a few notes. Another method for forming clusters is to take several notes that you might use in a voicing and play them as close together as possible.

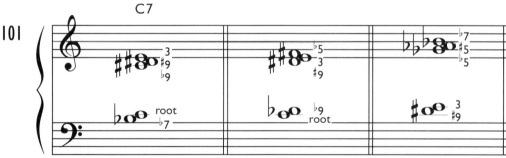

All of these devices can work to bring excitement and dissonance (but not chaos) into a solo or a comping pattern. Experiment. Horace Silver and Thelonious Monk used clusters often, sometimes creating a very dissonant effect, sometimes not. Cecil Taylor built much of his style from the use of clusters, often with a tremendous amount of dissonance. A broad range of possibilities exists.

Cecil's Revolution Blues was inspired by the brilliant Cecil Taylor, one of the most iconoclastic pianists in the history of jazz. The tune, a blues in B♭, revolves around the use of clusters. They range from two-note clusters to thick six-note cluster voicings. Give yourself time to adjust to the often-startling sound of clusters and experiment with them when you solo.

CECIL'S REVOLUTION BLUES

Track 67

The 1960s were a fertile time for compositional experimentation. Miles Davis had a quintet that included saxophonist Wayne Shorter and keyboardist Herbie Hancock, both of whom composed for the group and for records of their own during the same period. They didn't usually base their tunes on standard chord progressions full of ii-V's. Tunes like Herbie's *The Sorcerer* and *Dolphin Dance* and Wayne's *E.S.P., Nefertiti* and *Wildflower* used a lot of *non-diatonic harmony*, chords and progressions not based on a particular key center. The 1960s Miles quintet had an impressionistic, exploratory style, using tunes in this non-diatonic style to open up their improvisational concepts. Other musicians like saxophonist Joe Henderson, trumpeter Woody Shaw, pianist Andrew Hill and organist Larry Young were also playing and writing in this new style. Unlike modal music, there were changes going by but they weren't the sort of changes that bebop and bebop-inspired players used. Instead of ii-V's, you were more likely to see sus chords, Maj7#5 chords, and min/Maj7 chords often not relating to any particular key. For example, check out theses changes in the style of Joe Henderson's tune *Inner Urge.*

102

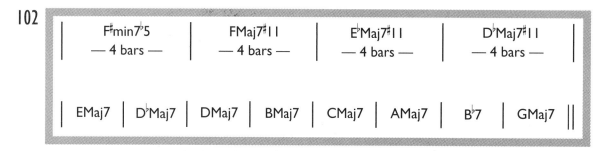

Notice there's only one dominant 7th chord, no min7 chords, and not once do the roots of the chords move downward in 5ths. This means that most of the typical ways to play over changes are less relevant. Playing tunes like this can be a great way to focus on issues of energy, intensity and development. This section will explore some techniques used to play these kinds of tunes.

*Here are some **Wayne Shorter** (born 1933) tunes from the 1960s that are well worth checking out:*

E.S.P.
Nefertiti
Footprints
Speak No Evil
Witch Hunt
Deluge
Yes and No
El Gaucho
Black Nile

Shorter But Hipper, dedicated to Wayne Shorter, is a non-diatonic tune that we will use to explore that style of jazz. Familiarize yourself with the tune (especially the changes) before moving on to the next couple pages.

SHORTER BUT HIPPER

Track 68

Now it's time that we take all the great devices we learned for making the changes and stick them in our back pocket. On a tune like *Shorter But Hipper*, the motion of the changes is not very conducive to such things as guidetones, and to simply arpeggiate the basic chord tones would be wasting a whole world of coloring possibilities. We're better off if we *play colors*. To "play colors," you focus on individual notes in the chords, generally extensions. Think of it as the opposite of the usual techniques of making the changes. Rather than emphasizing the chord tones, you're paying special attention to all the notes that aren't fundamental notes in the chords but sound good anyway. Check out this example over *Shorter But Hipper*, where the focal point in each bar is a non-chord color.

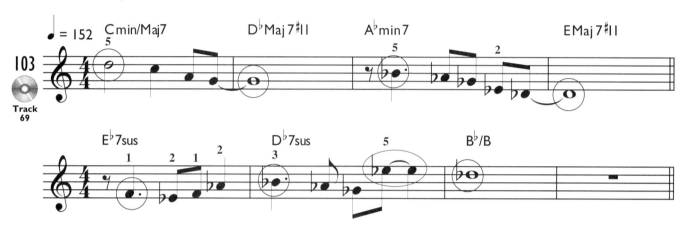

Along the same lines, shift your mind away from trying to find the nearest chord tone to make smooth transitions from chord to chord. Instead, look for any common tones and nearby tones that fit, chord tones or not. Pick a note and see how much you can use it throughout the progression and how little you can move whenever it doesn't fit. Here's an example of this approach with E♭:

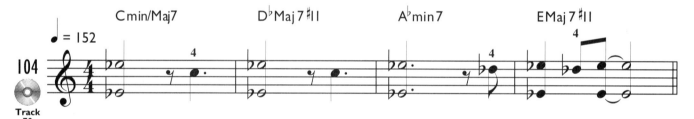

Here's another example, this time with B♭. Notice that B♭ doesn't fit over the first chord so we start a half step away on B natural and then move back to B♭ as we anticipate the second bar.

Try this approach with all twelve notes and see what you come up with.

Approaching a tune in this fashion allows you more freedom to think about other things, like melodic development. Rather than focusing on outlining every passing chord, we can hear a melody in our heads and squeeze it in wherever it fits, not worrying about things like how to get to the 3rd or 7th of the next chord. We adjust whatever notes we need to adjust to make the line compatible with the chord of the moment and flow with the melody. The funky scales we looked at in Chapter 4 come in handy here.

Here's an example of this, using an ascending melodic pattern to go through the changes at the beginning of *Shorter But Hipper*.

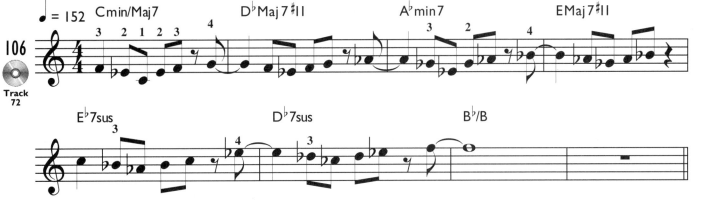

In actual performance, we would probably not replicate the same pattern so many times without changing it but practicing these kinds of techniques will help you get the hang of playing non-diatonic changes.

VOICINGS

As with soloing, colors take precedence in our chord voicings on this type of progression. It is the colors and their movement that define the sound and feeling of the harmony, not the voice leading of the 3rd and 7th like we so often find in diatonic harmony. Check out this example of comping over the first eight bars of *Shorter But Hipper* played without roots on the assumption that there's somebody else playing a bass line.

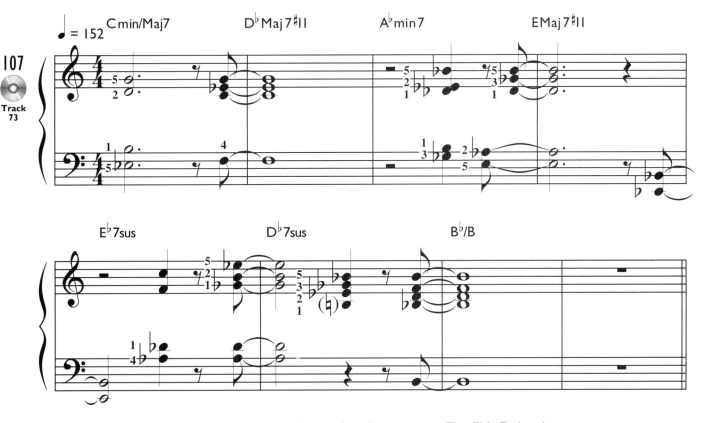

As you can see, extended colors are emphasized in the voicings. The EMaj7 chord is even voiced without a 7th. Try practicing the changes to this tune slowly, seeing how much color you can pack into each voicing.

Here is a two-chorus sample solo on *Shorter But Hipper*. In the first chorus, the scale choices are marked to help you understand where the notes are coming from. In the second chorus, the emphasis is melodic development. See if you can spot the melodic phrases and how they are repeated (usually in an altered form) to give the ear something to cling to.

SHORTER BUT HIPPER: *Sample Solo*

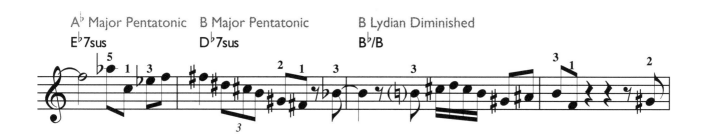

Now it's time for you to try your own solos. Try to think primarily about creating and developing lyrical melodies. Once you have that under control, it's just a matter of fitting them with the changes.

CHAPTER 8

Afterwords

As a reward for your hard work, here's *Maybe*, a tune to play that incorporates a lot of the things we examined in this book. The form and changes are in the style of the harmony to Wayne Shorter's *Yes or No*. Notice that the form is a little unusual. It's AABA form, but the A-section is fourteen bars long and the bridge is sixteen.

Fine

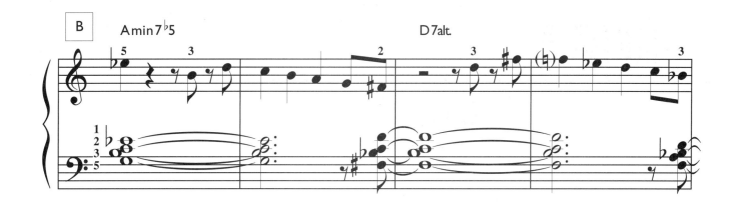

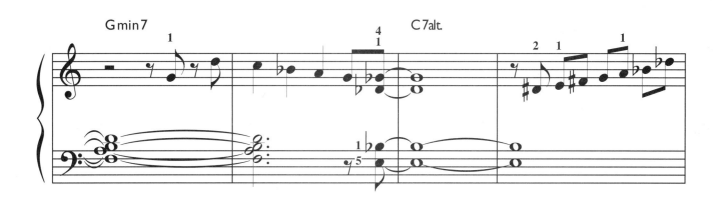

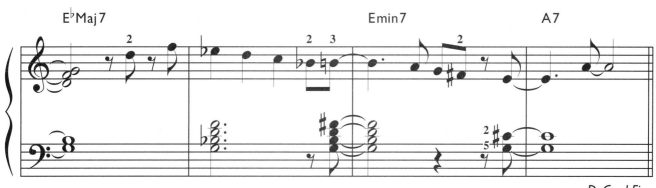

D.C. al Fine

Here's a sample solo chorus on *Maybe*. Dig into it and also try your own solos using the concepts we've learned.

MAYBE (sample solo)

Track 76

Now, create your own solo.

All the things we've examined over these three books should lay a solid foundation for any jazz keyboardist. They won't, however, prepare you for every situation you'll ever encounter. The nature of this music is that you learn quite a bit on the job and through your own practice and experimentation. The next few pages will quickly address a few issues not yet covered that you might want to be prepared for.

PLAYING WITH EXCELLENT MUSICIANS:

As you get out into the world of jazz, you'll invariably play with musicians who are far more skilled and experienced than you are. This is the fastest, most potent training you could possibly get as a jazz musician. Always remember this when you're in that situation. There's no need to be scared or intimidated. Just take some deep breaths, play your best, and keep your ears wide open so you can soak in everything you can. You may not instantly turn into Art Tatum, but if you're relaxed, you're bound to play far better than you usually do. When the musicians are at a high level and the energy is right, the music can draw things out of you that you didn't even know were there.

PLAYING WITH POOR MUSICIANS:

It stands to reason that the better you get, the more people there are who aren't at your skill level. Likewise, those people will want to play with you for the same reason that you want to play with people who are more advanced than you are. In these situations, don't let your ego get in the way. As a jazz keyboardist, it's your job to make any music you play sound as good as possible. If that means shredding *Countdown* at breakneck speed, so be it. If that means trying to hold *Autumn Leaves* together as the bassist loses the form, the drummer loses the time, and the saxophonist flubs all the changes, so be it. Obviously you don't want to seek out situations like these, but we all encounter them sooner or later. If you can get through these situations with class, it will only help the rest of your playing. It will also get you more gigs, by the way.

PLAYING DIFFERENT STYLES:

Now that you've made it this far, you've probably come to the realization that jazz is very challenging music. A musician must study and learn a tremendous amount of information to master the rhythm, harmony and improvisation of jazz. If you have done this, bravo! However, don't make the mistake that some jazz musicians make and become smug about it. Just because you can play jazz, that doesn't necessarily mean you're automatically a master of all other styles of music. For both artistic and financial reasons, jazz musicians often work in other styles, like blues, rock, funk and Latin. Some of these styles, like Latin jazz, closely and directly relate to our jazz studies. Others, like playing *You Light Up My Life* with a wedding band, don't. Either way, when you're playing in another style, give that style the proper respect and get into the music. If you can do this, you're bound to enjoy what you're playing and sound good doing it.

ODD TIME SIGNATURES:

Most of the music you've played in these books (and probably in whatever other playing you've done) has been in $\frac{4}{4}$ time. There have also been some tunes in $\frac{3}{4}$. More advanced players will sometimes use other time signatures as a musical challenge and change of pace. Through the work of artists like pianist Brad Mehldau, bassist Dave Holland and others, the expectation for fluency in less common time signatures has grown since the turn of the century. The most common among the uncommon time signatures is $\frac{5}{4}$.

Jazz in $\frac{5}{4}$ got its most famous exposure with Dave Brubeck's recording of Paul Desmond's *Take Five*. Other tunes have been written in $\frac{5}{4}$, and you can also take a standard tune and bend it into that time signature. When playing in an unusual time signature, the easiest way to keep track of the pulse is to divide it into smaller, more comfortable units. In the case of $\frac{5}{4}$, you can think of each bar as a bar of $\frac{3}{4}$ followed by a bar of $\frac{2}{4}$. Play the example below.

Another time signature you may encounter is $\frac{7}{4}$, used in such jazz tunes as Jymie Merritt's *Nommo* (recorded by Lee Morgan and Max Roach). In the case of $\frac{7}{4}$, you can think of each bar as a bar of $\frac{4}{4}$ followed by a bar of $\frac{3}{4}$.

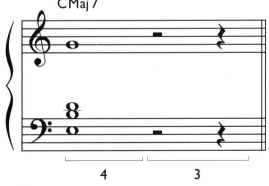

Any other uncommon time signature can be approached the same way, at least until you can hear it on its own terms. Figure out a way to break it down into smaller, more manageable units. The way the other players are interpreting the tune may suggest a specific way to break it down, and the tune itself may do the same.

FAST TEMPOS:

Since we've been looking at subtle details in the pieces in these books, not much attention has been paid to playing them fast. Jazz at fast tempos can be an intense and exhilarating experience for the listener and the player. At times it can also be a way for technically advanced players to flex their chops and test other players to see if they can do the same. You're very likely to encounter fast tempos in both of these contexts, often at the same time. The way to prepare for playing fast is simple: play fast. This doesn't mean you need to play a zillion notes a second. Quite the contrary, many great jazz soloists like Dexter Gordon, Miles Davis, J. J. Johnson, Thelonious Monk and Wes Montgomery can be heard playing convincing up-tempo solos without playing exceptionally fast phrases. The key is to relax and be comfortable with the tempo. Take a tune that is commonly played fast like *Cherokee, Bebop, Lover* or *Just One of Those Things*. Find a comfortable tempo and solo for a while, until your lines feel comfortable and flowing. Then kick the metronome up a notch or two and do it again. Keep doing this until you get to a challenging tempo. Just solo, solo, and solo, until your lines flow at that tempo and you feel relaxed. If you typically set your metronome to beat on the second and fourth beats of the measure, or on all four beats, you might want to change that on fast tempos. Setting your metronome to click on the first and third beats makes it much easier to keep track of the time — emphasizing the backbeat does little good if you're turning the beat around. Also listen to recordings of up-tempo tunes and see if you can easily hear where the beat is at all times.

LEARNING ON THE BANDSTAND AND THE IMPORTANCE OF GROWTH:

Preparing for a gig is something like preparing for a debate. If you're well prepared for a debate, you show up with a mastery of language, a thorough knowledge of the subject being debated and some idea of what ideas might be presented. If you're well prepared for a gig, you show up with your chops and theory in good shape, you know a lot of tunes and you've practiced the bandleader's favorite tunes extra hard. Debates and jazz gigs have another thing in common, though. In both cases you have only a general sense of what's going to happen, and your success depends upon your ability to gracefully handle whatever comes up.

Some jazz gigs are easy, some aren't. The uncertainty is one of the things that makes jazz so exciting to play. You may be completely on top of every tune that's called, or the bandleader may call tunes you've never even heard of, or call them in other keys. The rhythm section may be responsive and supportive, or they may drop out while you're soloing on *Giant Steps* to see if you can handle it by yourself. This is not meant to frighten you, quite the contrary. Every time you step onto the bandstand, you have an opportunity to learn something. No bad gig is the end of the world, and no good gig means that you're perfect. Whether you're playing new tunes in hard keys with amazing players or playing the same old tunes with the same old people, you have a chance to grow. If you look at legends of jazz like Duke Ellington, Dizzy Gillespie, Charles Mingus, Miles Davis and John Coltrane, their careers had something very important in common: they all sought to grow and to move forward from the beginning to the end. John Coltrane didn't think "Hey, wait a minute, I'm John Coltrane. People idolize me. If I'm so great, then why don't I just mellow out and stop practicing so much?" No, 'Trane spent his whole life striving to improve. We may not all be John Coltrane, but we can certainly all strive to keep learning and growing whenever we play.

RECORDINGS

The concepts explored in this book were broad and diverse. Likewise, the albums listed here are quite varied in style. Each album supports at least one of the concepts from this book, and each one is well worth checking out by any standards.

— *Art Blakey and the Jazz Messengers* (with Horace Silver on piano)
— Dave Brubeck: *Time Out* (includes the classic tune, *Take Five*)
— Jaki Byard: *Blues for Smoke*
— Ornette Coleman: *The Shape of Jazz To Come* (no keyboard — an album that proves that you can free up your improvisational thinking without sounding completely "out")
— John Coltrane: *A Love Supreme* (with McCoy Tyner on piano)
— John Coltrane: *Live at Birdland* (with McCoy Tyner on piano)
— John Coltrane: *Giant Steps* (with Tommy Flanagan and Wynton Kelly on piano)
— Chick Corea: *Now He Sings, Now He Sobs*
— Miles Davis: *E.S.P.* (with Herbie Hancock on piano)
— Bill Evans and Jim Hall: *Intermodulation*
— Bill Evans: *Everybody Digs Bill Evans*
— *The Bill Evans/Tony Bennett Album*
— Stan Getz and Kenny Barron: *People Time*
— Dizzy Gillespie: *Sonny Side Up* (with Ray Bryant on piano)
— Herbie Hancock: *Empyrean Isles*
— Dexter Gordon: *Ballads* (various pianists)
— *Earl Hines Plays Duke Ellington*
— Ahmad Jamal: *Awakening*
— Keith Jarrett: *Standards Vol. 1*
— Keith Jarrett: *The Koln Concert*
— James P. Johnson: *Original James P. Johnson*
— Charles Mingus: *Changes One* and *Changes Two* (with Don Pullen on piano)
— Thelonious Monk: *The Complete Genius (Complete Blue Note Recordings)*
— Thelonious Monk: *Thelonious Himself*
— Phineas Newborn, Jr.: *The Great Jazz Piano of Phineas Newborn, Jr.*
— Bud Powell: *Genius of Bud Powell*
— George Shearing: *Definitive George Shearing*
— Wayne Shorter: *Speak No Evil* (with Herbie Hancock on piano)
— Wayne Shorter: *Adam's Apple* (with Herbie Hancock on piano)
— Wayne Shorter: *Ju-Ju* (with McCoy Tyner on piano)
— Art Tatum: *20th Century Piano Genius*
— Cecil Taylor: *World of Cecil Taylor*
— Bobby Timmons: *This Here is Bobby Timmons*
— Lennie Tristano: *Intuition*
— McCoy Tyner: *The Real McCoy*
— Fats Waller: *At the Piano (Bluebird's Best)*
— Mary Lou Williams: *Free Spirits*
— Larry Young: *Unity*

CONGRATULATIONS!

You have now completed *The Complete Jazz Keyboard Method*. You deserve much praise for your hard word and all the skills and knowledge you've built up. See you on the bandstand!